Videostyle in Presidential Campaigns

Videostyle in Presidential Campaigns

Style and Content of Televised Political Advertising

Lynda Lee Kaid and Anne Johnston

Praeger Series in Political Communication

Westport, Connecticut
London

Library of Congress Cataloging-in-Publication Data

Kaid, Lynda Lee.
   Videostyle in presidential campaigns : style and content of televised political advertising / Lynda Lee Kaid and Anne Johnston.
      p. cm.—(Praeger series in political communication, ISSN 1062-5623)
   Includes bibliographical references and index.
   ISBN 0-275-94071-3 (alk. paper)
      1. Advertising, Political—United States. 2. Television in politics—United States. I. Johnston, Anne. II. Title. III. Series.

JK2281.K26 2001
324.7'3'0973—dc21   00-023311

British Library Cataloguing in Publication Data is available.

Library of Congress Catalog Card Number: 00-023311
ISBN: 0-275-94071-3
ISSN: 1062-5623

First published in 2001

Praeger Publishers, 88 Post Road West, Westport, CT 06881
An imprint of Greenwood Publishing Group, Inc.
www.praeger.com

Printed in the United States of America

The paper used in this book complies with the Permanent Paper Standard issued by the National Information Standards Organization (Z39.48-1984).

10 9 8 7 6 5 4 3 2

Contents

Contents

Series Foreword

Those of us from the discipline of communication studies have long believed that communication is prior to all other fields of inquiry. In several other forums I have argued that the essence of politics is "talk" or human interaction.[1] Such interaction may be formal or informal, verbal or nonverbal, public or private, but it is always persuasive, forcing us consciously or subconsciously to interpret, to evaluate, and to act. Communication is the vehicle for human action.

From this perspective, it is not surprising that Aristotle recognized the natural kinship of politics and communication in his writings *Politics* and *Rhetoric*. In the former, he established that humans are "political beings [who] alone of the animals [are] furnished with the faculty of language."[2] In the latter, he began his systematic analysis of discourse by proclaiming that "rhetorical study, in its strict sense, is concerned with the modes of persuasion."[3] Thus, it was recognized over twenty-three hundred years ago that politics and communication go hand in hand because they are essential parts of human nature.

In 1981, Dan Nimmo and Keith Sanders proclaimed that political communication was an emerging field.[4] Although its origin, as noted, dates back centuries, a "self-consciously cross-disciplinary" focus began in the late 1950s. Thousands of books and articles later, colleges and universities offer a variety of graduate and undergraduate coursework in the area in such diverse departments as communication, mass communication, journalism, political science, and sociology.[5] In Nimmo and Sanders's early assessment, the "key areas of inquiry" included rhetorical analysis, propaganda analysis, attitude change studies, voting studies, government and the news media, functional and systems analyses, technological changes, media technologies, campaign techniques, and research techniques.[6] In a survey of the state of the field in 1983, the same authors and Lynda Kaid found additional, more specific areas of concerns such as the presidency, political pools, public opinion, debates, and advertising.[7] Since the first study, they have also noted a shift away from the rather strict behavioral approach.

A decade later, Dan Nimmo and David Swanson argued that "political communication has developed some identity as a more or less distinct domain of scholarly work."[8] The scope and concerns of the area have further expanded to include critical theories and cultural studies. Although there is no precise definition, method, or disciplinary home of the area of inquiry, its primary domain comprises the role, processes, and effects of communication within the context of politics broadly defined.

In 1985, the editors of *Political Communication Yearbook: 1984* noted that "more things are happening in the study, teaching, and practice of political communication than can be captured within the space limitations of the relatively few publications available."[9] In addition, they argued that the backgrounds of "those involved in the field [are] so varied and pluralist in outlook and approach, ... it [is] a mistake to adhere slavishly to any set format in shaping the content."[10] More recently, Swanson and Nimmo have called for "ways of overcoming the unhappy consequences of fragmentation within a framework that respects, encourages, and benefits from diverse scholarly commitments, agendas, and approaches."[11]

In agreement with these assessments of the area and with gentle encouragement, in 1988 Praeger established a series entitled "Praeger Series in Political Communication." The series is open to all qualitative and quantitative methodologies as well as contemporary and historical studies. The key to characterizing the studies in the series is the focus on communication variables or activities within a political context or dimension. As of this writing, over seventy volumes have been published and numerous impressive works are forthcoming. Scholars from the disciplines of communication, history, journalism, political science, and sociology have participated in the series.

I am, without shame or modesty, a fan of the series. The joy of serving as its editor is in participating in the dialogue of the field of political communication and in reading the contributors' works. I invite you to join me.

Robert E. Denton, Jr.

NOTES

1. See Robert E. Denton, Jr., *The Symbolic Dimensions of the American Presidency* (Prospect Heights, IL: Waveland Press, 1982); Robert E. Denton, Jr., and Gary Woodward, *Political Communication in America* (New York: Praeger, 1985; 2d ed., 1990); Robert E. Denton, Jr., and Dan Hahn, *Presidential Communication* (New York: Praeger, 1986); and Robert E. Denton, Jr., *The Primetime Presidency of Ronald Reagan* (New York: Praeger, 1988).

2. Aristotle, *The Politics of Aristotle*, trans. Ernest Barker (New York: Oxford University Press, 1970), p. 5.

3. Aristotle, *Rhetoric*, trans. W. Rhys Roberts (New York: Modern Library, 1954), p. 22.

4. Dan Nimmo and Keith Sanders, "Introduction: The Emergence of Political Communication as a Field," in *Handbook of Political Communication*, eds. Dan Nimmo and Keith Sanders (Beverly Hills, CA: Sage, 1981), pp. 11–36.

5. Ibid., p. 15.

6. Ibid., pp. 17–27.

7. Keith Sanders, Lynda Kaid, and Dan Nimmo, eds., *Political Communication Yearbook: 1984* (Carbondale: Southern Illinois University, 1985), pp. 283–308.

8. Dan Nimmo and David Swanson, "The Field of Political Communication: Beyond the Voter Persuasion Paradigm," in *New Directions in Political Communications*, eds. David Swanson and Dan Nimmo (Beverly Hills, CA: Sage, 1990), p. 8.

9. Sanders, Kaid, and Nimmo, *Political Communication Yearbook: 1984*, p. xiv.

10. Ibid.

11. Nimmo and Swanson, "The Field of Political Communication," p. 11.

Acknowledgments

The videostyle concept evolved over a long time, and the research necessary to carry out a project of this magnitude involved many individuals. The authors are, first and foremost, indebted to the Political Communication Center (PCC) at the University of Oklahoma for access to the Julian P. Kanter Political Commerical Archive. This archive, with its unequalled collection of political spots, was a necessary resource without which the project could not have been accomplished. In addition, many individuals served as coders, helped with the video compilations, and assisted with data analysis over the years, including Robert Gobetz, Jane Garner, Lewis Mazanti, Karen Lane DeRosa, John Hilbert, Julia Spiker, Lori Melton McKinnon, Mei-ling Yang, Steve O'Geary, Holly Hart, Yang Lin, Mike Chanslor, Cindy Roper, John Ballotti, Gary Noggle, Dolores Flamiano, and Robin Bisha. More than any single individual, John Tedesco was a constant source of ideas and constructive suggestions. Those who aided the international aspects of the project are listed in Chapter 9.

In addition to the support of the PCC, the project also acknowledges the financial assistance of the PEW Trust, Curtis Gans and the Committee for the Study of the American Electorate, and the Media Content

Analysis Consortium (coordinated by Marion Just, Wellesley College). A portion of the research for this book was supported by the National Science Foundation under award #SBR-9729450 and SBR-9412529, Lynda Lee Kaid, Principal Investigator. The Council for International Exchange of Scholars (CIES), through the Fulbright Program, also provided assistance for the international phase of the project.

The Series Editor for Political Communication at Praeger/Greenwood, Robert Denton, also deserves our appreciation; he was endlessly patient and supportive.

Anne would like to thank Richard Cole, Dean of the School of Journalism and Mass Communication at the University of North Carolina, for his support and encouragement and the school's faculty as a whole for providing a supportive and collegial environment.

Family members, other friends, and colleagues provided support and encouragement, but none deserve more appreciation than Lynda's husband, Clifford A. Jones, and Anne's son, Alex Wadsworth.

Presidential Campaign Advertising on Television

Television and politics have always been bedfellows. From the time there were enough television sets available in the homes of the public, politics has been a part of the content of daily television fare. It is not difficult to understand why politicians, officeholders and candidates alike, have found television's near-universal penetration to be irresistible.

For presidential candidates the attraction developed quickly. When television became widespread enough to justify usage (1952), candidates recognized that advertising their message via television provided several advantages over other communication modalities. First, television reached larger numbers of voters simultaneously than any other campaign channel. A message distributed via television would reach millions each time it was broadcast, an audience that far exceeded the reach of a single campaign speech or other organized event, a draw that was unmatched by traditional print media. Second, the message was under the complete control of the sponsoring candidate—no need to worry about what a heckler in the crowd might shout in protest, no concern about an opponent's response in a debate, no pesky journalist to question or doubt the candidate's words. Third, not just the message but also its form of presentation were controlled by the candidate and media specialists. If the candidate was tired or looked haggard, recording could be postponed until another day or, perhaps better yet, makeup and lighting could hide most physical flaws. Postproduction editing could eliminate slips and stutters in speech, as well as unflattering gestures or other nonverbal behaviors.

For a candidate who always aims to put the "best foot forward" rather than "in the mouth," television advertising was truly an irresistible format. This book takes as its thesis the notion that candidates develop a way of presenting themselves to voters through the television medium, a "videostyle." This method of self-presentation has three main elements: a verbal or message component, a nonverbal component, and a television production component. This book attempts to chronicle the development of this use of television videostyle in presidential campaigns and to describe and interpret the patterns that characterize candidates and their styles.

The book is organized to provide an understanding of the role that television advertising plays in presidential campaigns and elections. This first chapter proceeds with a brief overview of the history of television advertising in presidential campaigns and the regulatory environment in which it exists in the United States. The second chapter reviews earlier research on the content and style of television spots and summarizes the evidence for the effects of political spots in election campaigns. In the third chapter, we provide a discussion of the concept of and theoretical underpinnings of videostyle, as well as a description of the methods used for the analysis of videostyle in this book. The remaining chapters draw on the data gathered and used to analyze videostyle, outlining the trends in videostyle across the years as well as the differences in videostyle attributable to candidate positioning, partisan affiliation, and advertising valence (negative versus positive strategies). Ethical aspects of videostyle, particularly as related to television production techniques, and media coverage of political ads are considered in separate chapters. Additional chapters describe the application of the videostyle concept to campaigns in other countries and summarize trends in videostyle.

EARLY USE OF TELEVISION ADVERTISING IN PRESIDENTIAL CAMPAIGNS

Until the twentieth century, presidential campaigns were conducted without the use of electronic advertising on radio or television. While it now seems difficult to imagine, candidates for the "highest office in the land" had to rely on printed messages (newspaper advertising, printed posters and billboards, brochures and handbills) and the even more old-fashioned public speaking, interpersonal communication, and political party organizations to make sure their ideas reached the voting public.

These earlier forms of political promotion, as well as the early uses of radio campaigning, are described in detail by other scholars (Diamond & Bates, 1992; Jamieson, 1984). However, it was the development of visual electronic media that transformed the way candidates communicate with voters. The earliest visual medium (film) did not, of course, have the kind of universal impact that was to be the purview of television. Nonetheless, there exist early examples of the use of film for political propaganda in the archival holdings of the Political Communication Center at the University of Oklahoma, the world's largest collection of radio and television commercials from political campaigns. One of the most interesting of these early examples is "Hell Bent for Election," the short animated feature produced for Franklin Roosevelt's 1944 re-election campaign. Longer than a traditional spot, the cartoon film was sponsored by a labor union and produced by Charles (Chuck) Jones, the Warner Brothers' animator later famous for the "Roadrunner" and other popular cartoon series. The promotional film embodies many traditional symbolic devices to pit the "good" Roosevelt and his "election express" train representing progress against the "evil" Republicans with their sinister and outdated train/ideas. The film also demonstrates many now-common devices for vilifying the opponent in political advertising, including the film version of morphing.

Although film would continue for many years to be the production medium of choice for much of television, in the 1950s the airwaves became the delivery mechanism by which politicians presented their messages to the voters. The first television commercials for political candidates were aired during the 1950 election cycle in a state race (Kaid, Haynes, & Rand, 1996). However, the 1952 presidential campaign of Dwight D. Eisenhower was the first to use television spots as an important aspect of the candidate's campaigning style.

Much of the credit for Eisenhower's strategic use of campaign spots goes to commercial advertising executive Rosser Reeves. A Madison Avenue guru who recognized television's potential for selling products like Anacin and M&Ms, Reeves also saw the possibilities raised by television for selling political candidates (Diamond & Bates, 1992; Wood, 1990) and devised a series of short, simple spots for Eisenhower. Labeled the "Eisenhower Answers America" series, these spots used a question-and-answer format in which Eisenhower is shown briefly answering a question put to him by one or more members of the public. A few longer spots varied this format by including war footage and pictures of Eisenhower meeting with European leaders during wartime. One such spot proclaimed Eisenhower the "Man from Abilene."

However, the best-known spot from the campaign was not produced in this manner by Reeves or anyone else on Madison Avenue. For the 1952 Eisenhower television effort, Walt Disney Studios produced and donated the only political commercial ever done by the Disney animators, an animated jingle often called the "I Like Ike" commercial, in reference to the repeated refrain of the background song. While no elaborate studies validate the effectiveness of this first presidential spot campaign, many observers believe the spots were instrumental in creating a warm and caring image for Eisenhower, softening his earlier reputation as a cold, military figure.

Eisenhower's opponent in the 1952 campaign was the Democratic nominee, Adlai Stevenson of Illinois. Stevenson did not particularly approve of "selling candidates like soap" and was reluctant to delegate his campaigning to television directors and producers. The Stevenson campaign chose not to fight Eisenhower on the airwaves, producing few spots for national distribution. The Illinois Democratic Party produced several musical and animated spots on behalf of the Stevenson campaign, but these did not receive national airtime.

The 1956 campaign was another Eisenhower-Stevenson matchup, but this time Stevenson decided to give television more of a chance. His campaign produced a series of spots to counter the claims of the "Man from Abilene." In Stevenson's "Man from Libertyville" spots, the former Illinois governor is seen talking from his home surrounded by books, helping his daughter-in-law with the grocery shopping, and talking foreign policy with Senator John F. Kennedy.

While most of Eisenhower's spots and the few produced by Stevenson in 1952 tended to be short spots, many only 20 seconds in length, the advertising of both parties in 1956 made extensive use of formats now considered very long, the 5-minute ad. But neither the longer format, the appearance of the candidate himself (as was the case in most Eisenhower 1952 spots), nor nostalgia for the television of yesteryear should fool anyone into thinking these spots were all positive, upbeat spots focused on the candidate's own ideas. In fact, as the data reveal in later chapters of this book, these spot campaigns were among the most negative in the history of American presidential campaigns.

In the 1960 presidential campaign, there was no hesitation on either side; both Democratic nominee John F. Kennedy and Vice-President Richard M. Nixon embraced television enthusiastically. In addition to the significance of the first series of television candidate debates (Kraus, 1962), both candidates produced an unprecedented number of spots of varying lengths and formats. Because there were so many more spots produced and used in this campaign (a combined total or more than 100 different ones), the potential for more and varied approaches was realized. Although not typical of the Kennedy spot arsenal that often featured the candidate speaking head-on in straightforward issue statements, the best-known Kennedy spot is a jingle spot in which the video appears animated (in fact, it is a form of pixillation) and consists mostly of signs with the Kennedy name and occasional still pictures, including Kennedy photos. There is no audio message other than a song under the video, which constantly repeats the Kennedy name: "Kennedy, Kennedy, Kennedy, Kennedy, Kennedy, Kennedy, Kennedy. Ken-ne-dy for me. Kennedy, Kennedy, Kennedy, Kennedy. Do you want a man for President who's seasoned through and through, but not so doggone seasoned that he won't try something new? A man who's old enough to know and young enough to do? Well, it's up to you, it's up to you, it's strictly up to you. Do you like a man who answers straight, a man who's always fair? We'll measure him against the others and when you compare, you'll cast your vote for Kennedy and the change that's overdue. So, it's up to you, it's up to you, it's strictly up to you. Kennedy, Kennedy, Kennedy, Kennedy, Kennedy, Kennedy, Kennedy for me. Kennedy, Kennedy, Kennedy, Kennedy . . . Kennedy!" People who see this spot today and are told that it is a classic "name identification spot," a spot designed to get the candidate's name out and remembered by the voters, are puzzled. They wonder why John Kennedy needed such a spot, forgetting, of course, that at this point in American history John Kennedy was a relatively unknown senator from Massachusetts.

Richard Nixon's spots in 1960 are a bit like his often-criticized television debate performance, high on substance but low on style and charisma. Many featured his foreign policy experience and tried to capitalize on the popularity of his running mate, Henry Cabot Lodge.

The 1964 campaign is often characterized as a watershed year in presidential campaign advertising because of its negativity. Incumbent president Lyndon B. Johnson did indeed embark on an ad campaign that attempted to vilify Barry Goldwater for everything from injudicious use of nuclear weapons to destruction of Social Security. The ads also marked the first time in which the candidate himself was virtually absent from the ad campaign. Although his voice is often heard as a voice-over on the video of a commercial, Johnson himself rarely appears in the 1964 ads. The most famous ad from this campaign is well known to scholars and political observers as the "Daisy Girl" spot. In it, a small girl counts as she picks the petals from a daisy; in the background a countdown is heard, and the camera zeroes in on the child's eye just as the countdown ends and a nuclear explosion occurs with the appearance of a mushroom cloud. The voice-over by Johnson says, "These are the stakes: to make a world in which all of God's children can live or to go into the darkness. We must either love each other or we must die." Only broadcast one time, on September 7, 1964, during NBC's *Monday Night at the Movies*, this spot is the most famous ad ever created for a political campaign at any level. By many standards, it also deserves the label of "infamous" (West, 1993, p. 65). The spot, although it does not use opponent Barry Goldwater's name, conjures up all manner of negative associations about Goldwater and what "he might do," seeming to validate the concerns of those who often changed Goldwater's campaign slogan, "In your heart, you know he's right," to "In your heart, you know he might." Despite producer Tony Schwartz's defense of the ad (Schwartz, 1973), the spot is a classic "fear appeal," designed to rely on emotion, not logic or rationality, in eliciting the "responsive chord" in voters that Schwartz believes all advertising must tap to be successful.

Unlike Johnson, Barry Goldwater chose to appear in many of his advertising messages, often long, 30-minute programs in which he expounded on his views and elaborated on his concern about morality issues. Also unlike the Johnson ad campaign, which expunged mention of the vice-presidential candidate, Hubert Humphrey; Barry Goldwater often referred to his running mate, Bill Miller, in his speeches and ads. Ironically, it was not Barry Goldwater's own appearances that would be remembered from his advertising campaigns; few can recall any particularly memorable spots. However, it was the outstanding performance by a celebrity endorser that would capture the attention of many political observers. In his first political appearances on television, actor Ronald Reagan gave stirring and convincing testimonials in defense of Goldwater and his intentions. In one ad, Reagan proclaims:

> I asked to speak to you because I'm mad. I've known Barry Goldwater for a long time. And when I hear people say he's impulsive and such nonsense, I boil over. Believe me, if it weren't for Barry keeping those boys in Washington on their toes, do you honestly think our national defense would be as strong as it is? And remember, when Barry talks about the way to keep the peace, when he says that only the strong can remain free, he knows what he's talking about. And I know the wonderful Goldwater family. Do you honestly believe that Barry wants his sons and daughters involved in a war? Do you think he wants his wife to be a wartime mother? Of course not. So join me, won't you, let's get a real leader, and not a power politician in the White House. Vote for Barry Goldwater.

So impressed with Reagan's performance were political leaders in the Republican Party that in 1966 he ran for and was elected governor of California and went on to star in his own presidential spots in 1980 and 1984.

By 1968 television advertising in presidential campaigns had become commonplace and an essential part of any campaign. It was unthinkable for any presidential candidate, however uncomfortable he might be with the medium, to shun the use of political television advertising. And so it has gone to the present, with television spots occupying an ever-increasing percentage of presidential campaign budgets.

THE COST OF CAMPAIGN ADVERTISING IN PRESIDENTIAL CONTESTS

One mark of how significant political advertising on television has become is the amount of money spent on it in each successive presidential election cycle. There are no completely accurate figures available on advertising expenditures in the earliest campaigns, but even the most liberal estimates would put presidential television advertising expenditures for both parties at a few million dollars. By 1964 the combined total for Republican and Democratic candidates had grown to $11 million, and by 1980 even that amount had tripled, to over $34 million (Alexander, 1983).

The most recent campaigns have been the most expensive, of course. In 1988 Michael Dukakis and George Bush spent a combined $65 million for radio and television advertising, supplemented by an additional $14 million from the Republican National Committee (RNC) and Democratic National Committee (DNC) and millions more from state parties (Devlin, 1989). The 1992 campaign saw even higher spending levels, with George Bush spending $48.8 million on ads (including $10.3 from the RNC) and Bill Clinton spending $35 million (including $9 million from the DNC) (Devlin, 1993). In addition, 1992 was a particularly expensive year because a viable third-party candidate, Ross Perot, did not take federal matching funds and instead spent his own money, including over $40 million for advertising on television (Devlin, 1993). The 1996 campaign proved even more expensive, partly because of the increased spending by the national parties on behalf of their presidential nominees. Bill Clinton spent $44 million in general election advertising, which followed $12 million in primary spending (although he had no opponent) and $42.2 million in post-primary/pre–general election spending by the DNC on his behalf, for total ad spending of over $98 million (Devlin, 1997). Bob Dole, on the other hand, spent a combined total of only $78.2 million in the primary and general election phases, including RNC money spent on his behalf (Devlin, 1997).

REGULATORY ENVIRONMENT OF POLITICAL TELEVISION ADVERTISING

One of the aspects of political advertising that seems the most troubling to many observers, even unbelievable to foreign observers of the

American system, is the basically unregulated nature of political television advertising. Political advertising in the United States operates under very few restrictions of any kind. Regulations that do exist fall into three basic categories: (1) spending limits on general campaign expenditures determined by the Federal Election Commission (FEC), (2) broadcast regulation rules for the sale/purchase of equal time according to the Access and Equal Time Provisions (312a&b) of the Federal Communication Act, as enforced by the Federal Communication Commission (FCC), and (3) statutory or case law that relates to advertising content.

Spending Limits

The first major campaign regulation law in the United States, the Federal Election Campaign Act (FECA) of 1971 (revised in 1974), set limits on the amount of contributions that individuals ($1,000 per candidate per election, with primary and general elections treated as separate elections) and multiparty committees or PACs ($5,000 per candidate per election) could give to political candidates. The original 1971 act tried to set limits in cents per voter on the amount of funds that could be spent on advertising, but this provision was eliminated as unworkable in subsequent revisions. Consequently, the law as it is now in place sets no limit on the amount of funds a presidential candidate may spend for television advertising. However, a candidate who agrees to take matching funds from the FEC must adhere to an overall spending limit for the campaign. This amount is set by the FEC for each presidential election. The limit does not include so-called soft money (money spent on behalf of a candidate by the candidate's political party organization or other such groups).

Independent expenditures (expenditures spent by an individual or non-campaign group on behalf of a candidate) are also not included in the federal spending limit, and the Supreme Court has ruled that there can be no regulation of or limitations on such spending (*Buckley v. Valeo*, 1976). If a candidate does not agree to accept federal matching funds, preferring instead to spend his or her own money or money raised directly by the campaign, he or she does not have to adhere to the federal spending limit set by the FEC. This was the case for Ross Perot's 1992 campaign, for instance, when Perot shunned federal funds in favor of using his own personal fortune.

It is important to note that this overall spending limit only indirectly influences advertising expenditures. A candidate could, in theory, spend all of the amount set by the federal limit and provided as matching funds on television advertising. In reality, most recent campaigns have spent well over half and sometimes over 75% of their total expenditure limit on electronic advertising (Devlin, 1989, 1993, 1997).

The federal regulations under the FECA law regulate campaign content in only one substantial way. The law requires that any communication advocating the election or defeat of a candidate through media (broadcast, billboard, newspaper, etc.) must state whether it is authorized or not authorized by the candidate and name the committee that financed it.

Broadcasting Regulations and Political Advertising

The Federal Communication Commission (FCC) administers the Federal Communication Act (FCA) of 1934 (and revisions), which requires under its access provision (312a) that a licensed broadcast station must provide reasonable access to or permit purchase of a reasonable amount of time for the use of the station by all legally qualified candidates for *federal* elective office (National Association of Broadcasters, 1988). The term "use" is defined as meaning that the candidate must appear on the air (in television this can be by picture or by voice or both). This requirement can be satisfied by the candidate being "readily identifiable to a substantial degree by the listening or viewing audience." Consequently, it is not necessary for the candidate to appear or play any substantial role in the commercial.

In addition, the FCA requires that in allocating time (or allowing its purchase) for candidates stations must adhere to the Equal Time Provision (312b), providing essentially equal-time access to all candidates. Stations must also sell this time at what is called "the lowest unit rate." This requirement, which is very unpopular with broadcasters, requires that the station must sell the advertising time to candidates at the lowest rate it has charged other commercial advertisers during the preceding 45 days, even if that rate is part of a discounted package rate.

Reinforcing the FECA requirement for sponsor identification in ads, the FCC also requires that political ads carry a "disclaimer" indicating the sponsoring entity. However, in administering the FCA, the FCC allows no station censorship of the content of political advertising. Although many stations have tried to gain exceptions to this principle, the FCC and the courts have generally held firm on this point, maintaining that the First Amendment to the Constitution prohibits any restraint on the content or format of political speech. For this reason, stations themselves are held to be exempt from any claim of libel or slander arising from an advertisement broadcast on their station.

Curbs on False or Misleading Content

The U.S. legal system permits virtually no limitations on political advertising content, primarily because of the fear of conflict with the

First Amendment guarantee of free speech. Although occasional objections have been raised to political advertising content on the grounds that the content itself is objectionable (as in the use of explicit abortion videos) or that the content makes a false claim about a sponsoring candidate's own qualifications (e.g., claiming a college degree where none exists), most concerns about political content have arisen out of attack advertising in which an opponent claims that the sponsoring candidate has made false or misleading statements about the opponent. Since so many laws explicitly or implicitly prohibit any regulation of political content, the only recourse most candidates have against false or misleading claims is to pursue action under libel laws. However, the courts set rigorous standards for proving libel for public figures, as candidates are generally interpreted to be. The attacked candidate must prove that the charge made against him or her was indeed malicious (i.e., knowingly false or with reckless disregard for the truth) in order to win such a suit (Albert, 1986). While such procedures offer legal remedies for extreme cases where the stringent burden of proof can be met, the judicial system is generally a slow and cumbersome remedy, the outcome of which cannot be expected to culminate in time to affect directly the outcome of electoral contests (Albert, 1986; Winsbro, 1987).

Laws in some individual states also prohibit candidates from making false or deceptive claims. These laws offer some protection against false affirmative claims by a candidate as well as false accusations against an opponent. For instance, Ohio has a detailed code that prohibits false claims of incumbency, untruthful qualifications (such as earned degrees or occupations), false endorsements, and false statements about voting records (Winsbro, 1987). These laws offer some hope for false advertising claims. While there will always be difficulty in distinguishing between truth and falsity (partly because of the difficulty in differentiating fact and opinion in a legal sense), the courts at all levels have usually been contemptuous of anyone who attempts to argue that false claims must be heard on free speech grounds. For instance, in *Gertz v. Robert Welch, Inc.* (1974) the court said "there is no constitutional value in false statements of fact."

Interestingly, the general public is quite naive about the protections enjoyed by political broadcast speech. A survey by Lang and Krueger (1993) found that most people incorrectly believe the government and broadcasters have the right to step in and prohibit politicians from running false or misleading ads.

The inability to regulate advertising content in political campaigns continues to trouble candidates, political interest groups like Common Cause, and concerned journalists. Such concerns have even led to arguments that political advertising should be regulated as product advertising is, according to "truth in advertising" standards applied by the Federal Trade Commission (Spero, 1980).

This continuing concern about false and misleading claims and the difficulty of regulating them under First Amendment strictures has led to other attempts to affect a candidate's "videostyle." While candidates once had free rein in what they said about themselves and their opponents, watchdog groups now scrutinize political spots, and newspaper and television journalists have begun to do "adwatches" as a way of curbing false and misleading spots (Broder, 1989). These attempts at informal regulation have reached new heights in the last three presidential campaign cycles (since 1988 in particular) and now have an impact on what candidates say and do in their television advertising.

2

Political Advertising Content and Effects

Presidential candidates face a daunting communication challenge. They must get their messages out to millions of eligible voters. This task is made more difficult by the fact that the communication is not one-sided. Each candidate seeks to shape voter impressions of both his or her own qualities and policy positions and those of the opposing candidate or candidates. The candidate does this, knowing that the opponent must seek to do exactly the same. Others seek to influence this communication dialogue as well. Journalists, interest groups, business and union associations, and all kinds of other specialized voices seek to have their own chance to communicate with voters and to influence their choices.

In this competition for the attention of the voter, television does not offer any candidate a unique channel, since all the competitors have access to television. What television does offer is the unique opportunity for a candidate to communicate his or her own personal style directly to voters in a format viewed by millions simultaneously. In a national campaign, no matter how hard the candidate works, no matter how many rallies are scheduled in how many states, the candidate can meet very few voters in person. Television, more than any other medium of mass communication, has offered the candidate a way to make every voter feel that he or she has personal knowledge of the candidate. As Alexander (1972) said over twenty-five years ago, "Television has bred a feeling of intimacy between voter and public official, an intimacy which has led voters to trust their own impressions of candidates rather than rely on the impressions of outside commentators" (p. 371). Voters can come to feel that they know as much about a presidential candidate, for better or for worse, as they do about the protagonists in their favorite situation comedy or the heroes of the police drama they watch each week.

Since television gives the voter a chance to see candidates in action and to get a feel for their style, it "has become the surrogate party worker, the vehicle for conveying candidate style, image, and issues" (Agranoff, 1976, p. 5). Some observers argue that the voting public can know nothing about a presidential candidate but what is experienced through television.

A presidential candidate from one of the two major political parties in the United States rarely lacks for media attention. However, only paid advertising provides the chance to make the communication link with the voter directly and in an unfiltered way. Political television ads can perform many functions for a presidential candidate (Sabato, 1981). Political television spots can help an unknown candidate become better known. In 1976, Jimmy Carter remained "Jimmy Who?" to many people until media coverage and television spots brought him into their own living rooms and made his name, his face, and his halting Southern drawl familiar.

Political spots can also help a candidate make his issue positions better known to the public. John Kennedy in 1960 made his issue positions known and placed himself squarely in the center of Democratic Party policy by concentrating a number of his spots on simple issues such as medical care and Social Security. Ross Perot tried to do the same in his famous "infomercial" format and gave the country lessons in economic and fiscal policy at the same time.

Ads can also allow a candidate to define or redefine his image and personal traits. Richard Nixon completely remade his image in 1968 through the use of commercials in which he almost never appeared but in which still and moving images were combined with his voice to give the impression of someone who cared about Vietnam and crime. Candidates can also use ads to convey a sense of belonging to and caring about specialized groups of citizens. In 1972 George McGovern's spots showed him in live interactions with factory workers and the elderly to communicate that he cared about these groups. In some spots this has extended to the production of spots in the Spanish language to attract voters with Hispanic heritage. President Bill Clinton used some spots with Spanish voice-overs in his 1996 re-election campaign, but the classic example must be the 1960 Kennedy spot in which an uncomfortable Jacqueline Kennedy does her best to pronounce the words of a scripted speech in Spanish. Of course, campaign spots can also perform many of these same functions in a negative way—that is, they can spell out the unpopular issue positions, the unflattering image characteristics, and the association with unpopular groups of the opponent.

Spots can also perform other less obvious functions for a candidate. Television commercials for a candidate can generate enthusiasm for a campaign, giving voters a sense of action and movement and inviting them to join the bandwagon. For political party and campaign workers and volunteers, the spots can also provide a sense of pride and reinforcement in their choice (Sheinkopf, Atkin, & Bowen, 1972, 1973).

With so many possible functions for spots during a campaign, it is important to understand more about how candidates present themselves through televised spots and how such spots really affect the voting public.

How presidential candidates present themselves on television, each candidate's videostyle, is difficult to evaluate or describe without understanding the overall findings on political advertising content and effects. While political commercials have been a part of campaigns for five decades, early analyses of political spot advertising were basically critical/interpretive and anecdotal. Like the later, more comprehensive historical overviews (Diamond & Bates, 1984, 1988, 1992; Jamieson, 1984, 1992b, 1996), early discussions centered around describing the context and situational aspects of the campaign and the content of commercials, attributing patterns or trends and effects on the basis of observer opinions or scholars' speculations. However, in the 1970s academic researchers began to explore the content and effects of political television advertising more systematically. These researchers began to discover and describe concrete patterns and effects in television advertising.

As social scientists in the 1970s began to break away from the pessimistic media-effects prescriptions of the "limited effects" model (Klapper, 1960), many discovered that the principles accepted by minimal-effects researchers did not apply as strongly to political television advertising as to other mass media phenomena. Even by 1981, when the first comprehensive review of the literature on political advertising (Kaid, 1981) was published in the *Handbook of Political Communication*, it was possible to say that researchers had discovered that political advertising had identifiable cognitive, affective, and behavioral effects.

The current body of literature on political television advertising falls into two basic areas, research on the content of the advertising and research on the various effects of the advertising.

POLITICAL TELEVISION ADVERTISING CONTENT

Systematic studies of the content of political spots are related directly to the study of videostyle because they seek to establish trends and patterns in the information contained in and conveyed by political advertising. Studies of advertising content from political campaigns have, however, been hampered by the difficulty of obtaining comprehensive samples of political spots for analysis. The first attempt at systematic analysis of spots across more than one campaign was undertaken by Richard Joslyn (1980), who was forced to rely on a "convenience" sample of 156 ads obtained from a media consultant and a private collector. Subsequent studies have often relied on more specific and specially constructed samples (for instance, women candidates or particular types of elections). More-comprehensive sampling has become possible since the establishment of the University of Oklahoma's Political Commercial Archive. Located in the university's Political Communication Center, this archive is the world's largest collection of radio and television spots from political campaigns, containing over 66,000 items (Kaid, Haynes, & Rand, 1996).

Studies of the content of televised political advertising are dominated by several key concerns about advertising content: (1) issue versus image content, (2) negative versus positive content, and (3) various other content considerations. The following sections address the research on these points. It should be noted, however, that the following analysis does not attempt to include content analyses that are intended to highlight differences based on candidate characteristics such as gender, nor is attention given to political spots in non-candidate issue or referendum campaigns.

Issues versus Images

No topic has been more dominant across the five decades of research on political advertising than the discussion of whether or not campaign commercials are dominated by image information or by issue information. This concern, of course, is rooted in the classic democratic voting model that insists rational voting decisions should be made on the basis of policy issues (Berelson, 1966), not on the basis of a candidate's image. One of the perennial criticisms of television advertising in politics is that it trivializes political discourse by concentrating more on candidate personalities and images than on issues. This has proven to be an unfounded concern, since research has shown that most ads, usually between 60% and 80% of them, concentrate more often on issues than on candidate images (Joslyn, 1980). Patterson and McClure's (1976) classic study of the 1972 presidential campaign found not only that issue information overshadowed image content but that the issue content of political spots outweighed the issue content of television network news during the campaign. Other work confirmed this finding in regard to the 1972 presidential race (Hofstetter & Zukin, 1979), and Kern (1989) reinforced these findings in her studies of spots in the 1980s. Findings on the last three presidential campaigns have also substantiated that issues are more frequently stressed in spots than are images (Kaid, 1991a, 1994, 1998). In analyses of the 1996 primaries, researchers have also discovered that candidate messages (advertising and speeches) were giving substantial attention to issues and were definitely more issue substantive by a margin of 3:1 than television news (Lichter & Noyes, 1996; Center for Media and Public Affairs, 1996).

Other studies at varying levels of races have found that issue content is predominant over image content in political television spots (Elebash & Rosene, 1982; Latimer, 1984), although some researchers have found that candidates for lower level races rely on a substantial amount of personal appeals in their spots. Typical of these findings are those by Latimer (1989a, 1989b), who found that Alabama state legislative candidates focused on image traits in their spots.

While this research debunks the notion that political television spots are dominated by image information, it is important to note that the concentration on issues does not always mean that candidates are providing substantial arguments or explaining complex policy issues. Even Joslyn's early analysis of spots indicated that the percentage of spots with specific policy issue information was much lower than the overall number of issue spots (Joslyn, 1980). In a later analysis of 500 spots from 1960 to 1984, Joslyn (1986) found that ads focusing on prospective policy choices were the least frequently occurring type. Payne, Marlier, and Baukus (1989) reinforced this notion in their analysis of 1988 presidential primary spots when they concluded that issues are treated more in the form of vague policy preferences and that spots are replete with emotional and cultural images and symbols. Darrell West (1993) analyzed sets of typical and prominent spots across a number of years and was equally critical of the lack of substantive, specific policy positioning by candidates, although he noted that spots have become more, not less, policy oriented in recent presidential elections.

One of the best-developed studies of issue and image content in political spots was conducted on the 1980 presidential primary spots by Leonard Shyles (1983, 1984a, 1984b). Shyles found a strong emphasis on defense and foreign policy in the 1980 primary ads. He also found that candidates in the presidential primaries used the spots to convey their image characteristics and that the choice of issue or image content also related to the presentational style of the spots (Shyles, 1984b). For instance, spots that focused on the candidate's image tended to be head-on candidate presentations with candidates in formal attire. A similar content analysis of the 1984 campaign spots found that the verbal portions of ads focused on candidate qualities such as competence, experience, and honesty.

Researchers have also noted the increasing difficulty in distinguishing between issues and images in campaign messages. Traditionally, issues have been viewed as statements of candidate positions on policy issues or preferences on issues or problems of public concern, while images have been viewed as the concentration on candidate qualities or characteristics (Kaid & Johnston, 1991; Kaid & Sanders, 1978). Many researchers acknowledge that this dichotomy is, in fact, a false one. As Rudd (1986) pointed out in his observation of spots from the 1982 Idaho gubernatorial campaign, issue spots are often used to bolster aspects of a candidate's image.

Negative versus Positive Ads

The controversy over negative and positive spots has raged most forcefully in the past two decades. Many media analysts seem to have "discovered" negative spots only in the 1980s, but analyses of spots over time indicate that negative spots have been a factor in all presidential campaigns (Kaid & Johnston, 1991). Johnson-Cartee and Copeland (1991, 1997) have also done a great deal to enhance our understanding of negative spots in their books, which categorize and analyze the strategies used in a wide variety of negative ads.

One of the clear findings about negative ads is that they tend to be more issue-oriented than do positive ads. Kaid and Johnston (1991) reached this conclusion from a study of over 800 presidential ads aired between 1960 and 1988. West (1993) concurred in his content analysis of typical and prominent ads: "It is somewhat surprising to discover that the most substantive appeals actually came in negative ads" (p. 51).

Other Content Considerations

Some researchers have been concerned about the types of claims and arguments used in political spots. In an analysis of logical claims in 1972 Nixon and McGovern ads, Buss and Hofstetter (1976) found that the use of logical fallacies was not a dominant strategy; instead, ads used cognitive maneuvers to identify issue stands or information about the candidate. On the other hand, Baukus, Payne, and Reisler (1985) have suggested that the arguments contained in spots are often so abbreviated that they are misleading and difficult to prove.

One of the most interesting aspects of spot analysis has been the determination of varying styles of spots associated with candidate and electoral position. For instance, in their original development of the videostyle concept, Kaid and Davidson (1986) identified differences in videostyles attributed to incumbents versus challengers in U.S. Senate races. Tinkham and Weaver-Lariscy (1995) have also determined that in 1982 and 1990 congressional ads incumbency was not a factor in using issue or image ads but did relate to negative attack ad usage. Futher consideration of these issues for presidential campaigns is contained in a later chapter of this book.

Another area that has been addressed with content analysis has been the ethical content of ads, although this is a difficult area for assessment (Kaid, 1991b). While some observers find the content of political spots so objectionable that they should be eliminated or at least severely regulated (Sinclair, 1995; Winsbro, 1987), others have simply analyzed the content of ads to determine what factors might contribute to false or misleading impressions. The only systematic content of ethical content in ads has focused on the technological distortions in the ads (Kaid, 1996) and is covered in more detail in a later chapter.

Finally, videostyle research has been concerned with the nonverbal and production aspects of spots, as well as with the verbal content. The analysis of prior work on these aspects of spots is reserved for the next chapter.

EFFECTS OF SPOTS ON VOTERS

There would be very little reason for analyzing spot content or for assessing patterns in videostyle if there were no evidence that political spots have identifiable effects on voters. Such evidence is not difficult to find, confirming that candidates who spend millions on advertising campaigns are not completely off the mark. Most of the effects studies rely on survey research or experimental designs to measure the effects of spots. The best-researched of these effects fall into three categories: (1) effects on voter knowledge levels, (2) effects on voter perceptions of candidates, and (3) effects on voting preferences.

Effects on Knowledge Levels

The American voter is not considered to be particularly well in-formed. Studies abound verifying that many cannot name their current congressperson, let alone the candidates for upcoming offices or the issues at stake in various electoral contests. Certainly the minimal effects tradition, with its emphasis on the significance of selective processes in thwarting media effects, had lowered expectations about the possibility that political advertising would be successful in communicating information to voters.

Nonetheless, this was one of the earliest surprises in political advertising research. Political television commercials do, in fact, do a good job of communicating information, especially issue information, to voters. One of the earliest research findings about political advertising was its ability to overcome selective exposure (Atkin, Bowen, Nayman, & Sheinkopf, 1973; Surlin & Gordon, 1976). This was a very important finding because it confirmed that spot advertising was successful in getting the candidate's message to all voters, not just those who already supported the candidate or party.

Subsequent research provided evidence that exposure to political spots affected candidate-name recognition (Kaid, 1982). In fact, in a study of the 1992 California U.S. Senate races, West (1994) found paid advertising exposure to be a better predictor of candidate recognition than either television news or newspapers.

A great deal of evidence now supports the claim that exposure to political ads can also influence voter recall about campaign issues and candidate issue positions (Atkin & Heald, 1976; Martinelli & Chaffee, 1995; Zhao & Bleske, 1995). Although Faber and Storey (1984) report that voters recall of political spots in the 1982 Texas gubernatorial race was only 34%, the split in the information they did recall was evenly distributed between issues and image information. Certainly, others have found that there are differences in the types and levels of information recalled from spots and that the type of information recalled can be structured somewhat by what viewers are cognitively attuned to or "seeking" from the ads (Garramone, 1983, 1986). The type of ad can also affect voter recall levels, with some research showing that image ads can produce greater recall of information (Kaid & Sanders, 1978), particularly when a candidate is less well known (Schleuder, 1990). However, negative ads generally produce higher levels of recall than positive ones (Basil, Schooler, & Reeves, 1991; Johnson-Cartee & Copeland, 1989; Lang, 1991; Newhagen & Reeves, 1991).

In fact, voters learn more about issues from television ads than from television news (Kern & Just, 1995; McClure & Patterson, 1974; Patterson & McClure, 1976) and more even than from televised debates (Just, Crigler, & Wallach, 1990), although more recent multivariate analyses suggest that television news is sometimes a better predictor of overall information acquisition in political campaigns (Zhao & Bleske, 1995; Zhao & Chaffee, 1995).

Receiver characteristics can also affect ad recall. Early research posited the notion that voters with low levels of campaign involvement were most likely to be affected by political spots (Rothschild & Ray, 1974), as are undecided voters and late deciders (Bowen, 1994).

Agenda-setting theory has also played a role in understanding the cognitive effects of political advertising. The issue content of ads has been shown to affect judgments of ad salience for voters (Bowers, 1977; Ghorpade, 1986; West, 1993; Williams, Shapiro & Cutbirth, 1983) and to affect the news agendas of media outlets (Roberts & McCombs,1994; Schleuder, McCombs, & Wanta, 1991).

Of course, findings about types and valence of ads and their content relationships to information recall about candidates and their campaigns relate directly to the study of videostyle, helping to explain the effectiveness of some strategies over others. Researchers have also demonstrated that the structure and design of ads can affect recall (Lang, 1991; Lang & Lanfear, 1990). Researchers also have shown that emotional aspects of a political ad can affect viewer recall (Lang, 1991). The presence of music in an ad can affect visual recall (Thorson, Christ, & Caywood, 1991a), and an ad's visual structure can affect content recall and candidate evaluation (Geiger & Reeves, 1991).

Effects on Candidate Evaluations

One of the most frequently confirmed effects of television spot exposure, in both experimental and survey research settings, has been the finding that exposure to political spots can affect a candidate's image evaluation (Atkin & Heald, 1976; Becker & Doolittle, 1975; Cundy, 1986, 1990; Hofstetter, Zukin, & Buss, 1978; Kaid, 1991a, 1994, 1997, 1998; Kaid & Chanslor, 1995; Kaid, Leland, & Whitney, 1992). Some of the most convincing evidence for the effects of spot viewing on candidate perceptions comes from multivariate analysis. West (1993) analyzed survey and voting data from 1972-1992, finding that (controlling for demographic variables such as political party, education, gender) seeing a candidate's ads still had a significant impact on judgments of candidate likability and information on candidate issues and traits.

As with the recall of spots, the type of spot may be related to the effect on candidate image evaluation. For instance, issue ads seem to be particularly effective in raising a candidate's image ratings (Kaid, Chanslor, & Hovind, 1992; Kaid & Sanders, 1978; Thorson, Christ, & Caywood, 1991a, 1991b). Viewer predispositions also can affect evaluations of candidates as a result of spot exposure (Donohue, 1973; Meyer & Donohue, 1973).

Usually, the effects of spots on candidate images have been in a positive direction, but sometimes the results have shown that the effects can also be negative, particularly as a result of spots attacking the opponent (Kaid & Boydston, 1987; West, 1994). Although a few studies have not found strong effects of spots on candidate evaluations (Meadow & Sigelman, 1982), others have found that the effects are often mixed. For instance, in a study of the 1992 California Senate races, West (1994) found that exposure to spots did not have a uniform effect on the candidates; some candidates' favorability ratings were not affected at all, and sometimes the effect was positive from exposure to the candidate's own ads and sometimes negative as a result of exposure to the opponent's attack ads.

In fact, there is now a substantial body of research that specifically addresses the effects on candidate images and voting behavior from exposure to negative or attack ads or comparing negative ad exposure to positive ad exposure. Early research suggested that those with low information-seeking habits were more likely to accept and be influenced by negative ads (Surlin & Gordon, 1977). Findings from experimental studies have suggested that positive ads are more effective than negative or comparative ads at affecting attitudes toward candidates (Hill, 1989; Kahn & Geer, 1994).

It should be noted that this does not mean that negative ads have proven ineffective, only that some experimental studies show them to be less effective than positive spots. One of the reasons negative ads have not proven as effective in some studies is that negative ads can produce a backlash effect on the image of the candidate sponsoring the ad (Garramone, 1984a; Merritt, 1984), but third-party or independent sponsorship can offset this problem (Garramone, 1984a, 1985; Garramone & Smith, 1984). Attacks that focus on the opposing candidate's issue positions are more effective than those attacking the character or image of the opponent (Kahn & Geer, 1994; Pfau & Burgoon, 1989; Roddy & Garramone, 1988). For a candidate who is the target of negative attack spots, rebuttals have proven helpful in blunting the effects of an attack (Garramone, 1985; Roddy & Garramone, 1988), and inoculation can also provide some advance protection against the effectiveness of opponent attacks (Pfau & Burgoon, 1988; Pfau & Kenski, 1990).

Effects on Voter Preferences and Behavior

There is also strong evidence that political television spots have behavioral effects. The most obvious of these are effects on voting decisions. Such effects have often been found in experimental and survey studies (Cundy, 1986; Kaid & Sanders, 1978; Mulder, 1979), and the effects seem to be especially strong for late deciders (Bowen, 1994). Hofstetter and Buss (1980) found that exposure to last-minute paid advertising was associated with late changes in vote decisions and ticket splitting. In his study of the 1992 California Senate races, West (1994) identified some effects of exposure to ads on vote preference for Barbara Boxer, but all other candidates were not similarly affected.

As with recall and image formation, receiver variables seem to play a role in advertising effects on voting behavior. Early studies suggested that the voting decisions of low-involvement voters were more easily affected by political ads (Rothschild & Ray, 1974). However, in the 1988 Minnesota Senate race, Faber, Tims, and Schmitt (1993) found that higher levels of enduring and situational involvement, as well as attention to television news, resulted in greater effects of negative ads on vote preference. In fact, many of the studies that have measured negative ad effects on recall and candidate image have also identified effects on voting behavior, leading to a clear conclusion that negative ads do affect voting preferences (Ansolabehere & Iyengar, 1995; Basil, Schooler, & Reeves, 1991; Roddy & Garramone, 1988).

The context in which ads are shown can also affect vote likelihood. For instance, negative ads are particularly likely to affect vote decisions when shown in a news environment (Kaid, Chanslor, & Hovind, 1992).

There has also been concern that political television spots may affect voter behavior in another way, other than actual voting decisions. Some have suggested that the voter negativity toward negative ads may turn voters off from voting at all, thus lowering turnout. The most publicized findings in this regard are those of Ansolabehere and Iyengar (1995), who suggest that exposure to negative ads reduces voter turnout by 5% (Ansolabehere & Iyengar, 1995; Ansolabehere, Iyengar, Simon, & Valentino, 1994). However, other studies have found little relationship between exposure to negative ads and intention to vote or lower levels of trust in government (Garramone, Atkin, Pinkleton, & Cole, 1990; Martinez & Delegal, 1990). Nonetheless, this concern continues to be a salient one, heightened by the high negativity and low voter turnout in the 1996 presidential campaign. New findings reported from that election indicate that exposure to Clinton and Dole spots increased levels of voter cynicism (Kaid, McKinney, & Tedesco, 2000), and Schenck-Hamlin, Procter, and Rumsey (2000) have found that exposure to negative "theme" ads may enhance cynicism by causing voters to hold politicians more responsible for the country's ills.

Political Advertising Effects in the Context of Voter Decisions

Overall, there is no question that political television spots have proven to be an effective tool for candidates at all levels. While this review has not attempted to break out all of the individual effects of spots, it has also made it clear that different types of spots may have different types of effects. Some spots are more effective at eliciting recall of information and providing voters with some idea of the salience of candidate issue positions. Other types of spots can build and sustain candidate images and communicate a candidate's strengths and weaknesses of character to voters. Both of these outcomes, on issue learning and on formation of candidate images, have some effect on voting decisions. Some spots seem to also have direct effects on vote likelihood.

For much of the twentieth century, scholars and politicians alike attributed most of the variance in voting behavior to partisan affiliations. The definitive work in the field of voting behavior attributed voting to a fourfold model (political party, issues, candidates, and groups) and declared political party to be the dominant component (Campbell, Converse, Miller, & Stokes, 1960). Even when issues or candidates were thought to rise to importance, the model believed that attitudes toward them were filtered through a partisan lens. Perhaps it is ironic that it was a real lens, television's actual lens, that changed all that. Media consultant Tony Schwartz, who produced the famous "Daisy Girl" spot for Lyndon Johnson in 1964, observed long before others seemed to understand what it meant that in the past, "political parties were the means of communication from the candidate to public. The political parties today are ABC, NBC, and CBS" (Schwartz, 1984, p. 82).

Although this comment may seem out of date in a media world that now offers not just ABC, NBC, and CBS but also CNN and scores of other independent and cable choices, the spirit of the comment is still important. Candidates do not rely on parties. They rely on mass media to carry their messages. Since television spots are the most direct way of doing that, providing them with proven effectiveness, it is easy to understand why candidates would choose television as their primary means of communicating with voters.

3

Videostyle: Concept, Theory, and Method

As the previous chapters document, political advertising has made its mark on national elections; our national elections do not occur without voters hearing and seeing numerous political ads. However, political advertising is not something that candidates *do* to voters. The messages and the images present in televised political ads are constructed using fears, myths, concerns, and narratives that exist in culture and in voters. In fact, political advertising, like all political communication in campaigns, "is an interactive process that constructs reality for voters" (Swanson, 1991, p. 11). The construction of this reality and the continuous negotiation of meaning that takes place during a campaign involve all media forms, not just television political advertising. News coverage, debates, brochures, and advertising inundate voters with symbols, information, events, and choices about the candidates and about the campaigns. But as the previous chapters have indicated, political advertising receives much attention from scholars and practitioners alike because of its brevity, effectiveness, and nature as completely controlled communication (completely controlled by the candidate and his or her "handlers," that is). While this aspect of political advertising has caused debate and concern over its merits, it also provides a way of closely studying the techniques, strategies, narratives, and symbols that political candidates and their consultants choose when they decide to construct a reality for voters.

This reality, then, as Nimmo and Combs (1990) argued, "is created, or constructed through communication, not expressed by it" (p. 3). Candidates and their consultants use communication to create a "reality" of their campaign and their vision for voters. In their discussion of consultants, Nimmo and Combs go on to say that these media managers attempt to link the candidate and his or her positions with "cherished cultural values" by using melodramas that will "tell a story of the candidate's vision for the office and the nation" (p. 177). In order to do this, consultants and candidates use a variety of avenues available to them in television, in culture, and within acceptable political practices.

How does this construction take place? How do candidates attempt to mediate in their messages some image of themselves, their campaign, and their vision for their campaign and the country? We believe that the "languages" of television have had growing influence on this process. Modern political candidates are trained to better adapt to television's dominance in politics. This training includes training in gestures, physical appearance, and speech (Maarek, 1995). Television personalizes the candidates for voters, and voters have come to expect a certain level of media competency in presidential candidates. That is, we expect our presidential candidates to be able to understand and use the conventions of television to communicate with us.

In this chapter, we argue that the techniques, strategies, narratives, and symbols that a candidate decides to use in television advertising make up a candidate's "videostyle." While every candidate has a personal style and occupies a particular position in an elective (incumbent/challenger) or partisan (Democrat/Republican) sense, candidates in modern campaigns seek to construct for voters through television an image that serves to represent the candidate. We label this presentation of the candidate through television "videostyle." This concept parallels in some ways a process of telepresentation that is similar to the process Goffman labels "presentation of self" in interpersonal communication (Goffman, 1959).

VIDEOSTYLE

The style of a candidate initially is revealed through a general communication style, a pattern of behavior that is apparent, consistent, and recurring. Such patterns of behavior "signal how literal meaning should be taken, interpreted, filtered, or understood" (Norton, 1983, p. 47). Although the personal style of a candidate could exist outside of mediated forms of communication, a candidate would necessarily adapt to the elements of television's languages to reach voters through televised political advertising. Therefore, patterns of techniques used and strategies employed (verbal, nonverbal, and television production) should be evident by looking at the candidate's political ads. Presentation of style is very important because it reveals something more than the content of the message; it reveals the context that one should use to interpret the content (Norton & Brenders, 1996).

Videostyle was first outlined in detail by Kaid and Davidson (1986), who argued that the "videostyle" of the candidate is composed of the verbal content, the nonverbal content, and the film/video production techniques used in political ads. This tri-component model is suggested by the fact that, while a candidate's style in his or her political advertisements would incorporate all of the traditional elements of "style," it would also include the style elements unique to television.

Verbal Components of Videostyle

The verbal content element of videostyle focuses on the semantic characteristics of the candidate's message. What is said in the ad, both in sound and in printed messages, makes up an important element of the communication a candidate uses to convey an image to voters.

The verbal content of an ad is composed of many different aspects. One aspect of verbal content in spots is frequently mentioned as "issue" or "image" content. The specific nature of the issues mentioned (foreign policy, the economy, crime) or the specific candidate characteristics attributed to an image (honest, competent, experienced, compassionate) may also be identified as verbal content.

Verbal content in an ad is also often characterized as either "positive" or "negative" content, depending upon whether it focuses on the candidate or on the opponent. Verbal content can also often be described according to the type of evidence or proof offered for a claim made by a candidate and by the explicit and implicit values conveyed in a spot.

Explicit strategies or tactics also may be labeled as verbal content in a political spot. In the verbal content of political spots, one important aspect may be the strategies and tactics adopted by candidates in relationship to their political positions. Partisanship, whether a candidate is a Republican or a Democrat, may be one such political position. Another is a candidate's status as an incumbent or challenger. Trent and Friedenberg's (1983) analysis of incumbent and challenger styles and strategies remains the corpus from which such candidate strategies are judged. They have identified eleven types of incumbent strategies: creating pseudoevents, making appointments for jobs and party positions, creating task forces, appropriating federal money, appearing with world leaders, issue manipulation, party endorsements, highlighting accomplishments, establishing an "above the trenches" stance, use of surrogates, and escalating foreign issues to crisis proportion. The challenger's style is typified by attacks made on the opponent's record, offensive stance on issues, emphasis on change and optimism for the future, appeals made to traditional values, middle-of-the-road philosophy, and use of surrogates to attack incumbents (Trent & Friedenberg, 1983).

Finally, even the language choices a candidate makes can be important elements of the verbal style of spots. Language that is particularly emotional or that conveys meaning in a dramatic way may convey a particular candidate style.

Nonverbal Components of Videostyle

More than 20 years ago, Nimmo (1974) argued that "what a politician says (content) may seem less important to an audience than the type of language (verbal or nonverbal) he uses and how (style) he says it" (p. 38). The nonverbal content of political ads includes the "visual elements and audio elements that do not have specific semantic meaning (sounds, voice inflections, etc.)" (Kaid & Davidson, 1986, p. 187). Goffman (1959) suggests a preeminent role for the nonverbal dimensions of a candidate's style. According to Goffman (1959), there are two dimensions to any presentation of oneself: the "verbal assertions," which are easily manipulated, and the nonverbal components of our behavior, which are not so easily controlled. Aspects of "performance" such as appearance, clothing, body movements, and eye contact must be looked at to understand the "message" of any television production (Metallinos, 1996). Because nonverbal components of behavior are "ungovernable," Goffman (1959) believes that people use these aspects of communication to check the validity of a message. More recent research supports this notion that when verbal and nonverbal messages are in conflict, the nonverbal communication is the more important in interpretation of the message (Knapp, 1978).

Nonverbal communication is important, particularly because it provides "a frame of reference for interpreting what is said verbally" (Burgoon, Buller, & Woodall, 1989, p. 9). Nonverbal behavior can repeat, contradict, substitute, complement, accent, and regulate verbal behavior (Knapp & Hall, 1992). In many cases, nonverbal cues are more trusted than verbal cues and can express what verbal cues are unable to express (Burgoon, Buller, & Woodall, 1989). All of the nonverbal categories of communication are important, and in politics some are used intentionally to set the stage for what will be said. For example, environmental cues that a president might use before giving a news conference (such as the flag and other symbols of power) set the stage for his conference (Burgoon, Buller, & Woodall, 1989). In addition, environmental factors such as music, lighting, colors, and music interact with language to provide an understanding of a situation (Knapp & Hall, 1992).

In several recent studies, researchers have found that nonverbal cues play a central role in personal and social interactions (Burgoon & Le Poire, 1999) and can influence the evaluation of a person's credibility, competence, composure, and sociability (Aguinis, Simonsen, & Pierce, 1998; Seiter, 1999; Seiter, Abraham, & Nakagama, 1998). In two studies, researchers looked at the impact of reactions on the evaluation of a debater in split-screen formats of TV debates. In one instance, Seiter (1999) found that nonverbally disagreeing with the speaker lowered the non-speaking debater's ratings of competence, composure, and sociability. In a different version of the study, researchers found that the speaker was rated more highly on composure, sociability, and competence when the non-speaking debater was shown constantly disagreeing with him (Seiter, Abraham, & Nakagama, 1998). Finally, Aguinis, Simonsen, and Pierce found that relaxed facial expressions and direct eye contact increased subjects' evaluations of a person's credibility.

Politicians must pay attention to how they appear and the language they use in their ads, because both influence the overall message of the ad and the audience's perception of them. Categories of nonverbal communication that appear to be influential in how someone interprets communication from a source include (a) kinesics, body movement, and gestures, (b) physical characteristics such as attractiveness, body height and weight, (c) touching behavior, (d) para language or how something is said, (e) proxemics or space, and (e) environmental factors such as settings and surroundings (Knapp, 1978). Although not all of these dimensions are included in a political ad, the overall nonverbal behavior of a politician, including dress, voice qualities, ad setting, body movement, and surroundings, might influence how his or her communication is interpreted and how his or her style is manifested in a political ad. Even the candidate's appearance (or absence) from a political spot sends a nonverbal message to voters.

Production Components of Videostyle

While Goffman discusses the relative importance of verbal and nonverbal components in the "presentation of self," videostyle suggests a third component of candidate presentation for evaluating television spots, television production techniques. Elements of television presentation influence how the candidate and his or her consultants will structure and construct messages and images for voters.

The video production or visual components of a television political ad are determined somewhat by the selectivity of the camera in film and television production. "Everything the camera sees, it necessarily interprets. It is innately selective" (Millerson, 1972, p. 198). By presenting an event from a variety of points of view, the camera can create an event or the feeling of a particular event by manipulating emotions and moods electronically (Zettl, 1976). But it is not just the camera that interprets the message for viewers. Rather, it is a combination of factors used in television and film production that guides the viewer through the narrative of a film, sitcom, or political ad. A premise about videostyle as a way of analyzing political ads is that the use of certain production techniques is not haphazard or accidental but rather designed with a particular effect or message in mind.

Numerous scholars have talked about the "ideology" present in all media. In his analysis of film, Nichols (1981) argued that ideology is present in the codes and symbols used in the film. Audiences are able to interpret these codes and images consistently over time because they rely on how culture and their own experiences have taught them to process these images. In other words, audiences are familiar with some of the conventions of television and film, and they interpret the images and messages they see and hear based on what they have learned culturally.

Televised political advertising also uses codes and symbols to help audiences interpret the message and the candidate. In an early work, Millerson (1972) argued that the rhetoric of production can be as persuasive and stimulating to the imagination as written persuasion. By using television production rhetoric, the artist can contrast two ideas, compare two ideas, link a variety of subjects, imply certain things in the production, show an unexpected outcome, create deliberate falsification or distortion, provide interpretation, and show repetition, irony, flashbacks, and double takes (Millerson, 1972).

Numerous researchers and practitioners have identified the meanings behind particular production techniques. Aspects of production such as camera angles and movement, color, editing, music and sound, lighting, camera shots, staging and setting, special effects, and other techniques can produce emotions or feelings, convey specific information, and cause us to interpret what we see in different ways (Edmonds, 1982; Metallinos, 1996; Millerson, 1972, 1990; Monaco, 1981; Primeau, 1979; Zettl, 1976, 1997).

Millerson (1990) and Zettl (1997) discuss at length the ways in which the camera, lighting, and sound can all be used to persuade the viewer of a particular feel, emotion, or interpretation of the message. Zettl (1997) notes that "the basic purpose of framing a shot is to show images as clearly as possible and to present them so that they convey meaning and energy" (p. 116). Millerson (1990) discusses how closer shots are used to show detail, emphasize, reveal reactions, and dramatize, while longer shots are used to establish mood, show where the action is taking place, show the positions of subjects, and allow the audience to follow broad movements.

Close-ups can also suggest intimacy with the subject, whereas a long shot removes the viewer from the subject and suggests a distance between the viewer and the subject (Edmonds, 1982; Zettl, 1997). Wide-angle shots exaggerate depth and make certain aspects of the scene appear more powerful and distinct (Zettl, 1997).

Camera angle can also be used to suggest the "meaning" of the images. For example, tilting upward with the camera is said to create feelings of rising interest and emotion or to give a sense of authority to the subject (Millerson, 1990). Tilting downward can convey disappointment, sadness, or critical inspection or minimize the authority of the subject (Millerson, 1990).

Perception of a person can also be influenced by the camera's height and angle in relation to the person. Low-angle shots (making it appear as if the viewer is looking up at the camera's subject) will make subjects appear stronger, more dominant, and more imposing, whereas high-angle shots (where the viewer is looking down on the camera's subject) make the subject look less dominant and give the viewer a sense of strength and superiority to the subjects (Edmonds, 1982; Millerson, 1972, 1990; Monaco, 1981; Zettl, 1997). The importance of a subject can also be manipulated through the amount of the frame that he or she fills: the larger the image of the subject in the frame, the greater the subject's importance (Millerson, 1972; Monaco, 1981).

The camera angle and shot tell the viewer what to focus on, what position or point of view might be taken, and what is important in the shot and convey certain emotions (Millerson, 1990). Lighting, sound, special effects, and editing also convey messages to viewers. Lighting techniques and sound are used extensively by television and film directors and producers to create moods and to elicit various psychological effects (Zettl, 1997). By placing lighting and shadows in certain places, one can give the illusion of a specific time or place. Lighting can also call attention to something in a particular shot by highlighting details of the picture (Monaco, 1981). Sound can also create a particular mood, like lighting. It can be used to suggest danger, happiness, or a calm feeling (Zettl, 1976, 1997). Millerson (1972, 1990) suggests that sound can function in several ways to direct attention and create a focal point for our attention. Certain sounds or sound effects can convey information, establish location, and provide interpretation for our ideas, thoughts, and feelings. Sound can identify for listeners certain places, moods, events, and people and can be used to link scenes and events together (Millerson, 1972, 1990). Music can also be used to evoke different emotions in the audience (Millerson, 1972, 1990).

General production techniques may also signal for viewers how to interpret the media content. The use of cinema verité in commercials (a "slice of life" look that appears unrehearsed or unplanned) seems to suggest that this program is "reality" or news, even if the program is actually an advertisement (Jamieson & Campbell, 1997).

The editing of the final product can influence the information received from the ads. Split-screen and double exposures can add to the importance of some shots (Monaco, 1981). A split screen can also be used to show the interaction of two events or to compare the appearance and behavior of two or more subjects (Millerson, 1972, 1990). Other editing techniques such as montage, fast motion, slow motion, and freeze frame may also be used to highlight particular scenes or parts of scenes in some productions (Millerson, 1972, 1990). Slow motion allows the image to be reinforced or allows details of the scene to be seen and studied. Freeze frames are used to evoke suspense, tension, and curiosity because an action is suspended. Superimpositions bridge two different events or circumstances by allowing one image to be placed on top of or merged with another (Metallinos, 1996).

Several studies have looked at how some of these visual dimensions of television can affect the impressions formed about the subjects on camera. In their book, *The Interplay of Influence*, Jamieson and Campbell (1997) discuss the ways in which television technology can influence the drama and persuasiveness of television news. For instance, the type of camera shot used on the anchor may influence the perceptions of the anchor.

Camera angle may also be related to perceptions of source credibility and attraction (Mandell & Shaw, 1973; McCain, Chilberg, & Wakshlag, 1977; Tiemens, 1970). Tiemens found that the "communicative ability" and "knowledgeability" of a televised newscaster were greater when the camera angle was low (signifying dominance and power) than when it was high and looking down on the newscaster (signifying submission and unimportance). Tiemens has also analyzed how camera framing and angles have influenced the images or impressions made in debates (1978). In an analysis of camera coverage of Ford and Carter in the 1976 debates, Tiemens (1978) found that camera framing and composition, camera angles, screen placement, and reaction shots seemed to favor Carter.

THE USE OF VIDEOSTYLE TO ANALYZE POLITICAL ADS

The concept of videostyle has evolved during the past two decades since Kaid and Davidson (1986) initially laid out the elements of videostyle and applied them to a series of U.S. Senate races from 1982. Their study, "the first attempt to describe systematically the style of political commercials" (p. 186), used verbal, nonverbal, and film/production techniques to code political spot ads. Adding to the original videostyle coding sheet to include content and types of appeals, types of negative attacks, and communication strategies identified by Trent and Friedenberg in the 1980s, Wadsworth (Johnston) (1986) used videostyle to analyze a set of presidential ads from 1952 to 1984.

These original coding categories have been augmented and refined, reflecting the changing literature and research on political advertising. In addition, videostyle has been used to study and make comparisons in the United States across time (Kaid & Johnston, 1991), in particular presidential elections (Kaid, 1994, 1998; Kaid, McKinney, & Tedesco, 2000; Kaid & Tedesco, 1999; Kaid, Tedesco, Chanslor, & Roper, 1993), between male and female candidates (Bystrom, 1995; Bystrom & Miller, 1999; Johnston & White, 1994), and between U.S. candidates and those in other democracies around the world (Holtz-Bacha, Kaid, & Johnston, 1994; Johnston, 1991a; Kaid & Holtz-Bacha, 1995; Kaid & Tedesco, 1993; Tak, Kaid, & Lee, 1997). In short, the consistent use of videostyle has now made it possible to make comparisons across various dimensions and to see how production styles of ads have changed, how negative advertising has evolved, and how rhetorical strategies have been altered. It has allowed an analysis of how culture and context of political campaigning, political positions, and personal style might be translated into the language of televised political advertising.

Videostyle has enhanced over the past several years an understanding of the ways in which televised political advertising has changed and evolved over time. By using videostyle we can now ask questions about presidential style patterns. What are some of the characteristics of styles used by incumbents and challengers and Republicans and Democrats over the past five decades of televised campaign ads? How have individual presidential candidates used their ads to suggest a particular vision of their candidacy for voters? Has the use of negative advertising changed over time? If it has, then how has it changed? What ethical issues may be raised by use of certain types of videostyle strategies? Are there differences among candidate videostyle portrayals beyond the boundaries of the United States? And finally, how have other media discussed political advertising over those years? In the following chapters, we use videostyle to try to answer some of these questions. In other chapters, we look at the relationship between the ads and the news media's attention to the ads.

METHOD OF APPLYING VIDEOSTYLE

To answer some of these questions, we analyzed all televised presidential ads from the general elections from 1952 to 1996. The ads for this study were obtained from the Political Commercial Archive in the Department of Communication at the University of Oklahoma. A complete set of ads was analyzed for each candidate in presidential races from 1952 through 1996. The total number of ads analyzed was 1,204.

We used content analysis as our method of analyzing these 1,204 political spots. The unit of analysis was the individual political spot.

The ads obtained for content analysis covered twelve presidential campaigns and include: Eisenhower/Stevenson, 1952; Eisenhower/Stevenson, 1956; Kennedy/Nixon, 1960; Goldwater/ Johnson, 1964; Nixon/Humphrey, 1968; McGovern/Nixon, 1972; Carter/Ford, 1976; Carter/Reagan, 1980; Mondale/Reagan, 1984; Bush/Dukakis, 1988; Bush/Clinton, 1992; and Clinton/Dole, 1996.

Ad Sample

Because so many ads can be made during a campaign, it was important to define clearly the boundaries for this study of what presidential ads from these races were included in or excluded from the analysis and why. Because the purpose of the study was to determine the style or strategy that the candidate wished to project to voters, several criteria were established for inclusion or exclusion of ads. Political advertising gives the candidate and his or her advertising consultants an opportunity for complete control of the content and the form of the message they wish to convey to voters. Therefore, in assessing the style the candidate was projecting or the strategies he or she was using in these ads, it was important that only ads known to be sanctioned by the candidate or the candidate's election committee be included in the study. For instance, although Adlai Stevenson did not run any national television ads in 1952, we included the ads produced and aired for him by the Illinois Democratic Party. Likewise, the ads produced by the Democrats for Nixon group in 1972 were included because they were approved by the Nixon campaign. However, after the 1971 and 1972 Federal Election Acts and the *Buckley v. Valeo* (1976) decision, the definition of what constituted approval by a candidate's committee became more formal, and we followed the legal rules that commercials paid for and identified as sponsored by independent or third-party groups whose expenditures were not attributable to a presidential candidate were not "sponsored" by that candidate.[1] No third-party candidates are included in our analysis.

Second, only ads from the general election campaign of the two major parties were included; ads used by the candidates during the primaries were excluded from the analysis. Finally, an attempt was made to include all ads produced or aired for presidential candidates during the general election phase of the campaign.[2] That is, if the candidate sanctioned the ads and asked a producer to make the ads for him, then the ads were included, even if they were shown only once or twice or were shown in only in certain regions of the country.[3] These ads still contain the strategies and styles that the candidate wished to project to voters.

Videostyle Categories and Coding

To apply the videostyle concept to the sample of 1,204 ads, a written coding instrument and codebook were developed to represent various aspects of the verbal, nonverbal, and television production components of videostyle. A copy of the codesheet is contained in the Appendix. While most categories called for the simple marking of the presence or absence of a particular characteristic of an ad, coders were sometimes asked to look for the *dominant* theme or content in the ads, as reflected by some appeal or format in the commercial.

Verbal content categories. In addition to simple categories like candidate name, party, and length and sponsor of commercial, the codesheet included categories that determined the issue or image focus of the commercial.[4] Spots were categorized according to the presence of partisan appeals, group appeals, personal qualities of the candidates, and type of issue content (general issue concern, vague policy preference, and specific policy proposal). If the spot was an issue spot, coders marked the specific issues contained in the spot from a list provided on the codesheet (see Appendix). Likewise, ads with image content were coded according to the presence of particular candidate qualities specified on the codesheet. This list of qualities was drawn from prior lists of image qualities used in the American National Election Studies coding by the University of Michigan (Rosenstone et al., 1997). Types of appeals or evidence were identified according to Aristotle's traditional categorization of types of proof: *logos, pathos,* or *ethos* (or logical, emotional, or ethical). Logical appeals use facts to make the ad's point, including the possible use of statistics, logical arguments, and examples. Emotional evidence includes the use of language and images meant to evoke feelings or emotions such as happiness, pride, patriotism, or anger. Ethical appeals or source credibility relies on good character to make its appeals, including the qualifications/integrity/trustworthiness of the candidate or of someone speaking on behalf of the candidate. The ads were also coded for the presence of fear appeals, a particular type of emotional appeal that tries to scare the viewer.

Finally, several of the strategies identified by Trent and Friedenberg as appropriate for incumbents and challengers were included. Coders also identified the focus of the ad as candidate-positive or opponent-negative. If attacks were made in the ads, the ads were coded for the purpose of the attack and for the techniques used in making the attack.

A set of categories was developed to measure the strategies used by incumbents and challengers. These were modeled after a list of such strategies suggested by Trent and Friedenberg (1983); they are discussed more fully in Chapter 5.

A final category of verbal content involved marking the presence or absence of a set of values contained in the spots. Two set of values were used. The first was based on Milton Rokeach's set of terminal values (Rokeach, 1973), and the second was a set of American values provided by Steele and Redding (1962).

Nonverbal content categories. The second area of categories related to nonverbal dimensions of the ads. Coders were asked to code for the setting of ads (formal or informal, outdoor or indoor). The candidate's overall eye contact, facial expression, body movement, fluency, rate of speech, pitch, and dress were also ascertained for each ad. Finally, all of the ads were coded for the dominant speaker in the ad, indicating whether the candidate or someone else was the major person delivering the message.

Television production content categories. Coders were asked to code for the dominant format as presented in the ad. Some formats previously identified include documentary, talking head, man-in-the-street, cinema verité, production idea spot, question and answer, humor and animation or gimmick ad, press conferences, minidocumentaries, attack ads, issue or argument ads, resolution ads, and biography spots (Devlin, 1986; Diamond & Bates, 1984; Sabato, 1981). From these various lists of ads, nine major formats that combined or incorporated several formats were selected, and others were added to form nine formats that included documentary, video clip/music video, testimonial, introspection, question and answer/confrontation, opposition focused, and issue dramatization.

Other production components of the ads included the presence of music in the ads and the presence of various techniques of production such as cinema verité, candidate head-on, and special production or animation. The ads were also coded in terms of the staging, sound characteristics, the dominant camera angle used, and the dominant type of camera shot used. Finally, the ads were also coded for the presence of a list of specific special effects (see Appendix).

Coding Procedures

The 1,204 ads were coded by trained graduate student coders. Training sessions explained the categories, applied them to political spots from other elections, and supervised practice coding sessions. At the conclusion of training sessions, intercoder reliability was determined on a set of sample ads (10%) drawn from the universe of ads used in the study. The intercoder reliability across all categories averaged +.86.[5] In succeeding chapters, we provide the results of this analysis of videostyle in presidential campaigns. In addition to overall trends in videostyle across time, we also provide particular analysis of videostyle in relation to negative campaigning, to political candidate position (incumbent versus challenger and political party representation), and to potential for ethical manipulation. We also provide a comparison of the videostyle of U.S. presidential candidates with that of their counterparts in other democracies around the world, and we discuss how the news media report about political campaign advertisements.

NOTES

1. This rule meant, for instance, that the 1988 ad called the "Revolving Door" was included as a George Bush campaign ad, but that the "Willie Horton" ad sponsored by a third-party group was not. Likewise, spots advocating election of a particular candidate but sponsored by the AFL-CIO or the National Rifle Association (NRA) were excluded.

2. The Political Commercial Archive at the University of Oklahoma does not have data on the airtime given to particular spots. In the case of early campaigns, it is sometimes not possible to determine whether a spot actually aired or was only produced by the candidate.

3. Until the last few presidential campaigns, many presidential candidates concentrated their media time-buying on national networks. However, over the past few campaign cycles the expansion of cable and satellite television and a deliberate strategy of making regional time-buys have changed the landscape for presidential television spot buying.

4. Issues can incorporate general candidate (or opponent) issue concerns, as well as specific policy preferences or proposals. On the other hand, ads that focus on images generally stress the candidate's (or opponent's) personal qualities, background, qualifications, traits, and the like.

5. In order to calculate intercoder reliability, we used the formula suggested by Holsti (North, Holsti, Zaninovich, & Zinnes, 1963). It is given for two coders and can be modified for any number of coders.

$$R = \frac{2(C_{1,2})}{C_1 + C_2}$$

$C_{1,2}$ is the number of category assignments both coders agree on, and $C_1 + C_2$ is the total number of category assignments made by both coders.

In the sample of ads used to calculate intercoder reliability, the overall reliability averaged +.86. Individual category reliability ranged from a low of +.67 for categories such as format of commercial to +.99 for focus of ad (positive or negative) and candidate eye contact.

4

Advertising Content and Styles Across the Years

The styles and contents of presidential ads have varied considerably since Eisenhower's first use of television spots in the 1952 campaign. For one thing, there have been great differences in the number of spots used by each candidate. The total number of ads in the sample analyzed here is 1,204 spots. As Table 4.1 shows, the small number of ads used by Eisenhower (35) and Stevenson (18) in 1952 (and an even smaller number in the sample used here for 1956) quickly increased in 1960 to 68 different spots used by John F. Kennedy and 48 different ads for Richard M. Nixon. The largest number of ads in any one year were used for Ronald Reagan in his 1980 campaign.

In looking at the components of videostyle in presidential ads across time, it is helpful first to consider the overall characteristics of the ads and then to look at trends across time and for individual candidates.

VERBAL COMPONENTS OF PRESIDENTIAL VIDEOSTYLE

The verbal aspect of videostyle encompasses the content of the spot. Verbal content can include the issue/image content of a spot, whether the spot is focused on the sponsoring candidate or on the opponent,

TABLE 4.1
Presidential Candidate Spots for Each Election Year (N = 1,204)

Candidate Name	Year	Number of Spots
Eisenhower	1952	35
Stevenson	1952	18
Eisenhower	1956	5
Stevenson	1956	12
Kennedy	1960	68
Nixon	1960	48
Goldwater	1964	37
Johnson	1964	27
Nixon	1968	41
Humphrey	1968	36
McGovern	1972	47
Nixon	1972	30
Carter	1976	53
Ford	1976	94
Carter	1980	77
Reagan	1980	173
Mondale	1984	28
Reagan	1984	66
Bush	1988	47
Dukakis	1988	71
Bush	1992	32
Clinton	1992	39
Dole	1996	43
Clinton	1996	77

what types of appeals are made in the spot, and the specific issues, values, or candidate qualities emphasized in the ad.

Type of Spot Content

One important and often discussed aspect of the content of a spot is whether the spot emphasizes issues or the character/image of a candidate. As mentioned earlier, issues can incorporate general candidate (or opponent) issue concerns, as well as specific policy preferences or proposals. On the other hand, ads that focus on images generally stress the candidate's (or opponent's) personal qualities, background, qualifications, traits, and so on. In coding spots to determine this emphasis, each spot was categorized according to the *dominant* content of the spot.

This means that, while a spot might include discussion of both issues and images, the spot was categorized according to which of these was the most important or dominant aspect of the spot.

As indicated in Table 4.2, most presidential spots are spots that emphasize issues. In fact, two-thirds (66%) of all presidential ads are issue spots, while only one-third concentrate on candidate images.

While many political observers have bemoaned a decline in issue discussions in national elections, the data from presidential ads do not support this conclusion. Not only is the overall emphasis of spots clearly on issues, rather than images, but this trend is generally consistent over time, as indicated in Figure 4.1. The campaign year with the highest percentage of issue spots was 1960 (84%), but similarly high percentages are apparent in 1964 (78%) and even in 1996 (79%). In fact, the only year in which issue content did not dominate the election was 1968, when personality or image content was dominant in 53% of the spots.

Looking at specific candidates, the highest individual percentages of issue spots were produced for Walter Mondale in 1984 (93%), Dwight Eisenhower in 1952 (91%), and Bill Clinton in 1996 (87%). Candidates with the greatest emphasis on image-oriented spots were Hubert Humphrey (61%) and Richard Nixon (46%) in 1968, Jimmy Carter in 1980 (46%), Ronald Reagan in 1984 (47%), and George Bush in 1992 (50%).

Although the dominant type of content in the presidential spots has been issue content, the question remains of how much of this content is

TABLE 4.2
Verbal Components of Presidential Videostyle: Type and Contents of Spots (N = 1,204)

	Number of Spots	Percentage
Type of Spot		
Image	406	34%
Issue	798	66
Dominant Contents of Spot		
Partisanship	54	5
Candidate Issue Concern	428	35
Vague Policy Preference	180	15
Specific Policy Proposal	82	7
Personal Characteristics of Candidate	406	34
Appeals to Groups	54	5
Focus of Spot		
Candidate-Positive	742	62
Opponent-Negative	462	38

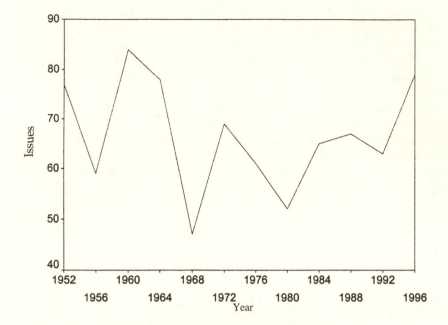

Figure 4.1   Issue Content in Political Spots, 1952–1996

in-depth and specific coverage of important issues. In order to examine this point more closely, spots that did not focus on candidate images were also grouped according to whether they (1) stressed partisanship issues (appealing to traditional accomplishments of the political party on an issue), (2) expressed a simple issue concern of the candidate or opponent (e.g., the candidate is concerned about the economy or unemployment), (3) indicated a vague policy preference of the candidate or opponent (e.g., the opponent is opposed to an increase in the minimum wage), or (4) provided a specific policy proposal (e.g., the candidate proposes to decrease income taxes by 15%).

It is clear from Table 4.2 that the most common type of issue spot emphasizes a general issue concern (35% of all spots take this approach). Dwight Eisenhower's set of spots from the 1952 "Eisenhower Answers America" series are a good example of this type of spot. In them, Eisenhower generally responds to questions from ordinary voters with general issue statements. In one spot from this series, a questioner comments to Eisenhower, "General, in order to make ends meet last year, I had to go into debt." Eisenhower answers: "You're not the only one. Last year fifty million Americans went into debt. And next year, they'll be in even deeper unless you help put the lid on Washington waste and extravagance." No real indication of a policy proposal or preference here; just a general statement of concern. A similar issue concern was expressed by Gerald Ford in his 1976 campaign in a spot where Ford proclaimed, "We all recognize the seriousness of inflation, particularly those who have a fixed income. Two years ago inflation was twelve to thirteen percent. Now it's between five and six percent. That's still too high, but it's going down, and if we can win the battle against inflation, it'll be good for everybody but particularly helpful to our senior citizens." As with the Eisenhower spots, this ad tells the voter nothing about how Ford wants to control inflation or what specific proposals he has for doing so, but it is meant to tell the voter that Ford recognizes the problem and wants to do something about it.

At the next level of issues are spots that tell the voter about the candidate's policy preferences. About 15% of presidential spots take this approach to issues. Eisenhower used some of his spots to make such preferences known, as this example illustrates:

> Voter: "I'm sixty-six. I can't live on my social security, nobody can."
> Eisenhower: "I stand for expanded social security and more real benefits. Believe me sir, if I am President I will give you older folks action, not just sympathy."

More specific yet are spots that actually lay out a specific proposal for what should be done about a particular policy issue. Only 7% of presidential spots are this specific. Kennedy's 1960 spots, however, often took this approach, as this example on the minimum wage indicates:

> Kennedy: "Mr. Nixon has said that a dollar twenty-five cents an hour minimum wage is extreme. That's fifty dollars a week. What's extreme about that? I believe the next Congress and the President should pass a minimum wage for a dollar twenty-five cents an hour. Americans must be paid enough to live."

In a 1976 spot, Gerald Ford makes a specific proposal about medical care: "Under the proposals that I recommended, no person would have to pay more than $750 a year for both hospital care and medical care. With that kind of protection then nobody really has to fear all of their resources being depleted. I say frequently, and I mean it, there is no reason somebody should go broke just to get well."

Appeals to issues on the basis of partisanship (5%) or groups (5%) have not been used frequently by candidates for president over the past five decades.

While the preceding discussion concentrates on the dominant emphasis on content in an ad, another way of looking at the verbal content of the presidential spots is to consider whether a particular type of content is *mentioned* in the ad. Obviously, an ad may have more than one type of content. In order to take full account of the videostyle of a candidate's ad, each spot was also categorized according to the presence of partisan appeals, group appeals, personal qualities of the candidates, and type of issue content (general issue concern, vague policy preference, and specific policy proposal). Using this breakdown, the presence or mention of each type of content in the 1,204 presidential spots was as follows:

Partisanship Appeals	168 (14%)
General Issue Concern	781 (65%)
Vague Policy Preference	510 (42%)
Specific Policy Proposal	140 (12%)
Group Appeals	231 (19%)
Personal Qualities	713 (59%)

While it is clear that issue concerns are still more frequent than are personal quality mentions, the gap is much smaller in this comparison. While only 40% of spots have images as their main or dominant content, 59% of all spots mention personal qualities or image characteristics of the candidate or opponent. An encouraging aspect of these data for those concerned about issue coverage in spots is that larger percentages of spots contain policy preferences (42%) and policy proposals (12%) than would be indicated by the dominant content categories in Table 4.2.

It is also interesting to consider these breakdowns of content mentions according to specific candidates. While partisan appeals do not make up a very large percentage of spot content, there has been a definite downward trend in this category over time. While only 14% of all spots from 1952 through 1996 mention partisanship at all, the percentages were much higher in the earliest campaigns, such as those of Eisenhower (34%) and Stevenson (61%) in 1952 and of Kennedy (37%) and Nixon (53%) in 1960 and in 1968 (29%). The percentage of spots using partisanship appeals declined substantially after 1968, a further indication of the much-discussed decline in political party loyalty among the American electorate. As party became less important to voters, candidates saw less need to emphasize it in their spots.

Appeals to specialized groups in the voting population also declined over time. Early spots made use of such appeals frequently. John Kennedy in 1960 used such appeals in 32% of his spots, such as this one about medical care for the elderly:

This is Senator John Kennedy, the Democratic nominee for the Presidency of the United States. One of the problems which concerns me most is our failure to meet the problem of medical care for our older citizens. Some of them are in ill health. Some of them are in your family. And yet under present laws, before they can receive any assistance in their medical bills, which may be expensive, they must take a pauper's oath, they must say they are medically indigent. I believe the way to meet this problem is the way Franklin Roosevelt met it in the Social Security act of 1935. I believe that people during their working years would want to contribute so that when they retired, when they reach the age of 65 for men or 62 for women then they can receive assistance in paying their bills. They pay their own way. They live in dignity. They get protection. This is the way it ought to be done. This is the sound way. And I can assure you that if we're successful, we're going to pass this bill next January.

The elderly is one group that has received considerable mention in presidential spots over the years (Kaid & Garner, 1995). The earlier example from the Ford 1976 campaign shows a similar concern for the elderly with its emphasis on the harms of inflation.

General issue concerns, of course, make up the highest category of mentions (65%). This has been a consistent trend over time. However, expression of a policy preference, even if a vague one, has also been seen in many spots over time (42%). Both Eisenhower and Stevenson scored high marks in this category in 1952 and 1956. John Kennedy also frequently mentioned policy preferences; 69% of his spots contained such mentions. Barry Goldwater's 1964 spots had the highest mention of policy preferences on issues since 70% of his spots made such points. Richard Nixon's 1972 spots (63%) and Bill Clinton's 1996 spots (64%) were also high in policy preference mentions.

However, not all candidates have placed a great deal of emphasis on policy preferences. The low scores belong to Hubert Humphrey in 1968 (19%), Ronald Reagan in 1984 (17%), and Bill Clinton in 1992 (28%).

Specific policy proposals are, of course, more risky for a candidate, since they may raise the ire of opposition groups. Still, candidates have been willing to make such specific proposals in 12% of their spots across time. The most courageous in this regard was Lyndon Johnson, who in 1964 made specific proposals in 30% of his spots. One example comes from this spot attacking opponent Barry Goldwater's stand on Social Security: "On at least seven occasions Senator Barry Goldwater said he would change the present social security system. But even his running mate William Miller admits that Senator Goldwater's voluntary program would destroy social security. President Johnson is working to strengthen social security. Vote for him on November third."

Walter Mondale was another candidate who stressed specific policy proposals in his ads; 25% of his spots took this approach. Other "high policy proposal achievers" have been Ronald Reagan in 1984 (17%) and Bill Clinton and Bob Dole in 1996 (each with 21%). Low marks for specific policy proposals would go to Goldwater who scored high on issue concerns and policy preferences (70%) but only proposed specific proposals in 5% of his ads. Nixon in 1968, McGovern in 1972, Gerald Ford in 1976, Jimmy Carter in 1976, and George Bush in both 1988 and 1992 were also very reluctant to make specific policy proposals in their ads; all mentioned such specifics in fewer than 10% of their ads.

However, very few candidates have been shy about mentioning their personal qualities and image characteristics. While the average across all years indicates that 53% of spots contain image mentions, some candidates have been particularly forthcoming about their own good qualities and the bad qualities of their opponents. In 1964 Lyndon Johnson had a lot to say about personal qualities, mentioning them in 74% of his ads. Most of these, however, were about the bad qualities of his opponent, Barry Goldwater. Johnson accused Goldwater of everything from being trigger happy with nuclear weapons to being irresponsible about Social Security.

Hubert Humphrey's ads, on the other hand, were more concerned with hyping the image qualities of Humphrey himself. In 78% of his ads Humphrey's personal qualities were mentioned. In various spots he was proclaimed to be "ahead of his time," "never known to be inarticulate," "captain of a team," "a man of new ideas," "very active," "a leader," "a strong man," one who has "initiative," "a really good person," and a "man of character." In 1980 Jimmy Carter divided the personal quality commentary in 86% of his spots between bad things about Reagan, who was accused of having a "shoot 'em dead attitude" from Western movies, and good things about himself, who was "respected for his humanity and good sense," "forward thinking," possessed of "intelligence and dignity," and "dedicated."

Specific Issue and Image Content

Issues in videostyle content. While the overall data and the examples give some idea of the issues mentioned by candidates, there are some interesting trends in the stress on specific issues across time. As Table 4.3 shows, and not surprisingly, the enduring issues stressed by candidates in their spots from 1952 through 1996 are (1) economic concerns, (2) taxes, (3) international/foreign affairs, and (4) military spending. While Stevenson concentrated on economic concerns in his 1956 spots (67%) and candidates in every year devoted some percentage of their spots to this topic, no candidate could match Ronald Reagan for the

TABLE 4.3
Issues Stressed in Presidential Spots (N = 1,204), in Percentages

	Total	E52	S52	E56	S56	N60	K60	J64	G64	N68	H68
Int'l/foreign affairs	12%	0%	6	40	0	38	9	7	54	29	6
Military/defense spending	8%	9%	0	60	0	19	1	7	16	32	6
Economic concerns	33%	9%	0	40	67	31	29	11	22	15	8
Deficit/balance budget	3%	6%	0	0	0	2	0	0	0	0	0
Crime/prisons/gun control	5%	0%	0	0	0	0	0	0	1	9	1
Drugs	3%	0%	0	0	0	0	0	0	0	0	0
Concern for children	3%	0%	0	0	0	0	1	2	0	2	0
Medicare/SS/Elderly	7%	6%	11	0	0	0	7	22	8	2	11
Other social policies	5%	20%	11	0	0	0	0	0	3	5	0
Abortion	<1%	0%	0	0	0	0	0	0	0	0	0
Environmental concerns	1%	0%	0	0	0	0	1	0	0	0	0
Health care	3%	0%	0	0	0	0	3	0	0	0	0
Probs. with immigrants	1%	0%	0	0	0	0	4	0	0	0	0
Smoking/tobacco abuse	<1%	0%	0	0	0	0	0	0	0	0	0
Taxes	11%	26%	6	0	17	2	1	7	5	0	3
Welfare Reform	2%	0%	0	0	0	0	0	0	0	0	0
Education	6%	0%	11	40	17	2	10	0	0	0	11
Civil rights/affirm. action	4%	0%	0	20	0	6	9	0	14	15	17

	N72	M72	F76	C76	C80	R80	R84	M84	B88	D88
Int'l/foreign affairs	17%	6	5	15	25	10	17	18	13	4
Military/defense spending	30%	11	9	0	21	8	0	29	2	1
Economic concerns	7%	19	29	32	26	61	73	29	15	10
Deficit/balance budget	0%	0	0	0	0	12	0	14	0	0
Crime/prisons/gun control	0%	9	3	0	0	0	2	0	6	8
Drugs	0%	4	0	0	0	0	0	0	0	6
Concern for children	0%	0	0	0	0	0	0	0	0	6
Medicare/SS/Elderly	0%	6	5	8	4	3	0	0	2	3
Other social policies	0%	0	10	6	10	0	0	11	4	3
Abortion	0%	0	0	0	0	0	0	0	0	0
Environmental concerns	0%	0	0	0	1	0	0	4	0	0
Health care	0%	4	3	0	0	0	0	0	0	4
Probs. w/immigrants	0%	0	0	0	0	0	0	0	0	0
Smoking/tobacco abuse	0%	0	0	0	0	0	0	0	0	0
Taxes	3%	13	14	15	9	6	6	14	4	0
Welfare Reform	7%	4	0	4	0	0	0	4	0	0
Education	7%	0	0	0	1	1	2	4	0	4
Civil rights/affirm. action	7%	0	11	0	14	1	2	0	0	0

TABLE 4.3 Continued

	B92	C92	C96	D96
Int'l/foreign affairs	16%	0	0	0
Military/defense spending	0%	0	0	0
Economic concerns	16%	79	43	23
Deficit/balance budget	3%	0	18	19
Crime/prisons/gun control	3%	0	28	9
Drugs	0%	0	23	21
Concern for children	0%	0	32	14
Medicare/SS/Elderly	0%	0	34	16
Other social policies	3%	0	29	2
Abortion	0%	0	5	0
Environmental concerns	3%	0	13	0
Health care	6%	8	13	14
Probs. w/immigrants	0%	0	6	7
Smoking/tobacco abuse	0%	0	8	0
Taxes	28%	8	31	53
Welfare Reform	3%	3	18	5
Education	0%	0	52	12
Civil rights/affirm. action	0%	0	3	0

sheer quantity of spots devoted to economic issues. In 1980, Reagan mentioned economic concerns in 105 of his 173 spots (61%), and in his 1984 re-election campaign Reagan's spots concentrated on economic issues again in 48 of 73 spots (73%). Of course, in 1980 Reagan's concern was that the economy needed boosting, but in 1984 the economy was important again because Reagan wanted to take credit for a strong and healthy economic situation he felt had improved "on his watch." Only the Clinton 1992 campaign placed such a high emphasis on the economy. The now-famous Clinton campaign motif—"It's the economy, stupid"—did truly characterize his spot content, since 79% of his general election spots in 1992 mentioned economic concerns.

Table 4.3 also shows that taxes were a consistent part of the verbal videostyle content of presidential ads across time. No candidate, however, gave so much weight to the tax issue, and unsuccessfully so, as Bob Dole, who mentioned it in over half of all his spots in 1996 (53%). A few candidates decided that taxes were not important to their campaigns; Stevenson in 1956, Nixon in 1968, and Dukakis in 1988 gave no spots over to this topic. John Kennedy in 1960 mentioned taxes in only one of his spots.

Foreign affairs and international issues have an interesting pattern, as well. Until the last decade of the twentieth century, almost all American presidential candidates felt some need to position themselves on foreign policy and military spending issues. Even Dwight Eisenhower, who needed little additional credibility in this area, mentioned military spending in 9% of his spots in 1952, and many of his longer, 5-minute spots in 1956 emphasized peace and military security issues. In 1960, Nixon, who thought foreign policy was a strength of his vice-presidential years, emphasized foreign policy issues in 38% of his spots and military/defense spending in 19%. Almost every candidate throughout the 1970s and 1980s also gave some attention either to foreign/international issues or to military spending or to both. However, in the 1990s, these concerns dropped out of the presidential campaign discourse in terms of spot emphasis. In the aftermath of the Gulf War and the fall of Communist regimes abroad, George Bush tried to remind the American people in 1992 that he and his predecessor, Ronald Reagan, deserved some points for the cessation of the Cold War in 16% of his spots. Clinton was silent on major foreign policy issues or military spending in both his 1992 and 1996 campaigns. Even military hero Bob Dole in 1996, while he mentioned his own background and his war injuries, did not use his expertise in foreign policy to discuss either international affairs or military spending in any detail.

Examination of specific issue concerns across time also tells an interesting story about some other popular issue concerns. Crime, for instance, is an issue that has risen and waned over the years in the consciousness of presidential candidates. Richard Nixon in his 1960 campaign was the first president to devote a substantial number of spots to the issue (9%). However, no candidate has talked more about crime and gun-control issues than Bill Clinton—nearly one-third (28%) of his 1996 re-election campaign spots were devoted to crime and gun-control issues. Related to the overall general crime issue is the question of drugs. Although the totals are not shown in the tables because so few candidates mentioned drugs specifically, it is interesting to note that only Mondale in 1984 and Dukakis in 1988 made even limited reference to drug problems; in the 1996 campaigns, both Clinton and Dole mentioned the topic in over one-fifth of their spots.

Other domestic policy issues have less clear patterns of increased and decreased emphasis. Problems of the elderly (Medicare, Social Security, etc.) received inconsistent mention across time. Although Lyndon Johnson mentioned such issues in 22% of his spots, the percentages in other years range from 0% (Eisenhower and Stevenson in 1956, Nixon in 1960 and 1972, Reagan and Mondale in 1984, and Bush and Clinton in 1992) to a high of 34% for Clinton in 1996. This is a topic to watch in future years, of course, as the "baby boomer" generation ages and brings more pressure to bear on such issues.

Education is another topic with inconsistent treatment across time. In 1956 Eisenhower appeared concerned about it and devoted time in two of his five spots (40%) to it. Most other candidates either did not mention education at all or mentioned it in one or two spots over the course of the campaign, but Bill Clinton's 1996 campaign again tops out the chart—over half of his 77 spots (52%) mention the education issue.

Many other topics that are often discussed in the news media never make it into the presidential candidates' own presentations of self. Apparently most candidates did not want to develop their videostyles around the abortion issue; no mentions were made by presidential candidates of this issue until Bill Clinton's campaign in 1996. Environmental concerns also pose risks to alternative constituencies and have gotten almost no mentions by candidates in their spots over time. No candidate saw a reason to dwell on smoking or tobacco abuse until Bill Clinton talked about it in his 1996 ads. In fact, a mark of how differently this topic was viewed in earlier years is the fact that some early spots actually feature actors and speakers smoking in the spots.

Images in videostyle content. Another aspect of the verbal content of a candidate's videostyle relates to the personal qualities the candidate seeks to convey in the spots. Here the verbal content is not so much a matter of specific words or phrases, although a candidate may sometimes proclaim himself to be "honest" or "qualified" in an overt and direct way. More often, the qualities of a personal image are conveyed indirectly through how a candidate presents his qualities or implies their relevance to his accomplishments, inviting the voter to evaluate him accordingly. We coded each commercial in which the candidate conveyed such information about himself according to the presence (or absence) of a series of personal qualities derived from those frequently mentioned to describe candidate images. Table 4.4 displays the percentages of spots for each presidential candidate in which such qualities are mentioned.

One of the first things that is noticeable in Table 4.4 is that candidates have increasingly found it important to overtly mention their honesty. In early campaigns (other than the high percentage in the small number of Eisenhower 1956 spots), most candidates did not think it necessary to stress their own integrity overtly. Goldwater in 1964 and Carter in 1976 thought it was important enough to their own self-concepts to stress it openly. However, in the twentieth century the honesty of our presidential candidates apparently became so important an issue that candidates felt they must address it directly. In 1992, George Bush mentioned it in 13% of his spots. While Bill Clinton left the issue alone in 1992, his 1996 re-election bid emboldened him to acclaim his integrity

TABLE 4.4
Candidate Characteristics Stressed in Presidential Spots (N = 1,204), in Percentages

	Total	E52	S52	E56	S56	N60	K60	J64	G64
Honesty/Integrity	5%	3%	0	40	0	0	0	0	8
Toughness/Strength	8%	3%	11	40	0	17	1	0	3
Warmth/Compassion	9%	0%	0	20	8	4	7	7	5
Competency	23%	11%	17	20	8	31	22	11	32
Performance/Success	18%	0%	6	40	17	10	0	15	3
Agressiveness	45%	49%	44	0	50	8	31	63	68
Activeness	15%	20%	0	0	17	19	22	11	30
Qualifications	9%	0%	6	20	0	21	0	0	3

	N68	H68	N72	M72	F76	C76	C80	R80	R84	M84
Honesty/Integrity	0%	3	3	2	6	11	4	5	0	0
Toughness/Strength	24%	6	3	4	2	6	0	5	0	18
Warmth/Compassion	17%	6	0	4	7	11	21	1	0	11
Competency	44%	14	10	19	26	32	27	13	17	25
Performance/Success	0%	8	23	0	30	6	25	3	74	4
Aggressiveness	20%	44	33	49	56	26	49	71	26	68
Activeness	29%	17	10	13	16	30	16	14	0	25
Qualifications	24%	11	3	0	9	21	10	6	0	4

	B88	D88	B92	C92	C96	D96
Honesty/Integrity	0%	0	13	0	21	30
Toughness/Strength	2%	1	0	0	53	23
Warmth/Compassion	9%	3	0	0	44	28
Competency	13%	1	6	3	74	19
Performance/Success	19%	8	9	67	77	16
Aggressiveness	21%	37	41	45	45	26
Activeness	6%	8	16	23	23	7
Qualifications	11%	3	6	39	39	7

in 21% of his many 1996 spots, perhaps because Bob Dole made it a hallmark of his own image in 30% of his television ads.

Perhaps the most surprising and recurring image trait candidates portrayed in their spots was their aggressiveness. Most candidates came across in their spots as assertive and determined. They wanted to be seen as on the offensive. This was particularly true for those in a challenger role, as we discuss more fully in Chapter 5, but it was a recurring theme for incumbents and challengers.

This emphasis on aggressiveness may help explain the low presentation of warmth/compassion in presidential videostyles. Few candidates have thought this to be the key to a successful image presentation.

One exception was Richard Nixon, who painted himself with a more compassionate image in 1968 in 17% of his spots but apparently found no need to mention it in his 1972 re-election effort. Another, more consistent exception was Jimmy Carter, who presented his compassionate side more overtly in both his 1976 (11%) and 1980 (21%) spots. No candidate, however, matched Bill Clinton's multifaceted presentations in 1996, when he presented himself as warm/compassionate in 44% of his spots, yet tough and strong in 53% and aggressive in 45%. Few other candidates have found a way to be so many different personalities convincingly at the same time.

Table 4.4 shows that the presentation of competency is also a consistent goal of presidential videostyle. Of all the presidential candidates over this time span, however, Michael Dukakis seemed to have the greatest difficulty conveying the competence factor; he only managed to bring it into one of his spots.

Values in Presidential Spots

Another aspect of the verbal content of presidential messages is the communication of values. Values are an important part of American culture and can mean many different things, but one accepted set of values is the list of "terminal values" identified by Milton Rokeach (1973) that describes overarching principles valued by individuals. We applied this list of values to the 1,204 ads of presidential candidates, indicating each spot that mentioned one or more of these values. Table 4.5 shows that the most frequently mentioned value in presidential spots from 1952 through 1996 was "a comfortable life." Nearly one-third of all spots (30%) by presidential candidates mentioned this value. A "sense of accomplishment" (24%), a "world at peace" (16%), and "family security" (13%) were also recurring values mentioned by American presidential aspirants.

There are, however, some differences in values over time, and some presidential candidates stressed some values more or less than others. For instance, while "a comfortable life" and "a sense of accomplishment" have been relatively stable (with a few exceptions) across time, other values have shown distinct peaks. Presidential candidates have not placed, in their spots at least, a high value on "national security" since 1968. An examination of particular presidential candidates shows some interesting highs and lows in value dimensions. The candidates who stressed "a comfortable life" the most strongly were Stevenson in 1956, Reagan in 1984, and Clinton in 1992. While Eisenhower and Stevenson made "family security" an important value in their spots in 1956, no presidential candidate stressed it very much after that until Reagan in 1984 and, even more strongly, Clinton in 1996. In fact, nearly

TABLE 4.5
Values Mentioned in Presidential Spots (N=1,204)

	Number of Spots	Percentage
*Terminal Values**		
Comfortable Life	365	30%
Sense of Accomplishment	285	24
World at Peace	196	16
Family Security	156	13
Exciting Life	32	3
World of Beauty	22	2
Equality	134	11
Happiness	65	5
National Security	122	10
Freedom	127	11
Pleasure	11	1
Self-Respect	122	10
True Friendship	32	3
Wisdom	72	6
*American Values***		
Change and Progress	660	55%
Material Comfort	359	30
Effort and Optimism	251	21
Patriotism	246	20
Puritan Morality	227	19
Science and Rationality	209	17
Value of the Individual	187	16
Efficiency, Practicality	155	13
Achievement and Success	130	11

*taken from list of terminal values outlined by Milton Rokeach (1973)
**selected from a list of American values presented by Steele and Redding (1962)

half of Clinton's 1996 spots (49%) stressed family security, almost twice as much as any other presidential candidate over the time of this study.

Another way of looking at values is to consider values associated particularly with American culture and mores. Steele and Redding (1962) defined a series of such values that can be considered applicable to American life, and Table 4.5 also shows the occurrence of a selected set of these values as portrayed in presidential spots. Here the particular significance of the American striving for progress can be clearly seen, since over half (55%) of all presidential spots mention the value of "change and progress." The value of "material comfort" garnered 30%

of mentions, showing consistency with the value of "a comfortable life" discussed earlier.

Presidential candidates also wanted to express values of "effort and optimism" (21%) and "patriotism" (20%) in their spots. A sense of "puritan morality" also pervades almost one-fifth of the spots (19%) and was strongest in the spots of Barry Goldwater and Gerald Ford. The values of "achievement and success" hit their highest marks in the spots of Kennedy and Nixon in 1960 and in Bill Clinton's 1996 ads.

Negative and Positive Spots

Another aspect of spots often compared between candidates is the degree to which the spots are "attack" or "negative" spots. A lot has been said about the use of these terms, but in videostyle analysis they basically mean the simple difference between a spot that is primarily focused on the candidate's good qualities, a candidate-positive spot, and one that is primarily focused on the opponent's alleged bad qualities, an opponent-negative spot. As with other content categories, the videostyle analysis deals with spots according to the *dominant* content in the spot. Thus, a spot is coded as either negative or positive. No comparative category is used, since a spot that contains some positive information about the candidate and some negative information about the opponent is coded according to the dominant aspect of the ad.

Across all five decades of political spots, the average percentage of candidate-positive spots has been 62%, as Table 4.2 indicates. Thus, only 38% of all spots have been negative ones. More details about the trends over time and breakdowns by candidate in terms of negative ads are provided in Chapter 6.

Appeals Made in Spots

Another aspect of the verbal content of a spot is the type of appeal used in making the claims in the spot. Most spots are trying to convince a voter to believe the candidate's claim. Whether it is an issue or image claim, the candidate usually offers some type of "proof" for the claim. As explained earlier, videostyle analysis considers these claims according to the classic categories of proof established by Aristotle (logical, emotional, ethical). For a more detailed explanation of these categories, see Chapter 3.

Table 4.6 lists the presence of these three types of proof in presidential spots. In the entire sample of presidential spots, logical proof is used in 70%, emotional proof in 84%, and ethical proof in 67%. More interesting may be the analysis of the *dominant* type of proof used in a spot. While a spot might contain multiple types of proof, this category assesses

TABLE 4.6
Verbal Components of Presidential Videostyle: Types of Appeals
(N = 1,204)

	Number of Spots	Percentage
Presence of Appeals		
Logical	843	70%
Emotional	1012	84
Ethical/Source		
Credibility	807	67
Dominant Appeal		
Logical	273	23
Emotional	531	44
Ethical/Source		
Credibility	400	33
Use of Fear Appeal	234	19

which type is the most important to the spot's claim(s). The analysis demonstrates that logical proof is actually the least used as the dominant form of proof in spots, while emotional evidence is the most common. In fact, 44% of all spots rely on emotional proof to make their point.

When these categories are examined over time, it is clear that this reliance on emotional proof is not a recent phenomenon. The following list shows the presidential candidates whose spots were particularly high in each type of proof:

Logical Proof	Emotional Proof	Ethical Proof
1952 Eisenhower (51%)	1960 Kennedy (53%)	1968 Nixon (51%)
1980 Reagan (37%)	1960 Nixon (71%)	1980 Carter (65%)
1992 Bush (47%)	1964 Goldwater (73%)	
1992 Clinton (44%)	1964 Johnson (71%)	
1996 Dole (44%)	1972 Nixon (57%)	
	1976 Ford (52%)	
	1984 Mondale (68%)	
	1984 Reagan (58%)	

It is clear that some of the most recent campaigns (1992 and 1996) have placed more reliance on logical proof than did some of their earlier counterparts. One example of logical proof is the use of statistical evidence, and many candidate spots in the high-logical-proof category relied on statistics to make their points. For example, Eisenhower answered a question in a 1952 spot about "how bad is the waste in Washington?" by working in a statistic with a bit of humor: "How bad? Recently just one government bureau actually lost $400 million dollars, and not even the FBI can find it. It's really time for a change."

Ronald Reagan has often been dismissed as an actor who relied on his "great communicator" skills to win and maintain power in the White House. However, while his 1984 spots relied on a great deal of emotional proof, his 1980 bid for the presidency was filled with logical and statistical argument. This short spot from 1980 is one example:

> Announcer: "Inflation has taken sixty-four cents out of every dollar since the Democrats got control of our economy. Vote Republican. For a change."

Another example of the combination of statistical evidence and proof by example is apparent in this 1980 Reagan ad:

> Announcer: "This is a man whose time has come. A strong leader with a proven record. In 1966 answering the call of his party, Ronald Reagan was elected governor of California, next to the President the biggest job in the nation. What the new governor inherited was a state of crisis. California was faced with a $194 million deficit and was spending a million dollars a day more than it was taking in. The state was on the brink of bankruptcy. Governor Reagan became the greatest tax reformer in the state's history. When Governor Reagan left office, the $194 million deficit had been transformed into a $550 million surplus. The *San Francisco Chronicle* said Governor Reagan had saved the state from bankruptcy. The time is now for strong leadership. Reagan for President."

Emotional proof is the most common form of evidence offered by presidential candidates, since 44% of all ads rely on it. The 1964 campaign provided a striking high in the category; both Goldwater and Johnson relied on emotional evidence in over 70% of their spots. The Johnson examples are well remembered. The famous "Daisy Girl" spot that invites the viewer to participate in a nuclear explosion is the best-known spot from that or any other campaign. However, the Johnson campaign used many other emotional appeals. Less well remembered are the poignant pleas with visually stirring pictures regarding children and poverty and criticisms about Goldwater's "risky" ideas on Social Security.

Barry Goldwater's campaign is rarely characterized as an emotional one, although his very slogan, "In your heart, you know he's right," relied more on moral overtones than logical interpretation. In some of his spots, often those attacking Lyndon Johnson, he used visual and verbal aspects of emotion to make his point, as this spot illustrates:

Announcer: "On February 11, 1964 in Washington, President Lyndon B. Johnson said 'We are a much-beloved people throughout the world.' We are a much beloved people throughout the world."
Goldwater: "Is this what President Johnson means when he says we are much-beloved? [Video of rioting and American flag desecrated.] Well, I don't like to see our flag torn down and trampled upon anywhere in the world. And I think most Americans agree with me on that. . . . All this results from weak, vacillating leadership. We must show the world that we are a mature and responsible people, aware of our rights, as well as our responsibilities."
Announcer: "In your heart, you know he's right."

The 1984 campaign also contained many emotional overtones in the spots of both Ronald Reagan and Walter Mondale. Reagan used soft and filtered visuals and emotional messages about how good things were for America in his simple spots that touted the American lifestyle. This example from the "Morning in America" series of spots illustrates the use of emotional proof:

Announcer: "It's morning again in America. Today more men and women will go to work than ever before in our country's history. With interest rates and inflation down more people are buying new homes, and new families can have confidence in the future. America today is prouder, and stronger, and better. Why would we want to return to where we were less than four short years ago?"

Another example appeals to concern about war and links it with an emotional concern for children. In this spot Reagan himself makes the plea:

In my lifetime we've faced four wars, and I want our children never to have to face another. A president's most important job is to secure peace for our children. But it takes a strong nation to build a peace that lasts. And I believe that America is stronger and more secure today, thanks to the determination of our people.

Many of Mondale's emotional pleas in 1984 also centered on the war and peace issue, as well as on children.

While Richard Nixon relied on emotional appeals in his 1960 and 1972 campaigns, it is interesting that he used a great deal of ethical proof in his 1968 campaign. Ethical proof relies on source credibility or "ethos" to substantiate a claim. It invites the voter to support the candidate because the candidate has "high moral" character and accomplishments or because others of high character support the candidate. For this reason, testimonials by respected individuals are often used in campaigns and are good examples of ethical proof. Nixon called on California Senator George Murphy for this endorsement:

> Well, I think Richard M. Nixon probably is more qualified in world affairs than anybody that I know. And I'm sure of one thing with Richard Nixon. He'll decide all these foreign policy matters on what's good for America, not what may be good for some other country in the world. And I think the time has come when we need this.

As part of his strategy to avoid speaking himself and relying on others to speak for him, the Nixon campaign called on a host of others to endorse the former vice-president in 1968, including Senator Hiram Fong of Hawaii, Senators Everett Dirksen and Charles Percy of Illinois, Senator Jacob Javits of New York, Senator John Tower and Congressman George Bush from Texas, Senator Howard Baker of Tennesse, and other visible political figures. He also used celebrity endorsers like singer Pat Boone.

Fear appeals are a particular type of emotional appeal that attempts to scare voters or raise their fears about specific issues or character traits. For this reason, fear appeals are often found in negative ads and are frequently combined with other types of evidence. Almost one-fifth of all presidential spots use some type of fear appeal (19%), as seen in Table 4.6.

Strong fear appeals were not used in American presidential spots until 1964. In that campaign, both Johnson and Goldwater made heavy use of fear appeals. The percentage of fear appeals in both their campaigns (48% of all Johnson spots and 52% of all Goldwater spots) was much higher than the average 19%. Of course, the "Daisy Girl" spot is a classic example:

> Over a shot of a small girl picking the petals from a daisy and counting: One, two, three, four, five, seven, six, six, eight, nine, a countdown is heard (Ten, nine, eight, seven, six, five, four, three, two, one, zero.) As the camera zooms in on the girl's eye, a nuclear explosion and a mushroom cloud are seen. Lyndon Johnson in voice-over says: "These are the stakes: to make a world in which all of God's children can live or to go into the darkness. We must either love each other or we must die."

Another fear appeal is easily recognized in an ad of a small child licking an ice-cream cone, while a voice-over says:

> Do you know what people used to do? They used to explode atomic bombs in the air. Now children should have lots of Vitamin A and calcium but they shouldn't have any Strontium 90 or Cesium 137. These things come from atomic bombs and they're radioactive. They can make you die. Do you know what people finally did? They got together and signed a Nuclear Test Ban Treaty and then the radioactive poison started to go away. But now, there's a man who wants to be President of the United States who doesn't like this treaty. He fought against it. He even voted against it. He wants to go on testing more bombs. His name is Barry Goldwater. And if he's elected, they might start testing all over again.

No matter how hot it may be, this spot does not make you want to rush down to the local ice cream parlor for a cone.

Given the high amount of emotional proof in Walter Mondale's 1984 campaign, twenty years later, it is not surprising that his spots also score high on fear appeals (64%). The fear raised still concerned war and peace issues, as this spot criticizing Reagan's endorsement of the "Star Wars" technology illustrates:

> Announcer: "Ronald Reagan is determined to put killer weapons in space. The Soviets will have to match us, and the arms race will rage out of control, orbiting, aiming, waiting. With a response time to fire so short there will be no time to wake a president. Computers will take control. On November 6th you can take control. No weapons in space by either side. Draw the line at the heavens with Mondale."

Fear appeals, which had played a much lesser role between 1964 and 1984, became quite prevalent in the succeeding campaigns. Some of the highest levels of fear appeals were seen in George Bush's 1992 campaign (56%) and in Bill Clinton's 1996 spots (48%). This George Bush spot in 1992 sought to raise fears about what would happen if Bill Clinton transferred his Arkansas governor's experience to Washington:

> Announcer: "In his twelve years as governor, Bill Clinton has doubled his state's debt, doubled government spending and signed the largest tax increase in his state's history. Yet his state remains the 45th worst in which to work, the 45th worst for children. It has the worst environmental policy, and the FBI says Arkansas had the biggest increase in the rate of serious crime. And now Bill Clinton wants to do for America, what he's done for Arkansas. America can't take that risk."

Bill Clinton was even more critical of Bob Dole in 1996 spots that proclaimed Dole was "Wrong in the Past, Wrong for our Future." He also successfully used children and fear of smoking to create this fear appeal ad called "First Time":

> Announcer: "These children are trying smoking for the first time. One will die from the habit. President Clinton says stop ads that teach our children to smoke. But Bob Dole opposes an FDA limit on tobacco ads that appeal to children. Says cigarettes aren't necessarily addictive. Some say milk is bad for kids too, Dole says. But 3,000 children start smoking every day. A thousand will die from it—1 of 3. Bob Dole or President Clinton: who's really protecting our children?"

NONVERBAL COMPONENTS OF PRESIDENTIAL VIDEOSTYLE

The nonverbal content of a spot consists of the elements of the spot that convey meaning outside the overt verbal content. Nonverbal content can include a candidate's voice intonations and speech patterns, the very presence or absence of a candidate, the candidate's dress style, the setting of the spot, and other facial and body characteristics. These aspects of a spot communicate to the voter the candidate's feelings and meaning in ways that are less overt and more subtle than verbal content.

Candidate as Speaker

One of the major components of the nonverbal meaning in a spot is conveyed by who is the major speaker in a spot. A presidential candidate can speak for himself or can rely on others to speak. When a candidate speaks directly to the voters, the candidate is providing the voter with direct and specific meaning about his personal qualities and his nonverbal characteristics. The voter, therefore, can judge the candidate in a complete manner. Such direct communication has, however, not been the norm in presidential spots. As Table 4.7 shows, the candidate has been the main speaker in only 37% of spots used in presidential campaigns. Candidates rely on "anonymous announcers" to carry the major point of the message in 40% of their spots. Other main speakers include government officials, celebrities, and spouses or family members.

Perhaps more disturbing than the overall percentage of candidates speaking in their spots is the trend over time. In 1960, for instance, Kennedy and Nixon were the main speakers in 59% of their spots. However, Figure 4.2 shows that by 1996 this had declined so dramatically that Clinton and Dole were the main speakers in only 5% of the

TABLE 4.7
Nonverbal Components of Presidential Videostyle: Candidate Speaking, Setting, and Dress

	Number of Spots	Percentage
Dominant Speaker (N = 1,204)		
Candidate	444	37%
Government Official	120	10
Anonymous Announcer	479	40
Non-government Celebrity	33	3
Spouse or Family Member	15	1
Combination or Other	113	9
Candidate Sound (N = 444)		
Sound-on/Candidate	384	87
Sound-over/Candidate	60	13
Setting of Spot (N = 1,204)		
Formal Indoors	397	33
Informal Indoors	158	13
Formal Outdoors	100	8
Informal Outdoors	99	8
Combination	84	7
Not Applicable	366	30
Candidate Dress (N = 444)		
Formal	358	81
Casual	61	14
Varied	25	5

1996 ads. The overall yearly numbers obscure some other low points. For instance, although the overall 1964 percentage of candidates as speakers is 42%, most of this is accounted for by Goldwater's direct style (60%). Lyndon Johnson appeared as the main speaker in only 18% of his spots.

When the candidate does speak, however, he generally speaks "sound-on" film/video—speaking on-screen, rather than as a voice-over. In 87% of the spots where the candidate is the main speaker the candidate appears in live, sound-on presentations.

Formality in Setting and Dress

The setting of a spot also conveys an impression to the voter. Table 4.7 indicates that most presidential candidates want that impression to

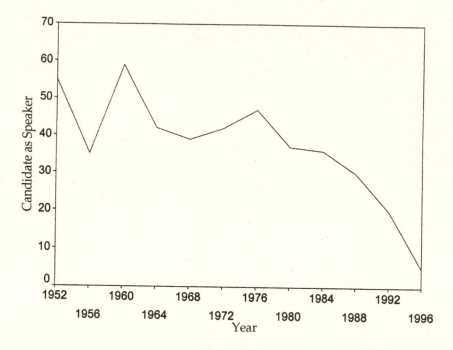

Figure 4.2 Candidate as Main Speaker in Political Spots, 1952–1996

be a formal one. Formal indoor settings account for 33% of all spots, while formal outdoor settings account for another 8%. Informal settings (both indoors and outdoors) account for another 21% of settings.

Formal indoor settings often work best for a candidate who wants to convey a sense of responsibility and trust. The trappings of an office, be it the Oval Office in the White House for an incumbent or another office setting, help the candidate portray a sense of serious attention to the work of the government.

Candidates also generally choose to dress formally when they appear in spots. In the spots in which the candidate is the main speaker, 81% of the candidates appear in formal dress. Only 14% of the time are the candidates dressed informally. Only Jimmy Carter in 1976 and Bill Clinton in 1992, both challengers seeking to convey a sense of warmth and caring, chose to use casual dress in any substantial number of their spots.

Candidate Speech and Body Movement

When a candidate does speak in his spots, it might seem likely that he would want to appear to be smiling and cheerful, an optimistic portrayer of his verbal message. This is not the case, however, as seen in Table 4.8. Most candidates do not wear a smiling face. In 85% of their spots, candidate facial expressions are primarily attentive/serious. Since this category, like others, was coded according to the dominant facial expression of the candidate, it is possible that candidates did smile at some point during a presentation, but only 11% of the time was this the dominant approach in the ad. Some candidates exceeded this norm, of course. Eisenhower was smiling in 51% of the spots in which

TABLE 4.8
Nonverbal Components of Presidential Videostyle: Speech & Body Movement (N = 444)*

	Number of Spots	Percentage
Facial Expression		
Smiling	48	11%
Attentive/Serious	376	85
Other	20	5
Eye Contact with Viewer		
Almost Always	219	49
Sometimes	50	11
Almost Never	103	23
Body Movement of Candidate		
Never	187	42
Moderate	205	46
Frequent	31	7
Candidate Speaking Fluency		
Fluent	414	93
Stumbling/Halting	30	7
Candidate Speaking Rate		
Slow	127	29
Moderate	309	69
Fast	8	2
Candidate Voice Pitch		
Monotone	23	5
Pitch Variety	340	77

*Not all sets of numbers and percentages add up to the total, since "Not Applicable" categories were excluded.

he was the main speaker, Dukakis in 1988 smiled broadly in 48% of his appearances, and, perhaps most surprising, 40% of Richard Nixon's 1972 spots show him smiling most of the time. John Kennedy in 1960, on the other hand, was one of the most serious/attentive of all speakers, displaying this facial expression in 77% of his spots.

When a candidate speaks in a spot, one mark of his ability to communicate directly with the voter is the extent to which he has eye contact with the voter (through the camera). Presidential candidates achieved this direct eye contact on a continuing ("almost always") basis in less than half of their spots (49%). In 23% of the spots, Table 4.8 indicates, the candidate, although the main speaker, "almost never" had eye contact with the viewer. Some candidates seemed to excel at this quality. John Kennedy, although usually serious, almost always had eye contact (in 60% of his spots). Barry Goldwater, another candidate known for a serious/attentive facial expression, achieved the highest level of all candidates for direct eye contact—"almost always" in 54% of his spots.

There were also differences in how candidates controlled their body movements during appearances in their spots. Most candidates struck a happy medium here, with 46% of spots showing candidates with "moderate" body movement. However, in 42% of the spots candidates "almost never" moved at all. Candidates with particularly high levels of a stationary body were Eisenhower in 1952, Nixon in 1960, and Dukakis in 1988. The latter finding lends some credence to the reputation Dukakis earned for being a "wooden" and nonexpressive candidate.

Table 4.8 also tells the story of candidate speaking voice characteristics. Speaking fluency did not differentiate many candidates from one another. Most candidates (93%) were judged to be "fluent," with only Carter in 1976 receiving any substantial number of ratings as a "stumbling/halting" speaker. Kennedy scored the highest on this category also, since he was categorized as fluent in 77% of his speaking appearances.

Most candidates also spoke with some pitch variety in their voices, avoiding a boring monotone. Eisenhower and Carter, however, sometimes were labeled as monotone speakers. Jimmy Carter also, particularly in 1976, was labeled as a "slow" speaker in 61% of his spots. His slow, drawling Southern accent placed him in the "slow" speech category much more often than the norm (29%).

PRODUCTION COMPONENTS OF PRESIDENTIAL VIDEOSTYLE

How a presidential candidate chooses to present himself in his spots via various technological and video production devices can tell a great deal about how the candidate and his media consultants want the audience to react to the candidate. One characteristic of candidate videostyle that falls into the production category is the length of a spot. A candidate who wishes to convey quick short messages may be telling the electorate that he does not want his ideas exposed to too much scrutiny or that he believes the voter cannot absorb a longer message. Whichever it may be, candidates messages have been getting shorter and shorter. Table 4.9 shows that the most popular length for political messages during the past five decades has been the 30-second spot, which comprises 57% of all spots. Spots 60 seconds in length made up 32% of the total, and longer formats of up to 5 minutes made up 12%.

However, these overall averages mask the changing trends over time. Spots have been getting shorter and shorter. Since 1980, the

TABLE 4.9
Production Components of Videostyle: Length, Format, Production Style (N = 1,204)

	Number of Spots	Percentage
Length of Spot		
15-30 Seconds	685	57%
60 Seconds	374	31
2-5 Minutes	145	12
Format of Spot		
Documentary Style	92	8
Video Clip/Music Video	108	9
Testimonial	191	16
Introspection	255	21
Issue Statement	24	2
Opposition Focused	250	21
Issue Dramatization	141	12
Quest/Answer/Confrontation	129	11
Other	14	1
Production Style of Spot		
Cinema Verité	322	27
Slides w/Print/Voice-Over	203	17
Candidate Head-On	283	23
Other Speaker Head-On	173	14
Animation or Special Prod.	116	10
Combination	107	9

majority of all spots have been 15-30 seconds long, and the 1996 campaigns were characterized by the highest percentages of short spots ever. In fact, 99% of Clinton's 1996 spots and 93% of Dole's 1996 spots were 30 seconds long or briefer. The last campaigns to make any substantial use of the 5-minute format were in 1980 and 1984, when both candidates used these longer formats to provide more information to voters.

Presidential Ad Formats

Another indication of a candidate's videostyle is the format of the commercial. Many different formats have been used, but some of the most common ones are shown in Table 4.9, along with the corresponding percentages of their usage in presidential spots. The most common formats have been the "Introspective" format, in which a candidate reflects on a problem, issue, character concern, or other campaign topic. This format was used in over one-fifth (21%) of all presidential spots. Many introspective spots are "talking-head" spots and use that form of production. John Kennedy in 1960 and Ronald Reagan in 1980 and 1984 were particularly skilled at this spot format. In one 1980 spot, Reagan uses this simple format to reflect on his feelings about peace and economic issues:

> Reagan: "Nancy and I have traveled this great land of ours many times over the past months and years. We've found that Americans everywhere yearn for peace just as we do. Our four children are grown now, we have one grandson, hopefully we'll be blessed with more. It is impossible to capture with words the feelings we have for peace around the world and how desperately we want it for our children and their children. By restoring an on-the-move economy, establishing a strong working relationship with our allies based on respect and understanding and by restoring that vital margin of safety which our military strength provides, America will be in position to negotiate a strong peace and to protect that peace from the whims of nations that would test our will and resolve. True peace is our dream, and I pledge to you, of all the objectives we seek, first and foremost will be the establishment of world peace."

Opposition-focused spots have also been a common format, also used in 21% of all spots. This category is actually a kind of multifaceted category for negative spots and may encompass comparative spots, spots that focus on contradictions in an opponent's statements, or spots that visually depict an opponent's weaknesses. Various types of opponent spots are discussed more fully in Chapter 6.

Testimonials have been a frequently used format (16%) since the very first presidential spot campaign in 1952. As mentioned earlier, they often constitute a convincing form of ethical proof, particularly when done by a respected or famous individual.

Nixon's extensive use of endorsements as ethical proof in 1968 was mentioned previously, but the trend was started much earlier. John Kennedy's campaign produced testimonial format spots from political figures like Adlai Stevenson, Senator William Fulbright, and Eleanor Roosevelt and from celebrities like Harry Belafonte, Henry Fonda, and Dr. Benjamin Spock. Richard Nixon responded in 1960 with President Eisenhower. In 1964, Barry Goldwater called on actors Ronald Reagan and John Wayne and used political testimonials from Eisenhower and Maine's Senator Margaret Chase Smith. In 1968 Hubert Humphrey used a Ted Kennedy endorsement, as well as celebrity testimonials from E. G. Marshall, Douglas Fairbanks, and Frank Sinatra.

It is important to note, however, that testimonials can also take the form of endorsements from family members. While Bob Dole in 1996 replayed the endorsement of Colin Powell from the Republican National Convention: "Bob Dole is the candidate most qualified by virtue of his beliefs, his character, and competence to be the next President of the United States of America," one of the most effective spots of the 1996 Dole campaign was Elizabeth Dole's testimonial about her husband's good qualities in a spot called "From the Heart":

> My husband is a plainspoken man from the heart of America, Russell, Kansas. In Russell, you say what you're going to do and you do it, the truth, first, last, always the truth. When Bob Dole says he'll cut your taxes 15%, he'll cut your taxes 15%. This is Bob Dole, he's a workhorse, not a showhorse and he knows whose money it really is, your family's.

Another type of testimonial is the "man-on-the-street" spot in which ordinary citizens appear to give spontaneous endorsements either in favor of the candidate or against the opponent. In 1968, Hubert Humphrey used this type of testimonial to enumerate his good points:

> Announcer: "These are critical times. Who do you want to be the next President?"
> Person in street: "As things stand right now I definitely feel that Mr. Humphrey would be the best, uh, uh, the best possible candidate for the presidency."
> Another Person: "This is a man who has had a very strong liberal background."
> Another Person: "He's not only a man of new ideas, uh, he's a man who is ahead of the times."

Another Person: "Cause I think he's the man who's ready for the job. He can handle it because he's very familiar with the problems, involved with the issues."

Another person: "He was very active and very much acquainted with the problems of the cities many years ago when we talked about civil rights and the poor people."

Another person: "Vice President Humphrey is without question the man that I feel that everyone in this country can trust."

Another person: "I think, sure Humphrey is a leader. He's one who can unite all the people behind him. He's just the best man for the job now."

Announcer: "People believe in Humphrey. The country needs him."

In 1976 Gerald Ford used the man-in-the-street format to get testimonials of another kind, negative evaluations of opponent Jimmy Carter's performance as former Governor of Georgia. This spot is an example:

Person on the Street (Atlanta): "I was here when Carter was governor and he made a lot of promises that he didn't keep."

Another person (Atlanta): "He increased the number of government employees in the state of Georgia substantially while he was in office. I don't know if that helped us or hurt us, but I know that it definitely increased the budget, and when you increase the budget, you have to increase the tax base."

Another person (Atlanta): "When I tell people here in Georgia that I'm going to vote for Ford they don't really understand why. It would be good to have a president from Georgia but not Carter."

While the testimonial format has remained a staple of political spots across time, the question-and-answer format has fallen out of use. Although 11% of all spots across time have used this format, it was most popular in the early years of presidential spots, when the format was relatively easy to produce. The original Eisenhower spots, of course, relied on this approach, and such spots made up 86% of Eisenhower's 1952 campaign ads. The decline in this format has been so great that no candidate has used a straight question-and-answer format in the last three presidential campaigns (1988, 1992, or 1996), and the percentages of such spots in 1984 and 1980 were, respectively, 1% and 2%.

Documentary formats were also not used a great deal in recent campaigns. The high point for this format was in 1972 and 1976. President Nixon particularly made use of this format in 1972 for his productions (many of them in the 5-minute length) on his historic trips to

Russia and China. Nixon used this format more than any other president; 40 of his 1972 spots were done in this format.

Issue dramatizations are another format whose use has ebbed and flowed. Issue dramatizations tell a story that points up a candidate's or opponent's position on an issue concern. This format is easily associated with the 1964 Lyndon Johnson campaign because it is the format used for the "Daisy Girl" spot and several other spots that highlight the dangers of Goldwater's ideas. Such formats were virtually nonexistent in the years from 1972 through 1980, but they began to be popular again in 1984. The 1988 campaign saw a great increase in issue dramatization, since 32% of all spots produced that year were in this format. One interesting issue dramatization from the 1988 Bush campaign features real footage of Michael Dukakis riding in a tank, looking extremely uncomfortable and a bit silly, while the voice-over recounts Dukakis's alleged opposition to defense programs:

> Announcer: "Michael Dukakis has opposed nearly every defense system we've ever made. He opposed new aircraft carriers, he opposed anti-satellite weapons, he opposed four missile systems, including the Pershing Two Missile deployment. Dukakis opposed the Stealth Bomber and a ground emergency warning system against nuclear attack. He even criticized our rescue mission to Grenada and our strike on Libya. And now he wants to be our Commander in Chief. America can't afford that risk."

Originally taken from news footage provided at a "photo-op" planned for Dukakis' campaign, this spot told a story that was reinforced strongly by the visuals of Dukakis, who looked as if he belonged anywhere but in a tank.

Production Styles of Presidential Spots

In addition to the actual format of a spot, production styles can tell a lot about a candidate. Table 4.9 shows that presidential candidates have used a lot of different production techniques. The most popular have been cinema verité (27%) and candidate head-on (23%). A candidate head-on production is not difficult to imagine. Such productions make the easiest and simplest way for a candidate to speak directly to voters. Another 14% of all spots have used this same production style but with someone other than the candidate as the speaker. Many testimonials, for instance, use this production technique. Political observers tout this production style as the most genuine and least susceptible to manipulation by the candidate and his media advisers. If this production style, the candidate speaking head-on, is to be valued for its directness and lack of manipulation, then the highest marks would go to Eisenhower; 80% of his spots used this production style. Others who used it more than the average of 23% include Kennedy (47%), Nixon in 1960 (46%), Goldwater (57%), and Carter in 1976 (51%). Low marks for avoiding directness would go to Nixon in 1968 (5%), and the lowest of all to Bill Clinton in 1996 (1%).

Cinema verité, the most common production format across the years, is designed to provide the viewer with a "slice of life," to appear to portray a realistic and naturally occurring event as it is happening. It was not particularly common in the early days of television production, and few spots used it until the 1968 campaign. This style reached its zenith in political spots under the direction of acclaimed media producer Charles Guggenheim, who produced some very real-life spots for the 1972 McGovern campaign. In many of these spots, McGovern is shown interacting with ordinary people in real events. Sometimes the interactions are actually confrontational, lending a sense of reality, rather than staging, to the spots.

Slides with print or voice-over are also frequently used in campaign productions. Across time, 17% of all spots have used this production style. The first really high use of such spots was in Richard Nixon's 1968 campaign, when producers chose this format as a way of creating motion and involvement, while avoiding the use of Nixon himself appearing in the spots (McGinniss, 1969). Over half of all Nixon spots in 1968 (51%) used this production style. But this production style, interestingly, fell into disuse after 1968 and was not particularly prevalent again until the 1996 campaign, when both Clinton (44%) and Dole (56%) used it a great deal.

The overall production style of a spot tells something about the candidate's approach to communication in a general way. The actual camera angles and shots applied to the candidate appearing in a spot might also provide information about the candidate's presentation style. Unfortunately, this aspect of videostyle analysis has not revealed much difference between candidates. As Table 4.10 indicates, there is a great deal of uniformity in these categories. Most candidates are shown in "straight-on" camera angles, rarely high or low. A few exceptions can be noted. Clinton in 1996 was shown from an unusually high number of "high" angles (9%, compared to the average of 2%). On the other hand, some candidates were frequently shown from low angles, including Carter in 1976 (15%), Mondale in 1984 (29%), Dukakis in 1988 (20%), and Clinton in 1996 (20%)—compared to the average across time of 4%.

Types of camera shots also do not provide for strong differentiations. Most candidates are shown in "tight" (head and shoulders) shots. Such shots were used in 63% of all spots.

TABLE 4.10
Production Components of Presidential Videostyle: Production
Techniques (N = 1,204)

	Number of Spots	Percentage
Presence of Music	443	37%
Presence of Production Techniques		
Computer Graphics	325	27
Slow Motion	118	10
Fast Motion	31	3
Reverse Motion	20	2
Freeze-Frame	124	10
Split Screen	35	3
Superimposition	195	16
Montage	31	3
Stop Motion	88	7
Stills	438	36
Candidate Dominant Camera Angle (N = 444)		
High Angle	8	2
Straight-On	392	88
Low Angle	19	4
Movement/Combination	25	6
Type of Dominant Candidate Camera Shot (N = 444)		
Tight (Head and Shoulders)	278	63
Medium (Waist Up)	105	24
Long (Full Length)	3	1
Combination	58	13

Music is another production technique that can create a strong effect in a spot. Over one-third of all spots (37%) use some kind of music. Almost every candidate has used music for creating emotion or excitement in spots. The 1952 campaign got this trend off to a rousing start with the use of the sung jingle in the "I Like Ike" animated spot created by Walt Disney Studios. Less well known are the singing spots for Adlai Stevenson's 1952 campaign. Less creative than the Eisenhower effort, some of these spots simply featured a woman singing little jingles such as:

"Dirksen, McCarthy, and Taft. Dirksen, McCarthy, and Taft, would you pardon me if I laugh? There's no sense in pointing out one single case. They are simply anti the whole human race. Dirksen, McCarthy, and Taft, forgive me if I cause a draft. Put these men in power and you will regret. I guess you saw Dirksen on your TV set? That look he gave Dewey is what we would get from Dirksen, McCarthy and Taft."

This one is hard to appreciate without hearing the music itself, but everyone can imagine the next one, by thinking of the familiar "Old MacDonald Had a Farm" tune:

Announcer: Let's Not Forget . . . The Farmer
Singer: Ole McDonald had a farm, back in thirty-one.
Politicians filled him with alarm back in thirty-one. Not a chick, chick here or a moo cow there, just broken down farm land everywhere. And farmer Mac doesn't want to go back to the days when there wasn't no moo or quack. To the days of 1931 when he didn't have bread when the day was done.
Farmer Mac knows what to do election day of '52. He's gonna go out with everyone in the USA. To vote for Adlai Stevenson to keep his farm this way. With a vote here and a vote there and a vote for Stevenson every-where. For if it's good for Mac, you see, it's good for you and it's good for me. All of America loves that farm. Vote Stevenson today.

Other examples from the Stevenson campaign are even more stilted and tortured, but they demonstrate a belief that the music could be used to help "sell" the candidate.

In 1960 Kennedy could not resist the musical jingle that highlighted his name with the intent to increase recognition. Mixed with pictures and posters with visual reinforcements of the Kennedy name, the jingle's words are reproduced in Chapter 1.

Both Gerald Ford in 1976 and Ronald Reagan in 1984 used music in their spots to create a strong mood of upbeat enthusiasm and patrio-tism. In some of these spots original music was written or new words were put to old tunes. In some spots well-known tunes were played and/or sung to emphasize visuals from the campaign spots.

Specialized Video Production Effects

A final aspect of production techniques considered in the videostyle analysis is the use of special production techniques. In the early years of spot production, spots were produced on film, an expensive process that required a lot of lead time for development and editing and allowed limited use of specialized production techniques. However, as video production came into widespread usage and electronic editing and later computerized production became possible, new and elaborate techniques were possible and affordable. Some of these specialized production techniques are listed in Table 4.10, showing the percentage of use of these techniques in presidential spots over the entire sample of presidential spots. The insertion and use of stills has been the most commonly used technique. Over one-third of all spots have used this technique in one way or another (36%). Of course, as mentioned previously, Nixon's 1968 campaign is famous for its use of still photographs, often juxtaposed and rephotographed to create the impression of movement. This technique was used to give life to Vietnam War pictures and create a lifelike immediacy to the images of war in Nixon spots.

Graphics, particularly computer-generated graphics, have also been used frequently; 27% of all spots have used them. The first noticeable use came in 1968 when Nixon ended his spots with a striking visual graphic of his name enlarging to proclaim: "THIS TIME VOTE LIKE YOUR WHOLE WORLD DEPENDED ON IT— NIXON." In fact, 85% of Nixon's 1968 spots used such graphics, the highest percentage ever.

Superimpositions were also frequently used for productions of presidential spots. Since superimpositions could be done in film as well as video, they date back to early spot production. However, their most striking and frequent use came from Bill Clinton's campaign spots, in 1996 when he repeatedly used a superimposition of Bob Dole and Newt Gingrich over Washington buildings to symbolize the alleged damage caused by their association and by Republican actions—60% of Clinton's spots used some such superimposition like this.

One important finding of the videostyle analysis is that the use of such special production techniques has been increasing dramatically. From 1952 through 1964, an average number of .68 uses of special effects per spot were used (just over one spot in two used such techniques). However, during the period from 1968 through 1984, usage had increased such that an average of 1.18 techniques per spot were in use (i.e., on the average every spot used at least some special effects technique). By the last three election campaigns, from 1988 through 1996, usage increased to a mean of 1.87. Thus, most spots used at least two such techniques on the average.

The visual aspects of spots are now a very important part of a candidate's videostyle. More than at any time in the past, the growing use of specialized production techniques and special production formats have changed the ways in which candidates communicate with voters. Not only do these differences in production provide more variety for candidates, they also open new possibilities for manipulation of the information provided to voters. More information on these possibilities is discussed in Chapter 7.

SUMMARY

This chapter has provided an overview of presidential candidate videostyle. By looking in a summary fashion at the elements of videostyle, it is possible to see trends and patterns in all three components of videostyle. Among the most interesting findings related to verbal content of spots is that presidential candidates have focused more on issues than images, although the number of policy preferences and proposals is somewhat less than the overall emphasis on issues would suggest. Candidates also have more often focused on positive than negative spots, although recent campaigns have shown a trend toward higher percentages of negative spots, particularly Bill Clinton's 1992 and 1996 campaigns. Presidential candidates also rely heavily on emotional appeals in their spots.

In terms of nonverbal components of videostyle, an important finding is that candidates do not often speak for themselves in their spots. Presidential candidates have also preferred formality in the setting of their spots and in their own dress. When they do appear in their spots, presidential candidates are usually serious/attentive in their facial expressions, not smiling.

The final component of production techniques varies considerably across the years, partly because of advancing technological developments. Spots have gotten shorter over time, candidates use a number of different formats for their productions, and the number of special effects in spots has increased in the past three election cycles.

While these findings give a composite look at presidential style in campaign spots, they do not outline particular styles that characterize individual presidents. The application of the videostyle components to individual presidents is provided in the concluding chapter of this book. The next chapter analyzes the videostyles associated with particular candidate positions, considering whether partisan affiliation or the position of incumbent or challenger affects a candidate's videostyle.

5

Videostyle and Political Candidate Positioning

Over the years, presidential candidates have found that different styles and strategies were more suited to their needs, to the culture, and to the climate and circumstances of the campaign. In addition, innovations in technology made some techniques easier to use on a regular basis. In this chapter a comparison of incumbents and challengers and Republicans and Democrats is offered to explore how political position and party may affect videostyle.

ADVANTAGES OF INCUMBENTS AND CHALLENGERS

Available Resources

The style of a communicator needs to be appropriate to the situation, the context, and the time. In a political campaign a candidate's running position is an important dimension of campaign strategy and, therefore, of style. Because style is dependent on the position and situation of the candidate and on the context of the election, it is important to consider the implications of a candidate running as the incumbent or as the challenger. Traditionally, the incumbent's position has been a more stable, ideal one for campaigning. In recent years, incumbency has become a more vulnerable and less secure position because of scandals and the growing affection for political outsiders. However, there still remains evidence of an incumbency advantage, particularly in lower-level elections, and scholars have argued that presidential incumbents also benefit from such advantages.

One explanation for incumbency advantage may be that voters are no longer using party identification as a voting cue and have substituted incumbency for party affiliation (Mayhew, 1974). Ferejohn (1977) suggests that because information is so costly in elections, voters tend to rely on simple decision rules in trying to determine how to cast their vote, and incumbency can serve as one such cue.

Incumbents may also have an advantage because they can advertise themselves and their work through their official duties. They are usually more visible and may be seen as more attractive alternatives to voters. They also benefit from being a known quantity and from their established reputations (Mann, 1978; Mann & Wolfinger, 1980; Mayhew, 1974).

The level of visibility and command of media attention have given incumbents increased contact with voters. In addition, congressional incumbents have been able to successfully focus voters' attention on areas of their job performance by sending them information about the projects they sponsor to help their districts (Fiorina, 1977; Jacobson, 1981; Mann, 1978; Mann & Wolfinger, 1980; Mayhew, 1974; Parker, 1980; Tinkham & Weaver-Lariscy, 1995). In recent years, distrust of incumbents has sometimes resulted in media scrutiny and questioning of use of the office for political gain in upcoming elections. However, even in the early 1990s, when the climate in the country was said to be "anti-incumbent," incumbents continued to have an advantage in congressional elections (Jackson, 1994).

For presidential elections, incumbency may not be as strong an influence, but it still offers definite advantages. Several factors have been tied to the incumbency advantage in presidential elections. One is the popularity of the president and voters' approval of the president's job performance (Brody & Sigelman, 1983; Sigelman, 1979). Presidential popularity ratings often affect election outcomes for an incumbent president. In addition, even when the incumbent president is not running for office, his popularity can influence how his party's candidate will do in the upcoming elections.

While some researchers have argued that incumbency is not a very salient issue for voters in presidential elections (Kessel, 1980), others have identified elements that make incumbency a powerful force in presidential selection. One advantage for presidential incumbents is that they carry the image of the president as "symbol of the nation" (Stovall, 1984). Whatever the incumbent president does during the election is seen as things that presidents must do, while challengers do things to help them win elections. Being able to use the position as symbol of the nation helps the president travel and make speeches that are not "intended" to be campaigning but, in fact, are (Polsby & Wildavsky, 1991). Tenpas (1997), in a study of presidents as candidates and their campaign styles, argues that presidential incumbents can use the "rose garden strategy" to maintain their presidential aura even while participating in a campaign. Because "the presidential aura is a powerful resource" (p. 105), she argues this may, in fact, be the most compelling advantage of all.

There are other advantages for presidential incumbents. Incumbent presidents have the power to control events, to control the political agenda, to control media attention, to use their ready-made campaign staff, to use their ability to build volunteer groups because of preexisting status and prestige, and to rely on the general belief in the president's ability to manage the nation (Bloom, 1973; Edelman, 1974; Minow, Martin, & Mitchell, 1973; Polsby & Wildavsky, 1991; Stovall, 1984; Tenpas, 1997). Other advantages, according to Tenpas, include name recognition, easy access to the media, ability to focus the nation on certain issues, ability to travel extensively on official trips, and the experience the incumbent has as chief executive.

Polsby and Wildavsky (1991) suggest there may also be liabilities in being the presidential incumbent. For example, disasters that occur in the country will be held up against the current president, and the incumbent does have to respond to and defend a record. The president may be able to detach himself from campaigning, or at least appear to, but he cannot detach himself from the office. The challenger, on the other hand, typically can attack the present system freely without offering viable solutions. One of the most difficult positions to be in in a presidential race is that of the vice-president. Being a former vice-president trying now to run for the office of president places this person in the position of defending an existing record that he or she may not support in its entirety (Polsby & Wildavsky, 1991). There are arguments that the vice-president can use the advantages of an assumed incumbency strategy. This strategy allows the vice-president to try to convince the media to legitimate his candidacy and to cover him as the front-runner, the probable winner and the likely choice for office (Powell & Shelby, 1981).

Communication Strategies

The differences between incumbents and challengers go beyond voter behavior and perceptions of these roles. The candidates themselves can assume a particular strategy in line with expectations of their positions or roles. Early research suggested that there may be strategies better suited for an incumbent while other strategies would work best for a challenger.

One suggested strategy for incumbent presidents is the "rose garden strategy," a strategy that involves sustained political silence and refraining from political campaigning, confrontation of adversaries, and nonpartisan issue-taking (Erickson & Schmidt, 1982). The rose garden strategy has given incumbent presidents the advantage of acting "presidential" and the appearance of going about the business of running the country without the political confrontations usually associated with campaigning.

An example of the rose garden strategy was perhaps Nixon's general approach to the campaign in 1972. Several researchers have suggested that Nixon used the strategy of appearing "presidential" in 1972 and that his consultants made a deliberate effort to connect Nixon with the trappings of the presidency and to emphasize his accomplishments (Trent, 1973). Tenpas (1997) also advises incumbent presidents when they run for office to capitalize on the trappings of their office, to respond to opposition criticisms, to set the agenda, to take advantage of surrogate campaigners, and to have a theme and a vision for their campaign.

For challengers, there also appear to be strategies suggested by their political position that work best for them. Usually, challengers should represent the middle ground of the party's beliefs, emphasize optimism and change for the future, and stay away from proposing specific solutions to problems. However, in particular campaigns, challengers have "violated" challenger strategies. For example, proposing specific solutions to problems worked well for Reagan in his role as challenger in the 1980 presidential campaign, according to Devlin (1982).

Attacking the incumbent may also be a necessary strategy for challengers in order to point out to voters what the incumbent's policies or performance have been. In using the attack strategy, the challenger should, according to some researchers, position himself or herself as a viable alternative to the incumbent and should inoculate the voters against possible negative attacks from the incumbent (Kitchens & Stiteler, 1979).

Trent and Friedenberg (1995) propose that the strategies used by incumbents and by challengers are typically very different. Incumbents typically use symbolic trappings to transmit the importance of the office, emphasize (in presidential campaigns) the legitimacy of the office, emphasize competency and the office, emphasize the glamour and excitement of the office, create pseudoevents to attract and control media attention, use their position to make appointments to jobs and committees, create task forces to investigate public concerns, appropriate federal funds, consult or negotiate with world leaders, use endorsements by party and other important leaders, emphasize accomplishments, maintain an "above the trenches" posture, and depend on surrogates to campaign for them.

There have been several studies examining presentational styles in ads as a result of the candidate's position as incumbent or challenger in the campaign, although most have not focused on presidential candidates. In a study of newspaper advertising in an Alabama election, Latimer (1984) found that challengers who won used lots of policy content in their ads, whereas winning incumbents used personal information about themselves more heavily than incumbents who lost. Payne and Baukus (1985) examined 101 senatorial ads from the 1984 election campaign and found different commercial patterns and strategies between incumbents and challengers. Findings showed that the argument spot was popular with both incumbents and challengers, while the attack style was more popular with the incumbents than with the challengers. Kaid and Davidson (1986) also present specific incumbent/challenger styles derived from their application of videostyle to U.S. Senate races.

Although incumbents and challengers may differ in style, sometimes other factors are found to be more significant in the styles used in the ads or the types of ads used in the campaign. Hale, Fox, and Farmer (1996) compared the influence of candidate type (incumbent or challenger), competitiveness of the campaign, and state population size on the use of negative advertising in recent U.S. Senate campaigns. The authors found that negative ads were significantly more likely to be produced by challengers, to come from hard-fought races, and to come from states with larger populations. They concluded that, while all three did have an influence, candidate status was less important than the competitiveness of the race and the state's population size.

In an analysis of 206 presidential televised campaign ads from the Republican and Democratic general election campaigns from 1980 to 1996, Benoit, Pier, and Blaney (1997) found that challenger ads were more likely to feature attacks than acclaims (ads that portray the sponsoring candidate or candidate's political party in a favorable light) and that incumbent ads featured more acclaims than attacks.

CLASSIFYING CANDIDATES BY POSITION

For the purposes of comparing political position, we classified presidential candidates from 1952 to 1996 according to their status as true incumbent (had served as president, even if for a short period), assumed incumbent (former vice-president or party had been in power in previous election), and challenger. In presidential elections where there was not an actual or true incumbent, then a former vice-president, a vice-president who took over the presidency for part of a term because of the death or resignation of the president, or a candidate whose party was in power during the preceding election was designated the "assumed" incumbent. Evidence has shown that a candidate who wishes to succeed an incumbent of his or her own party is often cast into the position of defending the administration's record even if he or she does not agree with it (Polsby & Wildavsky, 1980). These persons, because of the role into which they are cast, become identified as incumbents. The application of this classification to presidential candidates from 1952 through 1996, with appropriate designations for political party, is shown in Figure 5.1.

From the total number of 1,204 ads, 647 came from challengers and 557 were from incumbents or assumed incumbents. The analysis reveals that an incumbent style and a challenger style are indeed present in the way presidential candidates present themselves through their ads.

An analysis of the advertisements during these races allowed a look at several aspects of presidential political communication. First, the analysis provided a look at the differences (if any) between incumbent and challenger styles as manifested in political advertisements during the general elections. Second, because the ads span 12 elections and 44 years of presidential campaigns, the content analysis provides a look at the trends in the use of various styles and strategies by candidates for the two major parties. Finally, because during these campaigns several

Incumbent	Presumed Incumbent	Challenger
Eisenhower (R) 1956	Stevenson (D) 1952	Eisenhower (R) 1952
Johnson (D) 1964	Nixon (R) 1960	Stevenson (D) 1956
Nixon (R) 1972	Humphrey (D) 1968	Kennedy (D) 1960
Ford (R) 1976	Bush (R) 1988	Goldwater (R) 1964
Carter (D) 1980		Nixon (R) 1968
Reagan (R) 1984		McGovern (D) 1972
Bush (R) 1992		Carter (D) 1976
Clinton (D) 1996		Reagan (R) 1980
		Mondale (D) 1984
		Dukakis (D) 1988
		Clinton (D) 1992
		Dole (R) 1996

Figure 5.1 Incumbent and Challenger Roles of U.S. Presidents, 1952–1996

of the candidates ran as both challengers and true incumbents, the analysis offers a look at the relationship between style of the candidate and candidate position as incumbent and challenger; that is, how the same candidate running as a challenger in one election and as the incumbent in the next adapted or adjusted his style to fit the context of the campaign.

VERBAL COMPONENTS OF INCUMBENT AND CHALLENGER STYLES

Type of Spot Content

As Chapter 4 indicates, presidential ads over the years have emphasized issues, which is true for both incumbents and challengers. Table 5.1 shows that 70% of challengers' spots and 62% of incumbents' spots over the last 44 years of presidential campaigns have emphasized issues. However, the spots have tended to include broad statements of issue concerns or vague statements of policy preferences and did not address frequently specific issue proposals or ideas by candidates. Therefore, challenger and incumbent ads did not significantly differ on which content dominated the ads. There are some differences in how many challenger and incumbent ads actually mentioned certain issue and image appeals. Table 5.1 indicates that challenger ads were significantly more likely to mention general issue concerns in their ads (74%) than were incumbent ads (55%). Incumbents and challengers were equally likely to mention vague policy preferences or to mention a specific policy proposal in their ads. Challengers and incumbents were different in the percentage of the ads that mentioned personal qualities or characteristics, with incumbents mentioning them in 69% of their ads and challengers using them in 53% of their ads.

Although challengers and incumbents during the last 12 campaigns have spent a third of their ads trying to convince voters that they had the necessary positive personality traits to be good leaders, the majority of their ads have addressed, in some way, their issue concerns.

Issues in Incumbent and Challenger Ads

As Table 5.2 shows, the issue mentioned most frequently in challenger and incumbent ads was economic concerns, mentioned in 35% of challenger ads and 30% of incumbent ads. After economic concerns, incumbents addressed international and foreign affairs in the next highest percentage (15%). Taxes were the third most frequently mentioned concern for incumbents and were mentioned in 12% of

TABLE 5.1
Verbal Components of Videostyle by Political Position and Party (N = 1,204), in Percentage of Spots

	Challenger (n = 647)	Incumbent (n = 557)	Republican (n = 651)	Democrat (n = 553)
Type of Spot				
Image	30%	38%	62%	71%
Issue	70	62	38	29
Content of Spot				
Partisanship	15	14	12	17*
Candidate Issue Concern	74	55*	67	62
Vague Policy Preference	42	42	38	48*
Specific Policy Proposal	12	12	9	15*
Personal Characteristics of Candidate	53	69*	62	56
Appeals to Groups	16	22*	16	23*
Focus of Spot				
Candidate-Positive	61	63	66	57*
Opponent-Negative	39	37	34	43

*Indicates chi square is significant at $p < .05$ for difference between incumbent and challenger or Republican and Democrat.

their ads. These were also the top three issues for challengers, but challenger ads focused on taxes (11%) slightly more than they focused on international and foreign affairs (10%). Except for economic concerns, incumbents mentioned all of the issues in more of their ads than did challengers. When the issues are combined into some broader categories, it can be seen that incumbents mention military and foreign issues in a much higher percentage of ads than do challengers (26% to 16%), and challengers continue to focus more on broad economic issues that include taxes, deficit, and balanced budget (48%) than do incumbents (45%).

Candidate Characteristics in Incumbent and Challenger Ads

From 1952 to 1996, presidential incumbents and challengers have talked about their own qualifications and the characteristics that make

TABLE 5.2
Issue Content by Political Position and Party (N = 1,204) in Percentage of Spots

	Challenger (n = 647)	Incumbent (n = 557)	Republican (n = 651)	Democrat (n = 553)
Defense and Foreign Affairs	16%	26%	26%	15%
International Foreign Affairs	10	5	16	9
Military/Defense Spending	6	11	10	6
General Economic Issues	48	45	51	55
Economic Concerns	35	30	37	29
Deficit/Balanced Budget	2	3	2	3
Taxes	11	12	12	23
Crime and Safety	4	11	4	11
Crime/Prisons/Gun Control	2	8	3	7
Drugs	2	3	1	4
Issues Concerning Young People	6	14	4	16
Concern for Children	2	5	1	6
Education	4	9	3	10
Broad Social Issues	10	19	8	21
Medicare/Social Security/Elderly	6	8	4	10
Other Social Policies	4	11	4	11
Health Issues	2	3	2	5
Health Care	2	3	2	4
Smoking/Tobacco Abuse	0	<1	0	1
Other Issues	4	10	5	5

them suited for the presidency. As Table 5.3 indicates, the most desirable of these to challengers and to incumbents is aggressiveness. Over half of challenger ads and over a third of incumbent ads attempted to show that their candidate had this desirable trait. For incumbents, the next most-mentioned characteristic in their ads was the performance and success that the incumbent was having in his job (33%). This was unimportant to challengers, who tended to highlight their competency (17%) and their activeness (17%) in their ads. Competency was also important to incumbents after aggressiveness and performance/success and was portrayed in 29% of their ads.

TABLE 5.3
Candidate Characteristics by Political Position and Party (N = 1,204), in Percentage of Spots

	Challenger (n = 647)	Incumbent (n = 557)	Republican (n = 651)	Democrat (n = 553)
Honesty/Integrity	4%	6%	5%	5%
Toughness/Strength	4	12	6	10
Warmth/Compassion	6	13	6	13
Competency	17	29	20	26
Performance/Success	5	33	18	18
Aggressiveness	51	38	45	46
Activeness	17	14	14	18
Qualifications	5	14	8	11

Negative and Positive Spots

Although many of the challenger and incumbent ads used formats and strategies that allowed for negative attacks, the dominant focus of 63% of incumbent ads and 61% of challenger ads was "candidate positive," meaning they were focused on discussing the positive attributes of the candidates (Table 5.1). Over one-third of both challenger and incumbent ads were focused on making negative comments about the opponents. In ads that featured attacks on the opponent, there was no significant difference between incumbent ads and challenger ads in what aspect of the opponent was attacked or how the attack was made. For both incumbents and challengers, the most frequently made attack was on the opponent's issue stands and consistency (32% for challengers and 33% for incumbents). The next most popular for both was on the personal characteristics of the opponents (20% of incumbent ads and of challenger ads featured this type of attack). This overall finding contradicts what the popular perception has been about negative attacks made in presidential advertising. From 1952 to 1996, presidential campaign ads have focused the attacks made on opponents on issue stands, not on personal characteristics.

Both incumbents and challengers overall used negative associations most frequently in making their attacks (23% and 25%, respectively). The next most popular for both was the use of humor or ridicule in making the attack. Negative associations have over the years remained an important way of "attacking" either the personal characteristics or the issue stands of candidates. Through negative associations, ads can imply that opponents are responsible for a particular problem because of their behavior or past policies. Johnson's use of the potential for the use of atomic weapons to paint a negative view of opponent Barry

Goldwater in 1964 is a well-remembered example. Some of Reagan's 1980 challenger ads used graphics to depict the rising cost of food items and associated those images with Carter. Mondale in 1984 also used this technique, depicting images of nuclear dangers and tension and associating those images with Reagan. More recently, George Bush associated Michael Dukakis with crime in 1988, and Bill Clinton associated poor economic conditions with Bush in 1992 and budget gridlock with Bob Dole in 1996.

Appeals Made in Spots

In terms of types of appeals used by incumbents and challengers over the last 44 years of elections, spots differed significantly only in how frequently they used source credibility appeals. As Table 5.4 shows, logical appeals or appeals that emphasize evidence and facts about some issue or situation were used more by incumbents (72%) than by challengers (68%). The most popular type of appeal for both incumbents (86%) and challengers (82%) was an emotional appeal. Incumbents and challengers significantly differed in their use of source credibility appeals (74% and 61%, respectively). The *dominant* appeal used in ads for both incumbents and challengers was the emotional appeal, followed by source credibility and then by logical appeals.

Although fear appeals were not present in the majority of ads for either type of candidate, incumbents and challengers were significantly different in their use of fear appeals. Fear appeals were featured in 22%

TABLE 5.4

Appeals in Spots by Political Position and Party (N = 1,204), in Percentage of Spots

	Challenger (n = 647)		Incumbent (n = 557)	Republican (n = 651)		Democrat (n = 553)
Presence of Appeals						
Logical	68%		72%	73%	*	67%
Emotional	82		86	82	*	86
Ethical/Source Credibility	61	*	74	66		69
Dominant Appeal		*				
Logical	26		19	24		21
Emotional	45		43	44		45
Ethical/Source Credibility	29		38	32		34
Use of Fear Appeal	17	*	22	16	*	24

*Indicates chi square is significant at $p < .05$ for difference between incumbent and challenger or Republican and Democrat.

of the incumbent ads and in 17% of the challenger ads. While it may initially seem surprising that incumbents make such high use of fear appeals, it is the incumbent who must guard against the "call for change" issued by challengers. One persuasive way of guarding against change may be to raise fears of what may happen if change is adopted, particularly in line with the opponent's or the challenger's program. Thus, in 1964 Johnson's spots asked voters to be afraid not just of nuclear fallout but of losing Social Security benefits. Richard Nixon in 1972 wanted to enhance uncertainty by making voters fearful of reductions in defense spending advocated by George McGovern.

Incumbent and Challenger Strategies Used in Ads

As Table 5.5 indicates, incumbents basically adhered to strategies identified by Trent and Friedenberg (1995) as best suited to their position. Challengers, on the other hand, were not so likely to follow strictly

TABLE 5.5
Challenger and Incumbent Strategies in Spots (N = 1,204), in Percentage of Spots

	Challenger (n = 647)	Incumbent (n = 557)
Incumbent Strategies		
Use of Symbolic Trappings*	5%	27%
Presidency Stands for Legitimacy*	12	26
Competency and the Office*	47	73
Consulting with World Leaders*	6	12
Charisma and the Office	11	12
Using Endorsements by Leaders	15	12
Emphasizing Accomplishments*	16	50
Above the Trenches Posture*	17	28
Depending on Surrogates to Speak*	35	42
Challenger Strategies		
Calling for Changes*	71	14
Speaking to Traditional Values	44	49
Taking the Offensive Position*	51	34
Emphasizing Optimism	42	43
Representing Center of Party	17	16
Attacking the Record of Opponent*	47	37

*Indicates chi square is significant at $p < .05$ for difference between incumbent and challenger.

the strategies identified as best for them. Incumbent ads were significantly more likely than challenger ads to use the symbolic trappings of
the office, to emphasize the legitimacy of the presidency, to focus on the
incumbent's competency as manager of the nation, to feature the incumbent consulting with world leaders, to emphasize the incumbent's
accomplishments, and to feature an "above the trenches" posture taken
by the incumbent. The most popular incumbent strategy by far was the
emphasis on the incumbent's competence, used in 73% of incumbent
ads. In addition, half of all incumbents' ads emphasized accomplishments. By using these strategies, incumbents were able to remind voters
of their past accomplishments and of their ability to lead the country
competently. In 1972, Nixon's ads frequently displayed these strategies,
especially in his "China" ads, reminding voters of the Nixon
administration's accomplishments in foreign policy. Several of
Reagan's 1984 ads reminded viewers through video of Americans en-
joying the "good life," that "America was back" and was "prouder,
stronger, and better" economically and politically because of, according
to the ads, Reagan's competence as leader of the nation.

From the strategies identified — Incumbent presidents are often shown in their office, surrounded by
the trappings of the Oval Office, doing the work of the American
people. Their ads tie them directly to the symbols and trappings of the
office.[1] Even assumed incumbents attempt to connect themselves to the
entire "aura" of the presidency through the videostyle of their ads.
Incumbents also have to stand on their record as president or vice-president by emphasizing how competent they have been in office and how
much they have accomplished for the American voters. But incumbents
also need to appear presidential, which they do by consulting with
world leaders, depending on surrogates to speak for them, and appearing as someone who already occupies the office, not as someone trying
to win the office.

From 1952 to 1996, all challengers in the presidential campaigns were
less clear in their use of challenger strategies. Challengers did significantly differ from incumbents, using the following strategies more than
incumbents: calling for changes (71% of their ads used this strategy),
taking the offensive position on issues (51%), and attacking the record
of the opponent (47%).

"Calling for changes" is particularly well suited to the challenger
position during a presidential campaign. While incumbents can remind
voters of past accomplishments, challengers must remind voters of the
incumbent's failures and advocate changes in the existing
administration's policies. Many of the challenger ads featured some
type of a call for changes, but none so directly as Eisenhower's 1952 ads.
After responding to a question by an "average citizen," Eisenhower
ended many of his ads with statements such as "The day of reckoning

is sure to come unless we have a change," "It's time for a change," or even the more direct, "There's going to be a change next January."

NONVERBAL COMPONENTS OF INCUMBENT AND CHALLENGER STYLES

Candidate as Speaker

Incumbents were present in 58% of their ads, and challengers were present in 60% of their ads, although challengers were the dominant speakers more frequently in their ads (46%) than incumbents were in their ads (26%), as evident in Table 5.6. Incumbents relied on anonymous announcers in almost half of their ads (49%), while challengers

TABLE 5.6
Nonverbal Components by Political Position and Party: Candidate Speaking, Setting, and Dress (N = 1,204), in Percentage of Spots

	Challenger (n = 647)	Incumbent (n = 557)	Republican (n = 651)	Democrat (n = 553)
Dominant Speaker in Spot	*		*	
Candidate	46%	26%	37%	36%
Government Official	11	8	14	5
Anonymous Announcer	32	49	35	45
Non-government Celebrity	3	3	2	3
Spouse or Family Member	1	1	2	1
Combination or Other	7	13	10	9
Candidate Sound	*		*	
Sound-on/Candidate	62	48	59	50
Sound-over/Candidate	38	50	39	49
Setting of Spot			*	
Formal Indoors	36	30	32	34
Informal Indoors	13	13	12	15
Formal Outdoors	8	9	7	10
Informal Outdoors	8	9	7	10
Combination	6	9	9	5
Not Applicable	29	30	33	26
Candidate Dress				
Formal	50	44	42 *	53
Casual	6	7	6	7
Varied	1	1	1	2
Not Applicable	43	48	51	38

*Indicates chi square is significant at $p < .05$ for difference between incumbent and challenger or Republican and Democrat.

used them as the dominant speaker in only 32% of their ads. Challengers may have spoken for themselves in their ads more than incumbents because they hoped this strategy would help them achieve the same level of familiarity that the presidential incumbent enjoyed. In addition, challengers may feel the need to speak directly to voters about their issue positions and political philosophies. The incumbent gains less by speaking in the ad and looking like a contestant in the race and may in fact gain more by appearing in the ad looking presidential but allowing others to speak for him.

For both incumbents and challengers, the majority of the ads used live sound, as opposed to sound over film or tape, although there was a significant difference. A higher percentage of challenger ads (61%) used live sound than did incumbent ads (48%).

Formality in Setting and Dress

Table 5.6 also shows that both incumbents and challengers used a formal indoor setting such as an office or other institutional setting in their ads more frequently than any other setting (30% and 36% respectively). The second most popular setting for both was informal indoors such as a home or other non-institutional indoor setting.

Incumbents and challengers were both formal in their attire when the candidate appeared or was featured in the ad. Challengers wore coats and ties or suits 88% of the time when they appeared or were shown in the ads, and incumbents were dressed formally in 85% of the ads in which they appeared or were featured.

PRODUCTION COMPONENTS OF INCUMBENT AND CHALLENGER STYLES

Ad Formats for Incumbents and Challengers

There was no significant difference in the length of spots for incumbents and challengers. Fifty-six percent of challenger ads and 58% of incumbents ads are 20-30 seconds long.

One of the significant differences between incumbents and challengers was their use of ad formats. As Table 5.7 indicates, the most popular ad format used in incumbent ads was the opposition-focused ad (22%). The next two most popular formats used in incumbent commercials were testimonials (20%) and introspection ads (19%). The use of testimonials, which can include one person stating a reaction to the candidate or several "man-in-the-street" interviews, is not surprising for incumbents. Incumbents can certainly benefit from the use of citizens or political officials testifying to the job they are doing as president

TABLE 5.7
Production Components by Political Position and Party: Length,
Format, and Production Style (N = 1,204), in Percentage of Spots

	Challenger (n = 647)	Incumbent (n = 557)	Republican (n = 651)	Democrat (n = 553)
Length of Spot	*		*	
15-30 Seconds	56%	58%	60%	53%
60 Seconds	31	31	30	33
2-5 Minutes	13	11	10	14
Format of Spot	*		*	
Documentary Style	6	10	10	5
Video Clip/Music Video	8	10	7	11
Testimonial	13	20	20	11
Introspection	24	19	21	21
Issue Statement	1	3	1	3
Opposition Focused	20	22	20	22
Issue Dramatization	14	10	9	15
Question/Answer/Confrontation	15	6	11	10
Other	1	1	1	1
Production Style of Spot	*		*	
Cinema Verité	21	34	20	35
Slides/Print or Voice-over	17	17	15	19
Candidate Head-on	30	16	27	20
Other Speaker Head-on	14	14	18	10
Animation or Special Prod.	8	12	11	8
Combination	10	9	9	9

*Indicates chi square is significant at $p < .05$ for difference between incumbent and challenger or Republican and Democrat.

and to let viewers know the qualifications and personality characteristics that make them good presidents. While most of the presidents in this sample used testimonials from political leaders, testimonials for incumbents also came from celebrities. For example, Humphrey's 1968 candidacy was endorsed by Frank Sinatra and actor E. G. Marshall; Nixon received endorsements in 1972 from Mamie Eisenhower and Charleton Heston; and Leonard Bernstein and Mary Tyler Moore testified to Carter's qualifications in the 1980 campaign.

It is surprising that the most popular format for incumbents was opposition focused. Incumbents in the past and in earlier presidential campaigns have usually been advised to stay away from making direct negative attacks and rather to stand on their record and appear presidential. However, in the last several years, negative advertising has become so much a part of the televised campaign that it is hard to imagine that any presidential candidate, whether incumbent or challenger, would not use negative advertising. Opposition-focused advertising is considered the domain of challengers who need, by definition, to challenge the record of the sitting or assumed incumbent. And, in fact, challengers do use an opposition-focused format in almost the same percentage of their ads as do incumbents (20%), but it is not the most popular format for challengers. Challengers used the introspection format in 24% of their ads and more frequently than incumbents (19%). Introspection ads, which feature the candidate usually talking directly to the audience about the campaign, the issues, and why he or she is running, are important in allowing challengers the opportunity to define themselves for viewers. Even in a presidential race, where name recognition is high and information about both candidates is abundant, the incumbent president has had the advantage in being seen and heard in American living rooms. The introspection ad gives the challenger a chance to address the American public directly and gives the public a "close-up" view of the challenger's ideas and personality. The next most popular strategy for all challengers between 1952 and 1996 was the opposition-focused format (20%) and then question-and-answer/confrontation (15%), issue dramatizations (14%), and testimonials (13%). Issue dramatization ads also allow an opportunity for challengers to more subtly attack the incumbent. The issue dramatization format is one where a story is told about some issue or problem; the issue is "dramatized" rather than talked about. Typically, issue dramatization ads contain attacks on the status quo or even on policies of or concerns about the president. For example, the famous, "Daisy Girl" commercial used by Johnson in 1964 is an issue dramatization ad. In a 1984 Reagan ad known as "The Bear in the Woods," a bear wanders through a forest as the voice-over questions whether the bear (a symbolic representation of the old Soviet Union) is dangerous or not.

Production Styles and Special Effects for Incumbents and Challengers

Table 5.7 also indicates that incumbents and challengers differ in some of the production characteristics of their ads. Challengers used "candidate head-on" as the dominant production technique in their ads. Thirty percent of challenger ads and 16% of incumbent ads featured this technique. This production technique allows the candidate to address the viewers directly and is a good strategy for challengers who have not had the same opportunities as incumbents to directly address the public and who may not be as well known and visible. It is a neutral and impartial technique, using close-ups or medium shots of the candidate. In many ways it mimics a "talking heads" news format.

The most popular production style for incumbents is the *cinema verité* format (34%). This technique also has a news feel but features a more documentary style, in which the camera and therefore the viewer are allowed to follow the candidate as he performs the duties of a current or former office. Cinema verité may also be used to suggest a real occurrence, as in an issue-dramatization ad. Cinema verité (21%) is the second most popular technique for challengers.

Slides with print, movement, and voice-over (17%) is third. For incumbents, slides with print, movement, and voice-over (17%) is the second most popular technique. Incumbents use a candidate head-on style in 16% of their ads.

A neutral camera angle is used most frequently in both incumbent and challenger ads. Fifty percent of challenger ads and 45% of incumbent ads use a straight-on camera angle (Table 5.8). The most popular camera shot for both challengers and incumbents in past ads has been a head-and-shoulders shot, at 35% and 25%, respectively; the difference in frequency is significant. Medium shots are the next most popular for both types of candidates. Also, incumbents were significantly more likely to use music in their ads than were challengers (44% and 31%, respectively).

In general, challengers used more special-effect techniques in their ads than did incumbents. Challengers were significantly more likely to use computer graphics, freeze frames, montages, and stills than were incumbents. Incumbents were significantly more likely to use slow-motion and stop-motion photography in their ads than were challengers. The most popular special effect used for both types of candidates was the use of stills (39% for challengers and 33% for incumbents). Stills are typically used at the end of most of the ads showing a head shot of the candidate, but they are also frequently used throughout the ads with voice-overs and movement.

Because they used more special effects, challenger ads were sometimes more innovative and visually faster than incumbent ads. Challengers must develop interest and enthusiasm for their campaigns and candidacies; they must convince voters that upsetting the status quo is necessary and good. The use of special effects may help challenger ads create interest in the ad and may focus the voters' attention on particular details of a scene or allow an image to be reinforced over and over again. Montages and other quick cuts and freeze frames are all designed to emphasize scenes and to suggest motion and drama.

In 1968, Nixon used "montage" effects in several of his ads to dramatize failings of the Johnson administration and to tie former vice-president Humphrey to those failings. Several of Nixon's challenger ads combined a series of photographs or scenes from Vietnam or crime in

TABLE 5.8

Production Components by Political Position and Party: Music and Other Production Techniques (N = 1,204), in Percentage of Spots

	Challenger (n = 647)		Incumbent (n = 557)	Republican (n = 651)		Democrat (n = 553)
Presence of Music	31%	*	44%	36%		37%
Presence of Production Techniques						
Computer Graphics	31	*	22	25		29
Slow Motion	6	*	14	5	*	15
Fast Motion	3		2	2	*	4
Reverse Motion	2		2	1		2
Freeze-Frame	14	*	5	9		12
Split Screen	3		3	3		3
Superimposition	16		17	15		17
Montage	14	*	8	13		10
Stop Motion	4	*	12	9	*	5
Stills	39	*	33	48	*	23
Candidate Dominant Camera Angle		*			*	
High Angle	1		3	1		3
Straight-On	50		45	46		49
Low Angle	7		6	3		11
Movement/Combination	2		4	4		2
Candidate Not Present	40		42	46		35
Type of Dominant Candidate Camera Shot		*			*	
Tight (Head and Shoulders)	39		25	30		35
Medium (Waist Up)	16		20	14		22
Long (Full Length)	1		3	2		3
Combination	4		10	8		5
Candidate Not Present	40		42	46		35

*Indicates chi square is significant at $p < .05$ for difference between incumbent and challenger or Republican and Democrat.

the United States with dramatic music to highlight the failings of the Johnson administration in Vietnam and on law and order.

Summary of Incumbent and Challenger Videostyles

Given all of the different aspects of videostyle, it is helpful to look at some of the major elements in a summary form. Figure 5.2 provides a summary of the most significant elements of videostyle for both incumbents and challengers. As this representation shows, both incumbents and challengers focus on issues and take a candidate-positive approach

Incumbent Videostyle	Challenger Videostyle
1. Focuses on Issues	1. Focuses on Issues
2. Uses Candidate-Positive Spots	2. Uses Candidate-Positive Spots
3. Emphasizes More Personality Characteristics	3. More Emphasis on Economic Issues
4. Emphasizes More Group-Related Concerns	4. More Emphasis on Aggressive Personal Traits
5. Relies on More Ethical/Source Credibility Appeals	5. More Frequently Speaks for Self
6. Uses More Fear Appeals	6. Uses Candidate Head-on Production Style
7. Emphasizes More Social Issues and Foreign Policy	7. Uses Tight, Close-up Camera Shots
8. Uses Anonymous Announcers More	8. Uses Q/A Format for Spots
9. Uses More Testimonials and Documentary Formats	9. Uses More Special Effects in Production
10. Emphasizes Trappings of the Office and Accomplishments	10. Calls for Change
11. Uses Music More Often	11. Attacks Record of Opponent
12. Uses Cinema Verité Production	12. Takes Offensive on Issues

Figure 5.2 Major Elements of Incumbent and Challenger Videostyles

to their spots. Incumbents, however, are more likely to emphasize their personality qualities than are challengers. Incumbents also differ in their use of an anonymous announcer, whereas challengers speak more often for themselves. Challengers focus more on economic concerns and, as expected, they take an offensive position on issues, calling for change and attacking the opponent. Even so, they do not sponsor more negative or opposition-focused spots than do incumbents. Challengers also differ in their production styles, using more special effects for their spots, whereas incumbents rely more on testimonial and documentary formats.

VERBAL COMPONENTS OF REPUBLICAN AND DEMOCRATIC STYLE

Over the years, political position has been talked about more than party status in terms of benefits and liabilities in an election. However, we also wanted to explore if a presidential candidate's party would influence the style chosen. There were 651 ads for Republican presidential candidates and 553 ads for Democratic candidates.

Type of Spot Content

Over the last 44 years, Republican presidential candidates used fewer ads emphasizing issues (62%) than did Democratic candidates (71%). As Table 5.1 indicates, Republican candidates were more likely to mention their general issue concerns (39%) in their ads as compared to Democrats (32%) and less likely to talk even about vague policy preferences (10%) than were Democratic candidates (23%). Neither Republicans nor Democrats spent much time in their ads appealing to partisanship issues or to linking themselves with particular groups and their issue interests. However, Democrats were more likely than Republicans to do both, perhaps because, for much of the twentieth century, Democrats held the partisan advantage in the electorate and were also more inclined to take advantage of their appeal to voters in particular groups, such as labor unions.

Although discussions of issues dominated most of the spots for Republicans and for Democrats, appeals to the candidate's own personal qualities or characteristics dominated more of the ads for Republican candidates. Thirty-eight percent of the ads for Republican presidential candidates were image ads, as compared to 29% for Democratic presidential candidates. However, when the ads are examined in terms of *presence* of issue-related and image-related appeals, the number of ads that mention personality goes up. As Table 5.1 shows, over half of ads for Democratic candidates and almost two-thirds of those for Republican candidates mention the candidates' personal qualities or characteristics.

Specific Issue and Image Content

As Table 5.2 shows, Republicans and Democrats have emphasized different issues in their ads over the past 12 presidential campaigns. The issues mentioned most frequently in all Republican ads were economic concerns (37%), international and foreign affairs (16%), and taxes (12%). For Democrats, economic concerns (29%), taxes (23%), education (10%), and Medicare/social security/elderly (10%) were the most popular issues mentioned in ads. When issues are combined into broader categories (see Table 5.2), almost half of all ads for both Republicans and Democrats address general economic issues including concerns about the economy, taxes, deficit, and a balanced budget (45% for Democrats; 48% for Republicans). After broad economic issues, Republicans and Democrats part ways in terms of the issues they address in their ads. Republican candidates mention foreign affairs issues like military spending and international relations in 26% of their ads, almost double the frequency with which Democratic candidates mention those issues.

Democrats, on the other hand, feature issues addressing broad social concerns like social policy, Medicare, Social Security, the elderly, and welfare reform in 25% of their ads, more than double the percentage of Republican ads that mention those issues.

This finding suggests that although Republicans and Democrats have used their ads to talk about economic issues in equal amounts, their ads do support views of the two parties as being associated with certain issues: Republicans with foreign/military issues and Democrats with social policies.

According to Table 5.3, Republican candidates want to be seen as aggressive (45%) and competent (20%) and to focus on their performance and success in office (18%). Democratic presidential candidates have, according to their ads, emphasized the same candidate characteristics, with some additional attention and emphasis on competency (26%) and appearing as an active or "can-do" candidate (18%).

Negative and Positive Spots by Party

Republicans and Democrats were significantly different in the focus of the spots they have used over the past several decades of campaigning. Table 5.1 shows that Republican ads have been more focused on the sponsoring candidate's positive qualities (66%) than have Democratic ads (57%). But as the table indicates, most of the ads for both parties have not focused on giving voters negative information about their opponents.

In making the attacks, both parties have focused their attacks on issue stands and consistency and on personal characteristics of their opponents. In addition, the most popular strategies in making the attacks have been using humor and ridicule or through using negative associations.

Appeals Made in Spots by Party

Unlike the analysis of incumbent and challenger styles, Republicans and Democrats were very similar in the types of "proofs" or appeals they make in their advertising. Candidate ads for both parties running for office since 1952 have been dominated by emotional proof ads, rather than by either logical proof or facts and evidence or by appeals to the candidate's source credibility. As Table 5.4 indicates, the type of proof that dominates the ads, after emotional proof, is source credibility and then logical proof. As with the appeals to image dimensions and issue concerns, it is also important to note whether the ads *mention* these proofs at all, not just to look at which ones (logical, ethical, or emotional) dominate the ads. In that case, Republicans and Democrats are alike in their use of source credibility appeals (66% and 69%, respectively), but they are significantly different in what percentage of their ads mention evidence and facts or use emotional appeals. Ads for Republican candidates mentioned logical proofs in more ads (73%) than did ads for Democrats (67%). More ads for Democrats than for Republicans used emotional appeals.

Republicans and Democrats were significantly different in their use of fear appeals. From 1952 to 1996, one in every four ads for Democrats used fear appeals (24%), but Republicans used them in only 16% of their ads.

NONVERBAL COMPONENTS OF REPUBLICAN ADS AND DEMOCRATIC ADS

Candidate as Speaker by Party

Although the Republican and Democratic candidates were the main speakers in about the same percentage of their ads, Table 5.6 indicates Democratic candidates relied more on anonymous announcers (45%) and did not use in great numbers any other speakers to speak for them in their ads. Live sound is featured in more Republican ads (59%) than in Democratic ads (50%), with Democrats using voice-overs or sound-over in 10% more of their ads than did Republicans.

Formality in Setting and Dress by Party

Both Republicans and Democrats use formal indoor settings in their ads more than any other type of setting (32% and 34%, respectively). The parties differ in that Democratic candidate ads tend to use higher percentages of other varieties of settings such as informal indoor and outdoor settings (formal and informal) than do Republicans, as indicated in Table 5.6. In ads where the candidate appears or some visual of the candidate is shown, Republicans and Democrats are dressed in suits or coats and ties (86% for Republicans and 85% for Democrats).

PRODUCTION COMPONENTS OF REPUBLICAN AND DEMOCRATIC ADS

Ad Formats, Production Styles, and Special Effects by Party

As Table 5.7 indicates, ads for Republican and Democratic candidates have been more alike than different in terms of ad format over the 44

years studied. The top three formats for Republicans have been introspection ads (21%), opposition-focused ads (20%), and testimonials
(20%). Democrats have chosen opposition-focused ads (22%), introspection ads (21%), and issue-dramatization ads (15%) as their favorite
formats.

The most popular production style for Democrats over the years has
been cinema verité or "slice of life." Thirty-five percent of the ads for
Democratic candidates featured this technique, with another 20% of
their ads using candidate head-on. This style of production, featuring
a direct address to viewers and voters, was the most popular technique
for Republican candidates, who used it in 27% of their ads. The next
most popular style for Republican candidates was cinema verité, used
in 20% of the ads.

As with overall styles of presidential ads and of incumbents and
challengers, Republicans and Democrats have been similar and consistent in their use of camera angles and shots in their presidential campaign ads (Table 5.8). They have used straight-on camera angles and
either head-and-shoulders or waist-up shots when they appeared in the
ads. Intimacy and intensity are suggested by the use of the tight shots
by Republicans (30%) and Democrats (35%), but most of the angles and
shots used by the candidates are designed to give a sense of neutrality
and objectivity. This is certainly one of the components used by presidential candidates that is designed to mimic a neutral-observer perspective, such as featured in news programs.

Republicans and Democrats also did not differ in their general use of
special production effects in their ads over the years, although they did
differ in which effects were the most popular. The most popular special
effects for Democratic ads were computer graphics (29%). Republican
candidates used stills in their ads twice as much as Democratic candidates (48% and 23%, respectively).

Summary of Videostyle by Party

As with incumbents and challengers, it is helpful to look at the
various aspects of videostyle for Republicans and Democrats in a summary fashion. Figure 5.3 provides a summary of the major elements of
videostyle by party. Here there are more marked differences in the
verbal characteristics of the spots. Democrats use more negative spots,
more emotional and fear appeals, and more attacks on personal character of the opponent. However, they also offer more specific policy
proposals than their Republican counterparts, who rely on more general issue concerns to express their position on issues.

Republicans, according to Figure 5.3, are more likely to focus on
foreign policy, whereas Democrats emphasize social issues. Other dif-

Republicans	Democrats
1. More Positive Spots	1. More Use of Negative Spots
2. Use Issue-Oriented Spots	2. Use Issue-Oriented Spots
3. More Use of Logical Appeals	3. Use More Emotional Appeals
4. More Emphasis on Foreign Policy	4. Use More Fear Appeals
5. Shorter Spots (under 60 sec.)	5. More Attacks on Personal Character of Opponents
6. More Candidate Head-on Production	6. More Presentation of Specific Policy Proposals
7. More Government Officials Used as Speakers	7. More Emphasis on Partisanship
8. More Testimonials	8. More Group-Related Appeals
9. More Documentary Formats	9. More Emphasis on Social Issues
10. More Dependence on Surrogates to Speak	10. Longer Spots (2-5 minutes)
11. More Endorsements by Other World Leaders	11. More Cinema Verité Production
	12. More Use of Special Effects
	13. More Use of "Above the Trenches" Strategy
	14. More Use of Anonymous Announcer

Figure 5.3 Elements of Videostyle for Republicans and Democrats

ferences relate to production techniques and tend to show a different philosophy for communicating messages. Republicans, for instance, while they use a lot of head-on candidate presentations, also clearly favor a use of surrogates to speak for them, using more government officials and endorsements by world leaders.

INCUMBENT/CHALLENGER STYLE AND INDIVIDUAL STYLES

Dwight Eisenhower (1952/1956), Richard Nixon (1968/1972 for this analysis), Jimmy Carter (1976/1980), Ronald Reagan (1980/1984), and Bill Clinton (1992/1996) have all run both as challengers and as incumbents during the years of televised political commercials. Each man had his own style, which interacted with any political stance or posture from which he ran. But how does personal style interact with a candidate political position as an incumbent or challenger? Will the same man switch strategies—even if the strategies used before (as a challenger) were successful in bringing his message to the voters? As the following discussion indicates, the candidate's personal style seems to influence and sometimes override a candidate's use of the typical challenger and incumbent strategies.

Dwight Eisenhower

As the challenger in 1952, Eisenhower used shorter commercials and a question-and-answer format in all of his commercials (the "Eisenhower Answers America" ads). These ads were dominated by showing what was wrong with the opposition, primarily the Democrats in a generic sense. Almost all of his ads were focused on issues. He used candidate head-on as the dominant production technique, speaking for himself in the majority of his ads, and using logical evidence to make his point, usually about his issue concerns. In 1952, Eisenhower took the offensive position on issues and attacked the record and policies of the administration in power.

Eisenhower as the incumbent used longer commercials, used the documentary format in the majority of his ads, employed an emotional style, had a candidate-positive focus, and used a combination of the various production techniques in the majority of his ads. In 1956, Eisenhower's ads were dominated by source credibility appeals that generally dealt with his positive personality and character attributes. He used an anonymous announcer to speak for him in all of the ads studied and used typical incumbent strategies: using the trappings of his office, appearing with world leaders, emphasizing his accomplishments, using surrogates, and maintaining an above-the-trenches posture.

Of all of the incumbents studied here, Eisenhower most closely followed the typical challenger and incumbent styles in his ads. In some ways, Eisenhower's personality and personal style were secondary to his political position style. As the challenger, Eisenhower used most of the typical challenger strategies—question-and-answer format, candidate head-on production technique, an informative rhetorical style, attacking the record of his opponent, taking the offensive position on issues, using issue appeals, and speaking for himself in his ads. In 1956, President Eisenhower became the typical incumbent in his campaign ads, using a documentary format, more personal appeals, appearing less in his ads, relying on an anonymous announcer, and using an emotional rhetorical style in most of his ads. He also, as the incumbent president, emphasized his accomplishments, maintained an above the trenches posture in his ads, and used the trappings of his office to appear presidential in his ads.

Richard Nixon

Although Richard Nixon also ran for the presidency (as the assumed incumbent) in 1960, we compared only his run as a challenger in 1968 and his run as a true incumbent in 1972. In 1968, a question-and-answer format and a focus on his positive attributes, not on his opponent's (Hubert Humphrey) negative characteristics, characterized Nixon's ads. Challenger Nixon used fear appeals and source credibility appeals in his ads and focused on personality characteristics. Slides with print and somebody other than the candidate head-on were the dominant production techniques used in the 1968 ads. The most popular strategies for Nixon as challenger were using surrogates to speak, appealing to traditional values, calling for changes, and emphasizing optimism for the future. Nixon as the challenger also relied on endorsements from other political figures in his ads.

When Nixon ran as the incumbent president in 1972 against George McGovern he used longer commercials, more negative ads, and a documentary format in most of his ads. His ads used emotional appeals and generally emphasized issue concerns. As the incumbent, Nixon appeared in his ads more but spoke for himself less, using an anonymous announcer as the dominant speaker in many of his ads. The incumbent ads used a combination of production techniques, with cinema verité the most popular single technique. In 1972 Nixon used a combination of challenger and incumbent strategies in his ads. He appeared presidential in his 1972 ads by emphasizing the legitimacy of the presidency, showing his competency as a leader, consulting with world leaders, emphasizing his accomplishments, and maintaining an above-the-trenches posture. Incumbent Nixon ads also took an offensive position on issues and attacked his opponent, but they did this using an anonymous announcer to make the attacks and were generally attributed to other campaign organizations (Democrats for Nixon), not to Nixon's campaign organization.

Nixon, both as a challenger and as an incumbent, adhered in general to the basic styles for those positions. However, Nixon in both presidential elections stayed away from speaking directly to the camera or to voters in his ads. Many scholars have observed that Nixon was wary of television and of appearing on camera because of his unease with television and with media personnel (Bloom, 1973). This uneasiness was reflected in his ads for both campaigns. Nixon appeared in only 10% of his challenger ads, an extremely low percentage for a challenger. In 1968 Nixon relied on montage ads in which he did the voice-overs or on testimonials from other officeholders. In his 1972 ads, Nixon actually appeared more frequently than he had in his challenger ads (67%). However, even though he was "present" in the ads, he still did not appear speaking directly to the voters on-camera. Most of the incumbent ads where Nixon actually appears were documentary style ads that showed him carrying out his presidential duties.

Nixon, probably more than any other true incumbent, attempted to link himself intricately to the office of the presidency in his ads. He used many of the incumbent strategies designed to make him appear presidential and as the leader of the nation. When his ads used negative attacks or took the offensive position on issues, surrogates made the attacks for him so that he could remain "above the trenches" of politics.

Jimmy Carter

In 1976 as a challenger, Carter used an introspection format in most of his ads. The majority of the appeals made in his ads were emotional and focused on his issue concerns. He used candidate head-on and spoke for himself more in his challenger ads. His ads were dominated by a focus on his good qualities, and the most popular strategies in these ads were calling for changes, appealing to traditional values, and emphasizing optimism for the future. Challenger Carter also attempted to maintain an "above the trenches" posture in his ads, a typical incumbent strategy, but one that served Carter well in his stance as a political "outsider" in the aftermath of the Watergate scandal.

In 1980, President Carter used an opposition-focused format and an emotional rhetorical style in his ads. Carter's negative ads attacked the personality and issue stands of Ronald Reagan in 1980. He made source credibility appeals and focused on personality characteristics in his incumbent ads. As the incumbent in 1980, Carter was not seen as much in his ads, used an anonymous announcer to speak for him the majority of the time, and used cinema verité as a production technique. President Carter used traditional incumbent strategies—using trappings of the office, emphasizing his accomplishments and his competency, and using surrogates to speak for him. He did not make use of "maintaining an above-the-trenches posture" in his incumbent ads, using this incumbent strategy significantly more as a challenger than as the incumbent.

Carter, like the other true incumbents, adhered to the basic styles of a challenger and an incumbent when he ran in those positions. In fact, Carter deviated more in his use of challenger strategies in 1976 than in his use of incumbent strategies in 1980, although he and George Bush are the only full-term incumbents since 1952 who have lost to challengers. The combination of Carter's personal style and position style offers some evidence for why Carter's incumbent ads may not have been as successful as his challenger ads.

One way that Carter deviates from the other true incumbents is in his use of the incumbent strategy of maintaining an above-the-trenches posture in his ads. This strategy is typically used by incumbents to show voters they are removed from politics and are staying out of the political battle. This allows the aura of the president to remain intact and contributes to the view of presidential incumbents as above the fray of politics and as truly presidential. Eisenhower, Nixon, Reagan, and Clinton used this strategy significantly more as incumbents than as challengers. Carter, on the other hand, used this strategy significantly more as the challenger than as the incumbent.

For Nixon and Reagan, their personal style was consistent in their ads from one election to the next. Although they had basically adhered to challenger and incumbent styles, their own personal attributes modified their use of some of these strategies. Carter in 1976 established a "personal style" with viewers as a "nonpolitical" decent leader, untouched by Washington politics. As the incumbent, though, his use of certain techniques and strategies contradicted this personal style, and he did not continue the "above the trenches" posture that he had established as the challenger.

Carter also violated his personal style of "decent man" during his 1980 campaign through his use of negative advertising. In his incumbent ads, President Carter attacked his opponent's record more than any of the other true incumbents (except for the most recent usage by incumbents Bush and Clinton) and more than his own challenger ads in 1976. In addition, more of President Carter's 1980 ads were opponent-negative focused than in 1976 and more than his own challenger, Ronald Reagan, used in that election.

Ronald Reagan

Reagan's ads in 1980 were characterized by an opposition-focused or introspection format, attacks on personality flaws of his opponent, and the use of evidence, facts, and logic to make issue appeals. As the challenger, Reagan used more negative advertising and presented his messages in a candidate head-on production technique. Popular strategies with challenger Reagan were calling for changes, using surrogates to speak in the ads, emphasizing his competency, taking the offensive position on issues, and attacking the record of his opponent.

In 1984, President Reagan used introspection and opposition-focused formats and an emotional rhetorical style in his incumbent commercials. He made more emotional and source-credibility appeals and emphasized personality characteristics in these appeals. Reagan's incumbent commercials used special production techniques and candidate head-on and used more music and more special effects. In 1984, President Reagan generally adhered to typical incumbent strategies such as consulting with world leaders, emphasizing his accomplishments and his competence, emphasizing the legitimacy and the trappings of the presidency, and taking an above-the-trenches posture.

Reagan's unique style also influenced his use of challenger and incumbent styles. Because of his experience as an actor and as a past officeholder, Reagan was said to be very comfortable with television. This ease with appearing in front of the camera as well as his positive on-camera presence was reflected in Reagan's use of particular challenger and incumbent techniques. Reagan, in both his challenger and his incumbent ads, frequently speaks directly to the voters and to the camera. Candidate head-on was the most popular production technique for Reagan the challenger and the second most popular for President Reagan. In his incumbent ads, Reagan makes less use of an anonymous announcer and speaks more for himself than any of the other true incumbents. In terms of other strategies, Reagan, in general, adhered to the challenger/incumbent strategies and styles. He called for changes, attacked the record of Carter, took the offensive position on issues, and emphasized his accomplishments in his challenger ads in 1980. In 1984, President Reagan emphasized his accomplishments and competence and maintained an above-the-trenches posture in his ads.

Bill Clinton

Challenger Bill Clinton in 1992 used a negative focus in two-thirds of his ads, and most of his ads used an opposition-focused format. Clinton as challenger used very few fear appeals in his ads, although in his negative attacks he attacked Bush's associations and his issue stands and consistency. Three-fourths of Clinton's challenger ads were issue ads and focused on his general issue concerns. His 1992 ads used logical and emotional appeals almost equally, used cinema verité, and featured an anonymous announcer as the dominant speaker. Clinton as challenger mainly used two typical challenger strategies: calling for changes and attacking the record of the opponent. His 1992 ads also used two typical incumbent strategies: emphasizing his charisma and depending on surrogates to speak.

As the incumbent in 1996, Clinton's videostyle was very similar to his challenger style. Most of his incumbent ads were once again issue ads, but in this campaign they tended to focus on policy preferences. His ads were once again dominated by a negative focus, and attacks were made on Dole's issue stands and consistency and his associations (in particular, with Newt Gingrich). Clinton's 1996 ads also featured an anonymous announcer in most of the ads, and, although the ads used cinema verité again, the most popular production technique was slides with print and/or movement and voice-overs. In 1996, President Clinton used fear appeals in almost half of his ads and increased his use of source-credibility appeals (his challenger ads featured very few of them). As the incumbent, Clinton used more of the typical incumbent strategies, such as emphasizing his accomplishments, emphasizing his competency, using the symbolic trappings of the presidency, using an above-the-trenches posture, and speaking to traditional values. He also used two challenger strategies: attacking the record of the opponent and taking the offensive position on issues.

For Clinton, it is hard to see the interaction between personal style and political style because his videostyle remains almost the same from one campaign to the next. Clinton's challenger ads feature lots of negative advertising and attacks on his opponent, but this is not surprising because attacking the incumbent is a tried and true challenger strategy. Clinton's negative advertising is higher than other challengers, and perhaps this is because of the 1988 campaign in which Dukakis was criticized for responding too late to the attacks in Bush's advertising. This does not, however, explain why he used so many negative ads as the incumbent (and in the case of the 1996 election, his lead in the polls was always fairly good). Certainly Clinton's challenger ads had set a precedent for using negative advertising; therefore, Clinton (unlike Jimmy Carter) did not violate any expectations of his behavior when, as the incumbent, he once again used lots of negative advertising. Clinton's challenger and incumbent ads seem to reflect a basic style (negative and issue based) that was modified in 1996 to reflect his new political position as incumbent (the use of more incumbent strategies as the incumbent) and to address some of the circumstances of the campaign (the use of more source-credibility appeals because of character questions in 1996).

NOTE

1. Although categories such as incumbent/challenger style overlap with the nonverbal aspects of videostyle, we treat them with verbal components here in order to present the combined aspects of incumbent and challenger styles as outlined by Trent and Friedenberg (1983).

Negative and Positive Videostyle

Most of the discussion of videostyle in the preceding chapters has focused on the candidates' various approaches and strategies for enhancing their own images through political television spots. This chapter considers in more detail the interaction between this positive approach to image formation and the alternative, a negative videostyle. It is all too clear in modern campaigns that candidates must seek not only to enhance their own images but to use the tools under their control to mold and shape the images of their opponents. Negative videostyle, then, is the presentation of the opponent's undesirable characteristics and issue positions.

BACKGROUND ON NEGATIVE ADVERTISING

As must be clear to readers of earlier chapters in this book, negative advertising has been a feature of presidential campaigns throughout the periods covered in this analysis. While many observers point to the 1964 campaign as the nadir of negative spots, negative advertising seems to have become more prevalent in the 1980s, beginning a new era with the successful use of negative ads in 1980 by independent groups such as the National Conservative Political Action Committee (NCPAC) and concern that this negativity was "trickling up" to the presidential level

(Grove, 1988a, p. 18). By 1981 Sabato (1981) estimated that one-third of spots at all campaign levels were negative, and Joslyn's (1980) more systematic analysis of a convenience sample of advertisements at various levels indicated that 23% had a blame-placing focus.

The reasons for the trend toward negative advertising were originally based on purely pragmatic concerns by candidates and media consultants: Quite simply, negative ads appeared to work.

Political media consultants are virtually unanimous in their belief that negative ads can be successful (Taylor, 1989). The fact that negative ads appear to provide information to voters is one reason given for their success (Baukus, Payne, & Reisler, 1985), while others suggest that it is "easier to appeal to emotion than to logic" and that negative appeals are easier for voters to remember because they are oversimplified (Nugent, 1987, p. 49).

Scholars have also reinforced the possibility that appeals to emotion are a reason for the success of many negative ads (Kern, 1989). One easy way to build a negative videostyle for the opponent is to construct a fearful scenario of the consequences of choosing the opponent. Good examples are ads like the 1964 Daisy Girl spot, with the visual specter of a nuclear attack and the stark verbal message: "We must either love each other or we must die."

Voters are also affected by ads that engender uncertainty by exposing an opponent's inconsistencies, "flip-flops" on issues, or policy failures. For instance, Patterson and McClure (1976) reported that one of the most effective ads from the 1972 presidential campaign was the Democrats-for-Nixon ad that showed a representation of McGovern's head flipping while recounting inconsistent positions taken by McGovern on several major issues. Whatever the appeal (logic or emotion), it now appears that negative ads have become indispensable in competitive races, particularly for challengers (Kern, 1989).

Practitioners tend to measure the success of negative ads by pointing vaguely to winning and losing candidates. Scholarly researchers have looked to effects that can be measured more precisely, such as effects of negative ads on candidate images or perceptions of candidate issue positions. However, in the case of negative ads, much scholarly research has tended to confirm the instincts of media consultants about the success of negative ads. Researchers have found that negative ads do have direct effects on candidate images and evaluations, particularly when the negative ads are sponsored by independent sources (Garramone, 1984a, 1985; Garramone & Smith, 1984; Kaid & Boydston, 1987). However, Merritt (1984) and Garramone (1984a) have both identified some backlash effect from negative ads. Roddy and Garramone

(1988) have also noted that negative ads are more successful when they concentrate on issue attacks rather than image attacks.

NEGATIVE VIDEOSTYLE IN PRESIDENTIAL SPOTS

Although a great deal of attention has been focused on negative campaigns and negative advertising, very little research has recounted the actual content of negative advertising. Johnson-Cartee and Copeland (1991) have outlined a number of types and strategies of negative spots. Trent and Friedenberg (1983, 1995) have suggested that one distinction that might be applied is that challengers are more likely than incumbents to use attack strategies, and Kaid and Davidson (1986) used content analysis to verify this in their finding that several 1986 U. S. Senate challengers used more negative ads than their incumbent counterparts.

In an earlier look at negative and positive ad content, the authors (Kaid & Johnston, 1991) compared presidential ads from 1960 through 1988. While 29% were negative, challengers did not use more negative ads than incumbents, there were no differences in negative ad usage based on partisan affiliation of the candidate, and negative ads were more issue oriented than positive ads but relied more on emotional and fear appeals.

Overall Trends in Negative Videostyle

In the earlier discussion of overall trends in videostyle, the results indicated that across all years from 1952 through 1996 the number of negative ads was only 38%, just over one-third of all spots. The earlier discussion of videostyle categories also explained that the classification of spots into a negative or positive category was done on the basis of the *dominant* approach used in the spot. If the spot focused primarily on the sponsoring candidate's positive qualities or issue positions, it was classified as a positive spot. If the spot focused on alleged undesirable issue or image qualities of the opponent, the spot was classified as a negative one. A spot that contained some positive and some negative information was classified according to the *dominant* aspect of the spot.

As Table 6.1 shows, there have been considerable differences in the level of negative advertising used in specific presidential campaigns. The percentage of negative advertising has ranged from a low of 10% in the 1960 campaign to a high of 68% in the 1992 race.

It is clear from Figure 6.1 that there has been a definite increase in negative advertising during the past two presidential campaigns. In 1992 the percentage of negative spots was 68%, and the corresponding percentage for 1996 was almost as high at 65%. The surprising finding

TABLE 6.1
Positive and Negative Spots in Presidential Campaigns, 1952–1996

Year	Positive (N = 742)	Negative (N = 642)
1952 (53)	18 (34%)	35 (66%)
1956 (17)	13 (76%)	4 (24%)
1960 (116)	104 (90%)	12 (10%)
1964 (64)	34 (53%)	30 (47%)
1968 (77)	59 (77%)	18 (23%)
1972 (77)	52 (68%)	25 (32%)
1976 (147)	112 (65%)	35 (35%)
1980 (250)	161 (64%)	89 (36%)
1984 (94)	61 (65%)	33 (35%)
1988 (118)	63 (53%)	55 (47%)
1992 (71)	23 (32%)	48 (68%)
1996 (120)	42 (35%)	78 (65%)
Total	742 (62%)	462 (38%)

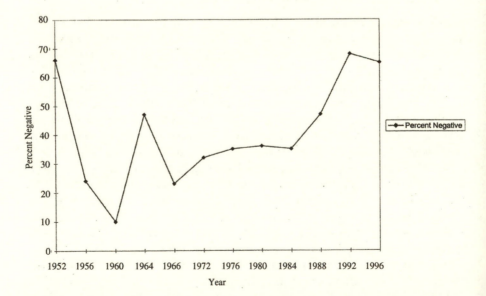

Figure 6.1 Percent of Negative Spots in Presidential Campaigns by Year

from the comparison over the years is that the 1952 campaign was also a very negative one, with 66% of the spots classified as negative.

Negative Videostyle in the Early Campaigns, 1952–1960

The look at the negative spot trends across years, however, masks some of the great individual differences in candidate videostyle. Table 6.2 indicates that some candidates took a much more negative approach than others. One surprise is that Richard Nixon's opponents in almost every one of his three presidential races used almost twice as many negative spots against him as Nixon used against them. Even in 1960, a low year for negative ads all around, Kennedy used 50% more negative ads than did Nixon.

TABLE 6.2
Individual Candidate Use of Negative Spots, 1952–1956

Name	Year	Percent of Negative Spots
Eisenhower	1952	66%
Stevenson	1952	67%
Eisenhower	1956	0
Stevenson	1956	33%
Kennedy	1960	12%
Nixon	1960	8%
Goldwater	1964	46%
Johnson	1964	48%
Nixon	1968	15%
Humphrey	1968	33%
McGovern	1972	40%
Nixon	1972	20%
Carter	1976	19%
Ford	1976	27%
Carter	1980	36%
Reagan	1980	35%
Mondale	1984	54%
Reagan	1984	27%
Bush	1988	36%
Dukakis	1988	54%
Bush	1992	66%
Clinton	1992	69%
Dole	1996	61%
Clinton	1996	68%

In the 1952 campaign, while two-thirds of the spots of both Eisenhower and Stevenson were classified as negative, the approach to
negative videostyle was very different between the two candidates. In
the Eisenhower spots, which were basically question-answer formats
("Eisenhower Answers America" series), Eisenhower never directly
attacks his opponent, Adlai Stevenson, or mentions his name. Instead,
Eisenhower delivers vague, sometimes oblique, criticisms of the opposing party, the Democrats. In one rather convoluted answer to the question, "The Democrats have made mistakes, but aren't their intentions
good?", Eisenhower responds: "Well, if a driver of your school bus runs
into a truck, hits a lamp post, drives into a ditch, you don't say his
intentions were good, you get a new bus driver." Certainly this is a
criticism of the Democrats, although it is difficult to imagine that the
former commander of the Allied Forces in Europe thought of himself as
a "new bus driver" for America.

Stevenson's spots were much more direct in their criticisms of Eisenhower, many used jingles and songs to criticize Eisenhower for his link
to Bob Taft, implying that, once elected, Eisenhower would turn things
over to Taft. In a humorous spot, the visual shows a cartoon-style heart
pierced with an arrow and showing Ike and Bob as the two implied
lovers. The voice-over starts with each saying the other's name as if
yearning for each other: "Ike . . . Bob . . . Ike . . . Bob . . . " and continues:
"I'm so glad we're friends again, Bob. Yes, Ike, we agree on everything.
Let's never separate again, Bob. Never again, Ike. Bob . . . Ike . . . Bob . . .
Ike." The announcer continues by posing the question: "Will Ike and
Bob really live happily ever after? Is the White House big enough for
both of them? Stay tuned for a musical interlude." This is followed by
a singing jingle at the end: "Reuben, Reuben, I've been thinkin'. Bob
and Ike now think alike. With the Gen'ral in the White House, who'd
give the orders, Bob or Ike?—Let's vote for Adlai—and John!"

The sharp contrast of the 1956 spots is largely due to the absence of
short spots from the Eisenhower sample. The five spots available for
Eisenhower in 1956 are 5-minute spots and therefore concentrated
mostly on scenarios that provided opportunities to praise Eisenhower
and his accomplishments. Stevenson, on the other hand, took his television style much more seriously in 1956—fewer jingles and musical
numbers and more straightforward attacks directly on Eisenhower. In
fact, in 1956 Stevenson began a trend that would intensify over the years
and reach new heights in the 1996 presidential race. Stevenson was the
first to take excerpts from his opponent's prior spots and use them to
attack his opponent. In a series of spots Stevenson took statements and
promises that Eisenhower had made in his 1952 spots and contrasted
them with his performance, using the slogan "How's that again, General?" to point up alleged failures. In this example, Stevenson's running

mate Estes Kefauver makes the complaint, as he does in all the spots in this series:

HOW'S THAT AGAIN, GENERAL?
Announcer: "How's that again, General? In the 1952 campaign, Mr. Eisenhower said this about Taft/Hartley:"
Eisenhower in clip from 1952 spot: "I know how the law might be used to break unions. That must be changed. America wants no law licensing union busting and neither do I."
Announcer: "How's that again General?"
Replay of Eisenhower statement: "I know how the law might be used to break unions. That must be changed."
Kefauver: "This is Estes Kefauver. That was one more promise Mr. Eisenhower didn't keep. During 4 years in office, the General did absolutely nothing about changing the union busting features of Taft/Hartley.
What's more, he stacked the National Labor Relations Board with anti-labor spokesmen. . . ."
Announcer: "Vote for Stevenson and Kefauver. Vote Democratic."

And so began the now-familiar technique of using the opponent's own words and indeed his own spot against him. By 1996 Clinton and Dole would take this strategy to new heights, using it over and over in repetitious sequences to reinforce the opponent's policy positions and personal flaws.

The 1960 campaign is the lowest in negative advertising in general; both candidates were also quite restrained in their attack strategies. Richard Nixon's 1960 spots had the lowest percentage of negative spots ever. Given current trends, with only 8% of his spots concentrating on the negative, it is unlikely that Nixon will ever lose this distinction. Nixon's negative ads were, in fact, quite mild, with many centered on rebutting charges from the other side. Kennedy was rarely mentioned by name, and sometimes Nixon even made the mild accusation himself:

Nixon: "I would like to talk to you for a moment about dollars and sense. Your dollars and sense. Now my opponents want to increase federal expenditures by $18 billion. How will they pay for it? There are only two ways. First, they will increase your taxes. That hurts everyone. The other is to increase our national debt, which increases your prices. Robbing your savings, cutting into the value of your insurance, hurting your pocket book everyday at the drug store, grocery store, and gas station. Is that what you want for America? I say no, I say that's a false doctrine, I say we can remain the strongest nation on earth only through continuing our program of strong government.

John F. Kennedy, however, was running from a less established position than vice-president of the United States, and his negative attacks were somewhat more direct. Instead of using Nixon's own words against him, he made use of a comment made in jest by President Eisenhower.

> Announcer: "Every Republican politician wants you to believe that Richard Nixon is quote experienced. They even want you to believe that he has actually been making decisions in the White house. But listen to the man who should know best, the President of the United States. A reporter recently asked President Eisenhower this question about Mr. Nixon's experience:"
>
> Reporter in recorded film clip: "I just wondered if you could give us an example of a major idea of his that you had adopted in that role as the decider and the final. . . ."
>
> Eisenhower: "If you give me a week I might think of one; I don't remember."
>
> Announcer: "At the same press conference, President Eisenhower said:"
>
> Eisenhower clip: "No one can make a decision except me."
>
> Announcer: "And as for any major ideas for Mr. Nixon. . . ."
>
> Eisenhower clip repeated: "If you give me a week I might think of one; I don't remember."
>
> Announcer: "President Eisenhower could not remember, but the voters will remember. For real leadership in the 60s, help elect Senator John F. Kennedy President."

This seemingly devastating attack was also the subject of a question asked by a reporter during the first Kennedy-Nixon televised debate in 1960. It was such a concern that the Nixon campaign produced several different rebuttal spots with Eisenhower providing an endorsement of Nixon and detailing his experience and qualifications.

Negative Videostyle Takes a Giant Leap: 1964

As Figure 6.1 and Table 6.2 clearly demonstrate, the 1964 election year does live up to its reputation as a very negative campaign year. However, this is not due only to the negative videostyle of Lyndon B. Johnson, whose percentage of negative ads reached almost the halfway point (48%). Opponent Barry Goldwater was not far behind, with 46% of his spots carrying a predominantly negative tone.

For Lyndon Johnson, an incumbent president who had come to the Oval Office by the tragic assassination of John F. Kennedy rather than by election, the choice to "go negative" seems a puzzling one. With the

1963 Kennedy tragedy so fresh and the polls showing Johnson with a continuous and wide lead, it is difficult to understand the drive for negativity. Whatever the motives—and some have suggested that fear of low turnout was the major reason—this was clearly the first campaign in which the construction of a negative videostyle for the opponent was the driving force behind the campaign messages. Goldwater did not make this a difficult strategy, since the Johnson advertising strategists were able to use Goldwater's own statements as fodder for their advertising cannons. In addition to the famous Daisy Girl ad and a plethora of other spots that made all-out nuclear war seem likely if Goldwater came anywhere near the White House, the Johnson campaign was able to use Goldwater's statements on Social Security to raise fears in the elderly. One humorous spot capitalized on an off-hand Goldwater comment about the East Coast:

> Announcer: "In a *Saturday Evening Post* article dated August 31, 1963, Barry Goldwater said, 'Sometimes I think this country would be better off if we could just saw off the Eastern seaboard and let it float out to sea.' Can a man who makes statements like this be expected to serve all the people, justly and fairly? Vote for President Johnson on November 3. The stakes are too high for you to stay home."

The visuals are perhaps the most effective part of this spot. As the announcer speaks, Goldwater's statement is visually implemented—a saw cuts off the eastern portion of a floating model of the United States, and the East Coast literally plops into the water and floats away.

Another Johnson negative ad tried to take on the image of Goldwater as a man of principle and high moral character by constructing an image of Goldwater as someone who abandons his principles for political expediency. In this ad an actor sits on the side of a water dam and reflects:

> Actor: "This is Arizona, Barry Goldwater's state. It's dry country out here; water's priceless. That's why they're building this dam. It's a federal dam; federal taxes built it. It was sponsored by Barry Goldwater. Now here's the funny part. Barry sponsored this dam for his state. But he wanted to sell the TVA dams in Tennessee. He voted against Hell's Canyon Dam in Idaho, against the Hanford atomic project in Washington, against public works all over the country. In Barry's book this sort of thing is creeping socialism. Except when it creeps into Arizona. President Johnson is president of all the people. Vote for him on November 3. The stakes are too high for you to stay home."

The Johnson spots hammered away at Goldwater until the dominant image of Goldwater was one of an impulsive, naive moralizer who did not have the experience or good judgment to run the country. Goldwater, of course, tried to create his own negative image for Johnson, but the ammunition just never seemed strong enough. This example shows the indirect and less than devastating attacks Goldwater relied on:

> Announcer: "On October 18, 1960, speaking in Shemokan, Pennsylvania, when he was running for Vice President, Lyndon Johnson said: 'I don't want some bearded dictator, 90 miles off, thumbing his nose at us,' end quote. Now to debate Mr. Johnson on this statement, here is Barry Goldwater, who calls him to account for this administration's colossal bungling on Cuba and Castro."
>
> Goldwater: "That same bearded dictator is still 90 miles off, thumbing his nose at us. And the Bay of Pigs has left us, not a monument to freedom, but a dark blot on our national pride. The United States must provide the leadership which will deal effectively with the problems of Cuba and which will stop the spread of Communism in the Western Hemisphere."

This attack was difficult to sustain, since most voters associated the Cuba and Bay of Pigs events with John F. Kennedy, not Lyndon Johnson, and the attack and link to Johnson were too oblique for most voters. To Goldwater's credit, he did deliver the attack himself, as he did many others during the course of the campaign.

More Positive Videostyles, 1968–1984

After the 1964 race, the percentage of negative ads in campaigns settled back to a more routine level. Nixon's 1968 campaign was another low percentage of negative ads (15%), as was his 1972 re-election bid (20%). His opponents, Humphrey in 1968 and McGovern in 1972, ran campaigns that were characterized by more positive videostyles. One of Humphrey's best-known attacks in 1968 was created by the man who also made the Daisy Girl spot for Lyndon Johnson, Tony Schwartz; the spot attacked, not the presidential nominee himself, but his running mate Spiro Agnew. The ad simply shows a TV screen with Agnew's name as vice-president followed by a question mark. The audio is merely a laugh track, which concludes with on-screen print: "This would be funny if it weren't so serious." While the ad does not provide any specific reason for the attack on Agnew, it fits very much in line with Schwartz's theory that the most important thing to do in targeting voters is to key off on their stored memories and evoke a "responsive chord" (Schwartz, 1973). The important thing to Schwartz was not what was said about Agnew in the ad, but what the question and the laughter would do to remind people of their own doubts and uncertainties about Agnew.

In 1972, George McGovern did attack Nixon repeatedly for the failure to end the killing in Southeast Asia. He, too, used Nixon's own words against him in challenging Nixon to debate:

> Announcer: "Presidential television debates were not designed to serve a candidate for office; they were designed to serve the public.
> 'Television debates prevent a candidate from waging a campaign based on special-interest appeals.
> 'Television debates give voters the opportunity to see the real, not the synthetic product of public relations experts.
> 'And they contribute to four major objectives which are in the public interest: a bigger vote, better informed voters, lower campaign cost, and, in the end, a better President.'
> The foregoing is a statement by Richard M. Nixon before he became President of the United States. Since the statement is as true today as when he wrote it, why does Mr. Nixon refuse to debate Senator McGovern?"

Of course, McGovern knew the answer to this question as well as anyone. Nixon would not take the chance of a repeat of the 1960 debates, which he believed he won on substance but lost on style. His videostyle was better served by creating a positive image of himself through other television presentation techniques. Surprisingly, McGovern spent very little time attacking Nixon for the one thing that would eventually bring down his presidency, the Watergate break-in.

While Nixon did not use a lot of negative ads, his best arsenal of negative spots came from a source not directly tied to his campaign. The Democrats for Nixon group, headed by soon-to-be-Republican John Connally, sponsored a series of negative ads aimed at McGovern. These are included in the totals for the Nixon negative ad category because it is clear that the spots were coordinated with and paid for by Nixon's own re-election committee. There were few of these ads, but they were very effective. Two of them, one on McGovern contradictions and one on McGovern defense policies, were particularly memorable and effective (Patterson & McClure, 1976). The spot on McGovern contradictions used a simple visual of a McGovern face, like a poster on a stick, and it turned from one side to the other as the contradictions were read, symbolizing a "turnaround" in McGovern's position on these issues:

> Announcer: "In 1967, Senator George McGovern said he was not an advocate of unilateral withdrawal of our troops from Vietnam. Now, of course, he is.

Last year the Senator suggested regulating marijuana on the same lines as alcohol.

Now he says he against legalizing it and says he always has been. Last January Senator McGovern suggested a welfare plan that would give a thousand dollar bill to every man, woman, and child in the country.

Now he says the thousand dollar figure isn't right.

Throughout the year he has proposed unconditional amnesty to all draft dodgers.

Now his running mate claims he proposed no such thing.

In Florida he was pro busing.

In Oregon he said he would support the anti-busing bill in Congress.

Last year, this year. The question is, what about next year?

The Democrats for Nixon spot attacking the McGovern defense plan featured visuals of toy soldiers, aircraft, and navy ships. As the voice-over recounted McGovern's plans to cut each area, a hand swept sections of the defense weaponry away, leaving the visual image of a depleted American military in disarray:

Announcer: "The McGovern defense plan. Cut the marines by one third. Cut the Air Force by one third. It cut navy personnel by one fourth. It would cut interceptor planes by one half. The navy fleet by one half, and carriers from 16 to 6.
Senator Hubert Humphrey had this to say about the McGovern proposal. 'It isn't just cutting into the fat. It isn't just cutting into the manpower. It's cutting into the very security of this country.' President Nixon doesn't believe we should play games with our national security; he believes in a strong America. To negotiate for peace from strength."
Democrats for Nixon

These spots, with their seemingly independent sponsorship, were among the earliest ads to capitalize on the enhanced credibility that voters awarded to spots that seemed to be emanating from a source other than the prejudiced camp of the candidate.

In 1976 both Carter (19%) and Ford (27%) used fewer negative ads than the overall average (38%). Carter adopted a more positive and straightforward style in many of his spots. A relatively unknown quantity before the campaign, Carter was anxious for his positive style to come across in a way that would attract voters to his personal qualities, as well as his issues. He reminded voters in his positive spots that he was a simple peanut farmer before becoming governor of Georgia:

I'm Jimmy Carter and I know what it is to make a living as a farmer. So you can judge how I feel about the Republican embargoes. I don't like them. I feel that in an economy such as ours we need to keep a healthy free market in grain both here in America and overseas. I can promise no future embargoes except in a national emergency. Under my administration farmers will not be deceived by government officials and farmers not the grain companies will receive the profits.

In another spot, Carter announces:

When I was elected governor, I went into office not as a politician, but as an engineer, a businessman, a planter, a farmer. We had 300 agencies and departments in the state government. We abolished 278 of them and set up a very simple economical structure of government. That saved a lot of money yes but more importantly it was so the people could understand it for a change and control it.

Carter did need to use some negative attacks. Ford had been in the White House only a short time, but he had a record as a congressman, which was one of the areas Carter zeroed in on:

Carter: "Gerald Ford voted against Medicare, against food stamps for the elderly, against adequate housing. Isn't it bad enough that older people are the worst victims and the easiest victims of hoodlums and criminals? Must they also be victimized by their own government in Washington?
I'm Jimmy Carter. I could not live in the White House without helping them."

Neither incumbent Carter nor challenger Reagan engaged in a very negative campaign in 1980. Both had a primarily positive videostyle. Reagan, however, faced a very strong negative attack from Walter Mondale in 1984; 54% of Mondale's spots were negative ones, compared to only 27% for Reagan. Reagan's 1984 campaign is often characterized as one of the most positive and effective re-election styles in history. Reagan was very successful in creating a positive videostyle that capitalized on his strengths and his ability to convey a vision of an America that was moving ahead and full of bright, shining hope. Often called the "Morning in America" commercials, many of his 1984 spots were full of colorful, optimistic scenes of ordinary Americans going about their lives, embodying the classic American dream. Shot through soft lenses, voiced by a soothing and optimistic announcer, and underpinned by comforting and hopeful music, these spots portray an appealing America for which Ronald Reagan took credit. One of these hopeful spots was listed in Chapter 4; the verbal message in another underscores the same points:

Announcer: "During the past year, thousands of families moved into new homes that once seemed out of reach. People are buying new cars they once thought they couldn't afford. Workers are returning to factories that just four years ago were closed. And America is back, with a sense of pride people thought we'd never feel again. Now that our country is turning around, why would we ever want to turn back?"
"President Reagan. Leadership That's Working."

When he did go on the negative, Reagan found it easiest to let an anonymous announcer remind voters of his predecessor's weaknesses:

Announcer: "Under Carter-Mondale the price of Connie McCoe's groceries went from $202 a month to almost $400 a month. Under Carter-Mondale the cost of a mortgage for Warren Bockus increased by nearly $500. And the weakest economy in recent history helped Edward Blair lose his job. Now Mr. Mondale says he wants to help Connie, Warren, and Edward again. If this is help, how much help can they afford to have?"
"President Reagan. Leadership That's Working."

Walter Mondale produced twice as many negative spots in 1984 as did incumbent Reagan (54% compared to Reagan's 27%), and they encompassed a broad range of strategies. One spot invited you to link Reagan with televangelist Jerry Falwell:

Announcer: "Reverend Jerry Falwell and President Reagan cordially invite you to join their party on November 6. Here's all you have to believe in.
A secret war in Central America.
All new Supreme Court justices must rule abortion as a crime. Even in cases of rape or incest.
No equal rights amendment for women.
No verifiable nuclear freeze.
Think about the people who have taken over the Republican party. They want their new platform to be our new Constitution.
Think about that."

Many of Mondale's negative ads focused on foreign policy concerns, an attempt perhaps to divert people from the rosy picture of domestic America painted in Reagan ads or to make them fearful of losing those dreams to war or nuclear attack. In addition to the "Star Wars" ad recounted in Chapter 4, Mondale emphasized Reagan's alleged foreign policy weaknesses in ads like this one:

1985
Announcer: "It's been four years and Ronald Reagan still hasn't even met once with the leader of the Soviet Union. The tough talk, the

political rhetoric, that's one thing. But no talk, that's dangerous. No conference, no meeting, and the nuclear arms race goes on and on. More nuclear warheads, more threats, but no meeting. If you're thinking about voting for Ronald Reagan in 1984, think of what could happen because of that silence in 1985."

Incumbent Reagan found little need for the negative style in his 1984 re-election bid. Only 27% of his spots were negative, and many were quite subtle. One that is often praised for its symbolism and subtlety is the spot known to many as the "Bear in the Woods." The visuals for this spot show a large bear roaming in the forest while a voice-over declares:

There is a bear in the woods. For some people the bear is easy to see. Others don't see it at all. Some say the bear is tame; others say it's vicious and dangerous. Since no one can really be sure who is right, isn't it smart to be as strong as the bear? If there is a bear?

Negative Videostyle Becomes Dominant, 1988—1996

As Tables 6.1 and 6.2 and Figure 6.1 all show, 1988 was the beginning of a new explosion in negative videostyle in presidential campaigns. Interestingly, many observers have attributed this intensification of negativism to George Bush's advertising in 1988, but the trends do not support this interpretation. Of the six candidates/campaigns in the three election years from 1988 through 1996, George Bush's 1988 campaign actually contains the fewest negative ads (36%). It is true, however, that Bush produced some very powerful negative ads, ads that were effective and memorable and that received a great deal of airtime.

George Bush's total arsenal of spots conveys a positive videostyle. Many of his ads focused on his long-term career and on his service in World War II and in numerous other government posts. One of his many positive ads begins with his taking the oath of office for vice-president, "I, George Herbert Walker Bush," and asks the question: "How does a man get to this point in his life? How does one man come so far?" The announcer continues:

Maybe for George Bush it began when he became the youngest pilot in the Navy. Or perhaps it began this day in 1944, when he earned the distinguished flying cross for bravery under fire. . . . Wherever it began, it continued when he took his family off to Texas and started and built a successful company. It continued when he was elected to Congress. Selected to serve as U.N. ambassador and U.S. emissary to mainland China, and later run the C.I.A. The more you learn how George Bush got this far the more you realize that perhaps no one in this century is better prepared to be President of the United States.

Another ad, labeled "The Future," uses family visuals and scenes from the Republican National Convention, while the voice-over incorporates excerpts from Bush's acceptance speech at the convention: "I want a kinder and gentler nation." An announcer proclaims, "It's the President who defines the character of America." And Bush continues: "I'm a quiet man, but I hear the quiet people others don't—the ones who raise the family, pay the taxes, meet the mortgage, and I hear them and I am moved." The announcer concludes: "The President, the heart, the soul, the conscience of the nation."

However, such was the power and effectiveness (and press attention) of Bush's negative ads that they have wiped the positive view from many people's minds. Most famous of the 1988 negative ads is, of course, the "Revolving Door" ad, often mistaken for the "Willie Horton" ad. The Revolving Door ad attacks Dukakis for a weekend furlough program for prisoners instituted in Massachusetts. Whatever an observer thinks of the message or the method of attack, this commercial was a brilliantly executed combination of verbal message and video production techniques. Using black-and-white footage to reinforce the sinister and harsh elements of the scene, the visual message in the ad showed a prison tower overlooking a "revolving" door which supposed prisoners of many ethnic backgrounds walked through. The announcer voice and on-screen printed message reinforced the haunting and frightening message:

> As governor, Michael Dukakis vetoed mandatory sentences for drug dealers. He vetoed the death penalty. His prison policy gave weekend furloughs to first degree murderers, not eligible for parole. While out many of them committed other crimes like kidnapping, and rape, and many are still at large. Now Michael Dukakis wants to do for the country what he's done for Massachusetts. America can't afford that risk.

An on-screen graphic proclaimed during the statement that "many of these committed other crimes while out" and that "268 escaped." Some have criticized the ad for implying that all 268 escapees committed crimes like kidnapping and rape while out, a statistic that would exaggerate the criminal happenings.

For the Bush campaign the furor over this spot was complicated by the appearance of an ad sponsored by an independent group, the National Security Political Action Committee, on the same topic. This ad, however, featured the picture and detailed story of an actual escapee from the furlough program, Willie Horton. The spot detailed Horton's criminal actions (including rape) while out on weekend furlough. Since Horton was African American, charges of racism began to haunt the Bush campaign.

Besides the Revolving Door ad, two other Bush campaign ads with a negative portrayal of opponent Michael Dukakis were particularly effective. One took advantage of an ill-conceived Dukakis photo-op that placed Dukakis in a military tank. The verbal message in this spot, an enumeration of Dukakis's alleged opposition to various defense programs, was scarcely necessary; Dukakis looked so out-of-place and silly (some likened his appearance to that of the cartoon character Snoopy) in the helmet and tank that it was almost impossible to envision him as commander-in-chief of American armed forces. A third ad accused Dukakis of allowing Boston Harbor to become polluted. All three ads were effective in combining a strong verbal and visual message, although the sponsoring candidate never appeared in them. Their strength, of course, was that they built a strong negative videostyle for the opponent.

Democrat Michael Dukakis developed a negative videostyle for his own campaign. With 54% of his spots focusing on the opponent, voters never got to know enough about Dukakis to feel they ought to vote for him. Although his attacks were more frequent than those of Bush, they were less powerful and less visually memorable. One of the problems with Dukakis's negative videostyle was that it was so diversified that it never really zeroed in on a few points that might have done damage. Many Dukakis negative ads were similar in format, attacking some past position of Bush's. The following example is characteristic of appeals delivered by an announcer:

> For 7 1/2 years, George Bush supported cutbacks in American education. He even sat by while college loans for working families were cut. Now suddenly George Bush says he'll be the education President. Michael Dukakis won't give us slogans. He's committed to a new national college loan program to make sure that any American kid can afford to go to college.

Dukakis also tried a series of negative ads referred to as the "packaging" series. These ads were dramatizations that suggested hypothetical campaign scenarios of Bush campaign handlers. The spots tried to convey the "managed" and packaged nature of the Bush campaign and ended with a tag line: "They would like to sell you a package. Wouldn't you rather choose a president?" These little "skits" focused on a number of topics, including Bush's alleged involvement with drug kingpin Noriega:

> Title: The packaging of George Bush.
> Bush campaign staffer: "Oh jeez. They're gonna kill us on this Noriega thing. Look at the headline, Panamanian drug lord."

Another staffer: "Yeah, it's a picture of Bush with Noriega."
Staffer: "They just won't let it go, will they?"
Staffer: "We need a lot better answer."
Staffer: "Something better than 'I don't remember.'"
Staffer: "Well I'm working on it, I'm working on it."
Staffer: "You better be."
Staffer: "Maybe we should just stick with 'I don't remember.'"
Announcer: "They would like to sell you a package. Wouldn't you rather choose a President?"

Dukakis also pounded away at Bush's choice of a running mate, making fun of Dan Quayle in this spot that showed an empty chair in the Oval Office:

Announcer: "The most powerful man in the world is also mortal. We know this all too well in America. One in five American Vice-Presidents has had to rise into the duties of Commander in Chief. One in five has had to take on the responsibility of the most powerful office in the world. For this job after five months of reflection, George Bush made his personal choice, J. Danforth Quayle. Hopefully we will never know how great a lapse of judgment that really was."

However, as with Humphrey's attempt to convince voters to abandon Richard Nixon in 1968 because of uncertainty over Spiro Agnew, Dan Quayle was not considered a risk sufficient to cause voters to choose Dukakis over Bush.

The 1988 campaign, however, was just a warm-up for the negativity of the 1992 and 1996 races, easily the most negative in modern times. Their negative advertising, directed at specific candidates, not general parties or past administrations, makes the simple and mild attacks of the Eisenhower 1952 campaign look quite Milquetoasty. In both years, both candidates came out swinging with negative videostyles. Clinton's 1992 campaign ads show the highest rate of negative advertising of any campaign in history (69%). Clinton pounded away at Bush in one spot after another. He was particularly effective in reminding voters that Bush had failed to keep his "no new taxes" pledge from 1988:

1988
Bush pledge: "Read my lips, no new taxes."
Announcer: "Then George Bush signed the second biggest tax increase in American history."
Bush: "Read my lips."

Announcer: "George Bush increased taxes on the middle class. Bush doubled his beer tax and increased the gas tax by fifty-six percent. Now George Bush wants to give a $108,000 tax break to millionaires—$108,000! Guess who's going to pay? We can't afford four more years."

And for voters who might remember the Reagan re-election campaign and think that things were still good in America, this spot tried to draw the contrast with "morning" in another place and time:

Announcer: "It's morning in Decaturville, Tennessee. But for 650 people who once worked here, there are no jobs. The Decaturville Sportswear factory closed and moved overseas.
Resident: "We were just family. It was a good place to work."
Resident: "It just hurts plum down to the heart."
Announcer: "It didn't have to happen. As *60 Minutes* reported, the Bush administration used your tax dollars to lure this sports factory to move to El Salvador. Tax incentives, low interest loans."
Resident: "That sign means nothing really. Not if the government's going to take it away from me."
Resident: "'Buy made in the U.S.A.' How can I buy made in the U.S.A, when I'm drawing unemployment?"
Announcer: "In the last four years, we've lost tens of thousands of textile jobs. Many here in the South. George Bush is using your tax dollars to help make it happen. Clinton, Gore ready to invest in America. Clinton, Gore for the people, for a change."

Perhaps instead of the famous sign in Clinton headquarters saying "It's the economy, stupid," the sign might have read, "It's the negative ads, stupid."

In 1992, however, George Bush was not lagging far behind in the use of negative ads (66%). He seemed to abandon any attempt to defend his own record. His accomplishments, indeed, had been more in foreign policy, and the world (America, at least) was not interested in foreign policy. The Cold War seemed to be over, never mind that the Republican administration had overseen its demise. As mentioned earlier, campaign spots for the 1992 and 1996 elections were virtually devoid of any foreign policy mentions. Bush seemed ill-equipped to fight on domestic policy grounds. He tried to attack Clinton's character and lack of consistency and truth-telling by depicting a dual Bill Clinton saying different things:

Announcer: "He said he was never drafted. Then he admitted he was drafted. Then he said he forgot being drafted. He said he was never deferred from the draft, then he said he was. He said he never received special treatment, but he did receive special treatment. The question then was avoiding the draft. Now, for Bill Clinton it's the question of avoiding the truth."

The draft issue, however, seemed a long time ago to most people, and it seemed more like a foreign policy issue than a domestic one. It also pointed up another problem that Clinton opponents in both 1992 and 1996 have had. They have focused a number of their attacks on Clinton's personal qualities, rather than on issues. Academic research, on the other hand, has shown that issue attacks are much more successful than attacks on an opponent's personal qualities (Kahn & Geer, 1994; Pfau & Burgoon, 1989; Roddy & Garramone, 1988).

The 1996 campaign was also very negative; both Dole (61%) and Clinton (68%) concentrated most of their efforts on negative portrayals of each other. Some have argued that the 1996 spots, particularly Clinton's efforts, were less negative and more "comparative" (Harwood, 1996). While many 1996 ads, particularly Clinton's spots, did attempt to blend some personal "credit-taking" with the negative attacks, the focus of most of these ads was quite negative. In fact, the ads of both candidates are even more negative than this "dominant focus" categorization would indicate, since a negative attack of some kind was made in 85% of Clinton's ads and 76% of Dole's ads, with the overall result that 81% of all ads in the general election campaign of the two major party candidates contained a negative attack in 1996.

Both Dole and Clinton used their negative ads to create negative videostyles of their opponents. The attacks in these spots were not just attacks on opposing policies; they often featured the opponent's own words and voice. Clinton used Dole's prior Senate record to savage him on old votes on Medicare, education, taxes, and family leave policy. This Clinton ad, called "Preserve" and illustrated with pictures of Dole on each side, is typical:

Dole: "I will be the President who preserves and strengthens and protects Medicare."
Dole: "I was there, fighting the fight, voting against Medicare, one of 12, because we knew it wouldn't work."
Announcer: "Last year Dole/Gingrich tried to cut Medicare 270 billion."
Dole: "Give children a chance in life. Give them an education.
Dole: "We're going to eliminate the Department of Education, we don't need it in the first place, I didn't vote for it in 1979."
Announcer: "Dole tried to slash college scholarships."
Dole: "Voting against Medicare."

Announcer: "Wrong in the past."
Dole: "We're going to eliminate the Department of Education."
Announcer: "Wrong for our future."

In his turn, Dole replayed footage of Clinton appearing on MTV in 1992 and suggesting he might have "inhaled" that marijuana if he had had the chance to do it again:

Announcer: "We send them off to school and we worry. Teenage drug use has doubled since 1992. And Bill Clinton, he cut the White House drug office 83%. His own Surgeon General even considered legalizing drugs. And in front of our children on MTV the President himself. . . ."
MTV Questioner: "If you had it to do over again, would you inhale?"
Clinton: "Sure, if I could, I tried before."
Announcer: "Bill Clinton, he just doesn't get it, but we do."

It was very difficult to find a positive message in the Dole or Clinton campaigns. Dole did fit in a biographic piece and the positive endorsements of his wife, Elizabeth. Clinton kept his wife completely out of sight and used some comparative messages to make his point.

DIFFERENCES IN NEGATIVE AND POSITIVE VIDEOSTYLES

Verbal Content Differences

Aside from the overall trends and the individual candidate usage of positive and negative videostyles, there are some interesting differences in the content of ads that use negative or positive styles. As Table 6.3 shows, one finding that should be heartening to those who find negative ads distasteful is that negative ads are significantly more likely than positive ads to emphasize issues. Of all negative ads across the years, nearly three-quarters (74%) have focused on issues and only 26% have focused on candidate image qualities. On the other hand, positive ads, while also focusing more on issues than images, only focus on issues in 61% of the total number of spots.

It is also apparent from Table 6.3 that candidates using negative videostyle presentations also are more likely to use logical proof. While positive and negative ads alike rely equally on emotional proof (44%), 33% of negative ads rely on logical proof as the dominant form of evidence, compared to only 16% of positive spots. However, negative ads do use fear appeals significantly more often (34%) than positive ads (11%).

TABLE 6.3
Appeals and Contents of Negative and Positive Spots

	Positive (N = 742)	Negative (N = 462)
Content of Ad*		
Issues	456 (61%)	342 (74%)
Image	286 (39%)	120 (26%)
Dominant Appeal in Ad*		
Logical	120 (16%)	153 (33%)
Emotional	328 (44%)	203 (44%)
Ethical	294 (40%)	106 (23%)
Presence of Fear Appeal*	78 (11%)	156 (34%)
Purpose of Negative Ad		
Attack Personal Characteristics		241 (52%)
Attack Issue Stands/Consistency		391 (85%)
Attack Group Affiliations		97 (21%)
Strategy in Negative Ad		
Humor/Ridicule		220 (48%)
Linking with Undesirable Ideas		279 (60%)
Name-Calling		66 (14%)
Guilt by Association		96 (21%)

*Chi square test is significant at $p < .001$

Table 6.3 also details the types of purposes and strategies used in negative ads. Consistent with the emphasis in negative ads on issues, 85% of all negative ads contain some kind of attack on the opponent's issue stands or consistency. Negative ads like the Democrats for Nixon ad that featured the McGovern "turnaround" on different issues is a good example of an ad in which the opponent's lack of consistency is questioned. Attacks on the personal characteristics of the opponent occur in 52% of negative ads. A few negative ads (21%) also focus on a candidate's group affiliations.

In analyzing negative videostyles, the ads that focused on a negative portrayal of the opponent were also coded for the type of strategy or approach taken to the criticism in the spot. The most common ones found are listed in Table 6.3. Nearly half of the negative ads (48%) strive to make their point with humor or ridicule. The "Ike and Bob" cartoon musical from Stevenson's 1952 campaign (mentioned earlier) is a good example of this strategy. Lyndon Johnson's anti-Goldwater spot about "sawing off the Eastern Seaboard" is also humorous.

Three out of every five (60%) of all negative spots use the strategy of trying to link the opponent with undesirable ideas. The Johnson spots linking Goldwater to nuclear explosions are obvious examples, as is George Bush's detailing of the bad effects from Dukakis's prison furlough program in the "Revolving Door" ad.

Name-calling is a strategy used less often; only 14% of negative ads employ this approach. One of the most common name-calling examples in American spots is the use of the dreaded "liberal" word. Dole tried unsuccessful to paint Bill Clinton with this term in 1996. One example is this spot, called "Sorry-Taxes," in which Dole tries to capitalize on Clinton raising taxes:

> Announcer: "The truth about Clinton on taxes. Remember? 'I will not raise taxes on the middle class,' but he gave the middle class the largest tax increase in history, higher taxes on your salary, gasoline, social security. Clinton even tried higher taxes on heating your home. Two hundred and fifty-five proposed tax and fee increases in all. Clinton says, 'but I don't think that that qualifies me as a closet liberal.' Sorry, Mr. Clinton, actions do speak louder than words. The real Bill Clinton, a real tax and spend liberal."

Guilt by association is another strategy sometimes used in negative ads. Over one-fifth of all negative ads (21%) use this strategy to attack the opponent. In this ad from the 1964 Goldwater campaign, the ad manages to attack Lyndon Johnson's running mate, Hubert Humphrey, for his association with the Americans for Democratic Action and do a bit of name-calling (left-wing radical) at the same time:

> Announcer: "Americans for Democratic Action organized by Hubert Humphrey in 1947 is so dangerous that even Governor John Connally has said, 'the left wing radical ADA and their cohorts stand for everything Texas doesn't.' Vote for Barry Goldwater. In your heart you know he's right."

During his 1996 campaign, Bill Clinton's most common technique for attacking Bob Dole was guilt by association—the association to be guilty about, of course, was House Speaker Newt Gingrich.

Clinton successfully used this attack strategy both verbally and visually. For many voters the most memorable visual image of the 1996 campaign may be the often repeated black-and-white footage of Dole moving behind Gingrich in slow motion. In fact, some version of Dole with Gingrich (always in black-and-white, usually superimposed over the Capitol, and often with Dole crossing behind Gingrich in slow motion) appeared in over half of Clinton's ads. In three of these ads

("Target," "Twice," and "Wrong in the Past"), the producers managed
to work a version of this visual representation of guilt by association
into the ad on four different occasions.

While most attacks on the opponent have featured issues, there are
some spots, of course, where the attack is directly focused on the
personal qualities or image of the opponent or where the main thrust
even of the issue attack is to call into question some aspect of the
opponent's character. Table 6.4 displays the same image qualities we
analyzed in Chapter 4 on how a candidate presents his own videostyle
to voters, but here the focus is on what qualities the candidate is using

TABLE 6.4
**Opponent Characteristics Stressed in Presidential Spots (N =
1,204), in Percentages**

	E52	S52	E56	S56	N60	K60	J64	G64
Honesty/Integrity	3%	0	0	8	4	0	7	24
Toughness/Strength	0%	0	20	0	10	0	0	3
Warmth/Compassion	0%	6	0	17	0	10	22	3
Competency	14%	11	20	17	13	13	33	32
Performance/Success	14%	0	20	75	2	18	15	38
Aggressiveness	0%	0	0	0	0	0	0	0
Activeness	3%	6	0	0	0	7	0	3
Qualifications	0%	11	20	0	6	0	0	0

	N68	H68	N72	M72	F76	C76	C80	R80	R84	M84
Honesty/Integrity	5%	14	17	17	9	9	16	13	13	14
Toughness/Strength	2%	0	3	0	7	8	0	7	6	4
Warmth/Compassion	0%	3	0	2	0	9	10	2	0	7
Competency	24%	14	27	15	14	21	29	18	8	21
Performance/Success	24%	22	13	32	12	25	12	40	14	75
Agressiveness	0%	0	0	0	0	0	0	0	0	0
Activeness	2%	11	0	4	6	13	0	3	0	0
Qualifications	10%	6	0	0	17	0	14	0	5	4

	B88	D88	B92	C92	C96	D96
Honesty/Integrity	15%	18	50	51	44	45
Toughness/Strength	2%	0	0	5	12	1
Warmth/Compassion	0%	1	0	0	7	34
Competency	6%	13	19	3	19	9
Performance/Success	26%	20	28	67	70	61
Aggressiveness	0%	0	0	0	0	6
Activeness	0%	0	0	3	19	26
Qualifications	9%	3	13	3	7	22

to attack the opponent. In other words, how is the candidate using the spots to structure the videostyle character or image of the opponent?

In the earliest days of television advertising for presidential campaigns, candidate attacks appear to have focused mostly on the opponent's competence and performance/success in office. However, by 1964 the attacks began to take a somewhat different approach. To be sure, Lyndon Johnson did frequently question Barry Goldwater's competency, but Table 6.4 also shows that he criticized Goldwater for a lack of warmth and compassion. In fact, over one-fifth of all Johnson spots attacked Goldwater on this characteristic. On his side, Goldwater was critical of Johnson's competence and performance in office, but he also put great emphasis on attacking Johnson more personally for his lack of integrity. Not until the heated attack campaigns of the 1990s were the opponent attacks again so focused on the integrity issue. However, in the 1992 and 1996 campaigns both candidates made the personal integrity and honesty of their opponents substantial aspects of their opposition attacks.

Although, as we mentioned in Chapter 4, most candidates were anxious to be perceived as aggressive in their own self-presentations, presidential candidates do not want to criticize their opponent for insufficient aggressiveness. No candidate gave substantial emphasis to this characteristic in an opponent until 1996, when Bob Dole suggested in a few commercials that Bill Clinton had not been aggressive enough in some policy areas.

Taken together, the data in Table 6.4 seem to confirm other impressions that the nature of attack advertising has become more personal in recent years. While earlier campaigns, in addition to the focus on issue attacks, tended to attack an opponent's performance in office or his competence at the tasks required, there has been an increase in attacks on a candidate's personal integrity and on qualities of warmth and compassion.

Nonverbal and Production Differences

One important nonverbal difference in the positive and negative videostyle approach, regardless of candidate and year, is that the candidate is rarely the speaker in a negative ad. In negative ads, the candidate is the speaker in only 17% of the ads. Anonymous announcers make most attacks. In positive ads, the candidate is the main speaker in almost half (49%) of the spots. A chi square test shows that this is a statistically significant difference. This lack of appearance by the candidate in negative ads also makes it difficult to analyze other aspects of nonverbal style in negative ads. Thus, no attempt is made to do that here.

It also appears that there are some production style differences be-tween negative and positive spots. For instance, negative spots tend to be significantly shorter than positive spots. Nearly 75% of negative spots are very short, 30 seconds or less. On the other hand, positive spots have more varied lengths: 46% are 30 seconds, 37% are 60 seconds, and 17% are a greater length, such as 5 minutes. There are also signifi-cant differences in the production techniques used to produce positive and negative ads. Obviously the candidate head-on format is much more popular in positive spots (30%) than in negative ones (13%), in keeping with the fact that the candidate is rarely the main speaker in a negative ad. While positive spots rarely use slides with voice-over (9%), this format is the most popular for negative spots (30%), providing information with anonymity.

Negative spots are also more likely than positive spots to take advan-tage of special production techniques. Negative ads use more computer graphics and more slow-motion, freeze-frame, and fast-motion shots.

Differences on Political Positions of Candidates

Although mentioned in Chapter 5, it is also interesting to put the differences in negative and positive ads in the context of the candidate's electoral positions. The position of the candidate as an incumbent or challenger is one aspect of electoral races that have been analyzed earlier. As noted there and shown again in Table 6.5, it is surprising to note that there are no substantial differences in the percentages of positive and negative ad use by incumbents and challengers. Incum-bents used 63% positive ads and 37% negative ones, while challengers relied on 61% positive spots and 39% negative ones.

This analysis classified every candidate as either a presumed incum-bent or a presumed challenger, using logic similar to that proposed by

TABLE 6.5
Comparison of Political Positions in Use of Negative and Positive Spots

	Positive (N = 742)	Negative (N = 462)
Partisan Affiliation		
Republican	427 (66%)	224 (34%)
Democrat	315 (57%)	238 (43%)
Electoral Position		
Presumed Incumbent	349 (63%)	208 (37%)
Presumed Challenger	393 (61%)	254 (39%)

Powell and Shelby (1981). This means essentially that when there is no true incumbent, either one candidate is designated the incumbent based on a prior position (such as being the current vice-president) or presumed incumbency is designated according to the political party in possession of the White House. When races are classified without the presumption of incumbency into true incumbents, true challengers, and open-seat candidates, there is still no difference between incumbents and challengers in their use of negative and positive ads. True incumbents use 40% negative ads, while true challengers use 41%. Open-seat candidates, however, do provide a different comparison. Such candidates use 67% positive ads and only 33% negative ones, perhaps indicating that an open seat creates a somewhat less negative atmosphere for both candidates.

A final analysis provided in Table 6.5 is between negative and positive ad use according to political party. This analysis suggests, unlike those comparing earlier years (Kaid & Johnston, 1991), that there are indeed differences based on partisanship. Democratic candidates are far more likely to rely on negative ads (43%) than are their Republican counterparts (34%). This difference, not apparent when the earlier years of 1960–1988 were compared, is likely due to the extremely negative campaigns of the last two Democratic presidential candidates, the negative campaigns of Bill Clinton in 1992 and 1996.

7

Videostyle and Ethics in Televised Political Advertising

One of the recurring concerns about television advertising's use in political campaigns is whether or not such use creates ethical questions. Many political theorists have suggested that the use of television marketing and advertising techniques to "sell" a candidate to the electorate is itself an unethical practice. This point of view would make all attempts by a candidate to use a videostyle in an election campaign an unethical practice. While this seems like a rather extreme point of view that raises many free speech issues, it is not unreasonable to ask if particular political advertising techniques may be unethical.

Of course, any aspect of political campaigning can be judged unethical if it fails to sustain a truthful message to voters. Johannesen (1990) has suggested that all communication should meet basic tests of honesty and promise-keeping, politics being no exception. In politics concern about ethical messages is a direct result of the belief that the ideal democratic process requires voters to have accurate information and to make rational judgments in choosing between competing candidates (Kelley, 1960; Regan, 1986). Franklyn Haiman (1958) has placed communication messages in a similar context by saying that communication should encourage the human ability to reason logically, thus creating what Kelley called an "informed electorate." A rational electorate able to make informed choices between candidates and parties must be able to count on information that is true, accurate, unambiguous, and unclouded by emotion. Political advertising fails this test for many observers, including Spero (1980), who has charged that political advertising "is without peer as the most deceptive, misleading, unfair, and untruthful of all advertising" (p. 3).

ISSUES IN POLITICAL ADVERTISING ETHICS

Political advertising on television certainly has no unique hold on false or misleading claims in the political campaign process. However, political advertising on television does pose some particular issues that concern many political observers. In an earlier discussion about ethics in political advertising in general, one of the authors of this book suggested,

> Several factors account for this increased salience of ethical issues, including the high cost of buying television time, the wide and instantaneous reach of television messages, the possible inherent predisposition of television to the dramatic and visual, and the seeming ability of technology to alter reality. (Kaid, 1991b, p. 1)

This first concern, that voters can be bought because television advertising costs a great deal of money, has certainly been disproved by many historical cases. Certainly, as pointed out in Chapter 1, presidential campaigns cost a great deal of money, and political advertising makes up a great deal of that cost. It is true that sometimes one candidate or party spends much more money than the opposing side on television advertising and wins the election. However, election paths are just as full of candidates who spent much more money than their opponents and lost. There is no justification for concluding that televised political advertising is unethical just because campaigns in general and ads in particular cost a lot of money. In fact, Diamond and Marin (1989) have maintained that if a campaign is supposed to educate voters, "then perhaps we should ask whether *enough* money is being spent in the U.S." (p. 387). Penniman (1985) has even suggested that, compared to other democracies on a per voter basis, U.S. elections are a "bargain."

The bigger question, which the 1996 campaign has forced the American democratic system to confront, is how to treat a situation in which a candidate or party raises funds to pay for advertising outside normal legal channels. Federal election laws were designed to regulate the sources and disclosure of campaign funds that could be raised for advertising or any other campaign expenditure. However, the fact that some candidates and parties may raise funds outside the law is not inherently the fault of political advertising.

The second concern, that television has a large and instantaneous reach, seems more of an advantage than an indictment. Not only does this mean that messages reach many more voters than would be possible through other information conduits, but the spontaneous and far-reaching spread of television acts as a deterrent to candidates tailoring contradictory messages to competing publics.

The third concern, that television is predisposed to dramatic and visual imagery, is often pointed to by many observers as resulting in political advertising's emphasis on images and emotion at the expense of issues and logic. The concern about issues hardly seems justified in light of the findings reported here about presidential videostyle. Candidates generally spend much more of their advertising dollars presenting issue information to voters than they do promulgating images. It may be true that television political advertising can be accused of favoring the dramatic and of relying on emotional messages, but such concerns must be judged against many things, including whether the emotional cues are justified by the factual basis in an ad.

The last concern, technology's ability to alter reality, raises more serious concerns in light of modern campaign techniques. This aspect of political advertising ethics is related directly to videostyle because it is centered in one of the three components of videostyle, the production techniques by which a candidate chooses to be presented.

TECHNOLOGY AND ETHICS IN CANDIDATE VIDEOSTYLE

Concern about the use of technology to create false or misleading impressions has been a legitimate ethical problem for political advertising in all mass media channels. In the print media, photographs taken from certain angles, cropped in certain ways, or resulting from deliberate superimpositions or fakery have been used to create political ads that leave false impressions with voters. In the audio channel, voice editing can easily give an erroneous impression, and voice compression can alter the sound of a candidate or opponent's voice for use in either audio or video commercials. The latter technique is particularly effective in making a candidate with a slow, halting delivery sound forceful and dynamic.

The issues faced by political television advertising in regard to these new technologies is not unlike that faced by journalists and product advertisers. New video and computer technologies have confronted journalists with ethical considerations in the selection of camera angles, arrangement of pictures, editing of video material, staging of events, and similar issues (Koop, 1980; Rivers & Mathews, 1988; Rivers, Schramm, & Christians, 1980).

Video technology today provides many opportunities for ethical abuse. As Rose (1983) suggests, the ability of technology to alter or reproduce voiceprints, to make undetectable deletions, and to fabricate authentic-appearing messages "raises profound questions about the integrity of future communication" (p. 15).

Today most ethical concerns in this area center around television's capabilities for altering or enhancing reality. Among the most common concerns with use of television technology are (1) editing techniques, (2) special effects, (3) visual imagery/dramatizations, and (4) computerized alteration techniques. Each has the potential to interfere with the ability of an informed electorate to make rational choices.

The use of *video editing techniques* to create a false impression is not difficult to conceive (Diamond & Bates, 1984; Sabato, 1981). An often cited example is the 1968 Nixon ad that interspersed scenes of a laughing Hubert Humphrey with horrifying Vietnam War footage. Messaris (1990) suggests that use of video technology in this way may be unethical because it creates "misleading syntax" for the viewer. The juxtaposition of two or more images creates a falsehood that misleads the viewer. Another good example of the misleading use of such juxtapositions is given by Jamieson (1986), who describes a 1960 Kennedy commercial that lifted unrelated footage of Nixon nodding in the Kennedy-Nixon debates and juxtaposed it with a Kennedy statement to imply Nixon agreement with Kennedy's position. Although applied to broadcast reporting rather than advertisements, Leroy and Smith (1973) have verified that even politicians consider such video splicing and editing techniques to be unethical.

The use of *special effects* techniques takes many forms in televised political media. In the first Eisenhower campaign, the Walt Disney studios produced the well-known "I like Ike" animated ad, complete with catchy music and classic cel animation techniques. Subsequently, politicians and their media advisers have utilized every technique from cut-out animation to slow motion and backward motion to computerized "Star Wars" sequences. Some observers decry such special effects for their inherent inability to contribute to the political reasoning process, maintaining that the use of special effects in political ads does "not seem to amplify or to expand upon a point already made, but rather to evade the requirement of rational argumentation altogether" (Winsbro, 1987, pp. 915-916). The use of such techniques in political advertising is quite high (Angell, 1988). In fact, Kaid and Johnston (1991) report that 385 of the 930 television ads (41%) used in presidential campaigns from

1952 through 1988 contained special effects; and from the discussion of special production techniques in Chapter 4, it is clear that these devices played a big role in recent videostyles of presidential candidates.

Similar concerns are raised by those who see television's predisposition toward *drama and visual imagery* as inherently bad and thus contributing to unethical political advertising outcomes. While some observers find nothing positive for the Democratic system in talking cows (which appeared in a famous ad for Montana's Senator Melcher) or fish puppets (a protagonist in an ad during Nelson Rockefeller's 1966 New York gubernatorial re-election campaign), others would argue that such dramatizations are not harmful in any way but merely serve to focus voter attention on important issues or candidate qualifications. However, when dramatizations are used to "stage" actions in a way that presents as authentic visuals that are just not true, then ethical concerns about the use of video technology to achieve these ends are serious (Messaris, 1990).

The first three of these television technology concerns (editing, special effects, and dramatization) can easily be viewed as techniques whose ethicality is dependent upon the nature of the usage, the *intent* of the source, and the degree of misperception and harm caused. After all, political speech has always employed whatever technology was currently available to it, from classical times to the present, from posters and billboards to satellite distribution. Television did not invent unreasoned political discourse (Shannon, 1990). Nonetheless, these uses are frequent enough and have demonstrated sufficiently misleading applications to warrant attention in any consideration of unethical uses of technology in political advertising.

Certainly the other technology concerns raise much clearer ethical questions. New *computerized video technologies*, such as "Scitex," now make it possible to alter real moving video images (Sheridan, 1990). Not only can a candidate's actual visual image be altered, but all types of alterations can take place to change live video footage and its components. Computer digitizing is already widely used to alter visual images in commercial advertising (Parker, 1988). As long as candidates still make some live or news-covered appearances, concerns about makeup, hair color, and smile brilliance are not likely to give way to computerized solutions, but the ability to manufacture and alter "live" video has created new questions for ethical concern. The ability to make "undetectably false pictures" (Sheridan, 1990, p. 6) is a technology twist that politicians should leave to entertainment and fantasy programming; it has no place in politics. The particular danger of all types of technological tricks in political advertising is that, from an ethical viewpoint, such devices often have the ability to *conceal* from the casual viewer the fact that the device has even been used. Video image alteration, for instance, may be virtually undetectable, at least to the non-expert.

Given these concerns about the potentially unethical uses to which technology can be put in modern television videostyle, it seems worth asking questions about how ethical the uses of technology have been in presidential videostyle.

MEASURING TECHNOLOGICAL ABUSES IN PRESIDENTIAL SPOTS

In order to measure the occurrence of these types of problem technologies in presidential campaign ads, it was necessary first to develop a set of guidelines to direct the analysis. This was done by assembling a panel of experts on communication ethics and developing a set of guidelines to apply to political television spots in order to pinpoint those that might be ethically suspect.[1]

After meetings, discussion, and the viewing of many spot samples, this panel formulated a series of guidelines,[2] which were then developed into a series of categories for coding the presidential television spots. This process worked similarly to that described in Chapter 3 for the videostyle coding process, except that the codesheet focused more specifically on particular types of technology and on the use of such technologies in ways that might raise ethical concerns. Particular attention was given in the coding system to the presence or absence of various technology-related techniques (examples of these categories included misleading editing techniques, superimpositions, special effects, voice compression or acceleration, computerized alterations of video images) and to the purpose or use of the technological technique (to create a false or misleading impression, to create fear, to ridicule, to unfairly stereotype, etc.). As with the earlier videostyle analysis, coders were trained graduate students, and samples were checked for intercoder reliability.[3] This research was part of a larger project that was supported by the National Science Foundation.[4]

The sample of spots used in the evaluation of potential distortions in the video production aspect of videostyle was somewhat different from the one used for the other analyses in this book. The major difference is that the universe to which the guidelines for identifying abuse was applied was an expanded one that included presidential primary spots from the years 1952–1996, as well as a few spots from non-presidential campaigns. The total number of spots to which the guidelines were applied, to isolate those that might contain abuses, was 2,504.

FREQUENCY OF VIDEO DISTORTIONS IN SPOTS

When the guidelines formulated by the expert panel were applied to the expanded sample of 2,504 commercials, the coders identified 475 spots that used video or computer technology in a way that seemed to distort, or to mislead voters. The first observation about this type of technological abuse in the production element of videostyle is that it happens quite frequently—almost one-fifth (19%) of all of the spots analyzed had some type of misleading or distorted aspect in the video or audio information presented to voters. As Table 7.1 shows, these distortions are primarily a characteristic of commercials in the past two decades. Only 8% of the 475 spots containing such distortions occurred from 1952 through 1960, and only 10% were aired in campaigns between 1964 and 1976. However, 82% were from spots broadcast after 1980.

The 1992 and 1996 presidential campaigns, both primary and general elections, are responsible for particularly high percentages of such distortions. Table 7.2 shows that, of 240 spots analyzed for the 1992 primary and general elections, 42% (100) were identified as having video abuses that mislead viewers. A similarly high percentage (43%) of the 290 spots from the primary and general elections in 1996 also had problematic uses of video production techniques.

The 1996 general election spots were particularly troublesome. Of the 77 spots produced for the Clinton general election campaign, 88% contained some type of technological distortion. Among the most com-

TABLE 7.1
Characteristics of Ads with Technological Distortions (N = 475)

	Percentage
Time Periods	
1952—1960	8%
1964—1976	10
1980—1996	82
Political Party Sponsorship	
Republican	46
Democrat	52
Independent	2
Type of Commercial	
Image	27
Issue	73
Focus of Commercial	
Positive	22
Negative	78

TABLE 7.2
Characteristics of 1992 and 1996 Presidential Ads with
Technological Distortions

	1992 (n = 100)	1996 (n = 124)
Political Party Sponsorship		
Republican	45 (45%)	73 (59%)
Democrat	54 (54%)	51 (41%)
Independent	1 (1%)	—
Type of Commercial		
Image	24 (24%)	18 (15%)
Issue	76 (76%)	106 (85%)
Focus of Commercial		
Positive	19 (19%)	27 (22%)
Negative	81 (81%)	97 (78%)

mon abuses in the Clinton ads were the changing and shading of Dole's image, the use of slow-motion sequences of Dole and Gingrich superimposed over Washington backgrounds, and the use of black-and-white footage to create sinister and fearful images. The Dole campaign was not innocent of such abuses, since over half of the Dole general election spots (56%) also contained a troublesome distortion.

Obviously, these findings indicate a clear trend toward more and more distorted technological abuses in modern ads. These percentages for 1992 and 1996 (42% and 43%) are much higher than the 19% of all spots analyzed across the period from 1952 through 1996 (even though these spots are themselves included in the larger analysis). The new technologies have proved too tempting for candidates and their producers.

TYPES OF SPOTS WITH DISTORTIONS

It is not surprising that Table 7.1 also shows that most spots with technological distortions are issue spots. This is true across all time spans, as shown in the 1992 and 1996 breakdowns in Table 7.2, simply because most spots are issue spots to begin with.

However, another clear trend in the use of technological distortions in spots is that the distortions occur much more frequently in negative spots. This situation is quite different from the distinction in issue and image spots, of course. Across the total time span, the percentage of positive spots is much higher than the percentage of negative spots, as demonstrated in Chapter 6. Nonetheless, of the 475 spots identified as

distorted in Table 7.1, more than three-fourths (78%) of them are negative spots. This is also true for the more recent time spans analyzed in
Table 7.2—for example, most of the distorted spots in 1992 and 1996
were also negative ads.

The trends in partisan sponsorship of ads with distortions do not
provide a great distinction among the parties. That is to say, both
Democrats and Republicans use the distortion techniques. The overall
sample across time (Table 7.1) indicates a somewhat higher use for
Democrats (52% of the 475 distorted ads) than for Republicans (46%).
This trend was also apparent in the 1992 ads but was reversed (Republicans had a higher percentage of distortions) in 1996. These trends were
probably a result of the heavily contested Republican primary in 1996,
which caused the overall numbers for 1996 to push the Republicans
ahead in distortions, even though Clinton's general election ads were
more distorted than Dole's spots.

FROM EDITING TO SPECIAL EFFECTS

The types of abuses seen in the production aspect of videostyle are
wide and varied. They range from simple editing techniques that create
a false impression for the viewer to computerized alterations that
change a candidate's (or opponent's) real features. Table 7.3 shows
some of the most frequently occurring types of distortions in the 475
spots identified as troublesome from 1952 through 1996.

Almost one-third of the spots (30%) used editing techniques to distort
the information conveyed to voters. Early examples come from the
Eisenhower 1952 campaign. In the simple question/answer format

TABLE 7.3
Technological Techniques Used for Distortion (N = 475)

	Percentage*
Editing Techniques	30%
Visual Imagery/Camera Techniques	24
Computerized Alterations in Video	56
Special Effects	41
Specialized Audio Techniques	37
Dramatizations	22
Audio and Video Mismatches	8

*These percentages are based on the occurrence of these techniques in the sample of 475
commercials and represent the percentage of commericals in which each technique was
judged to create an ethically suspect distortion. These categories are not exclusive and total
more than 100% because a given commercial might contain more than one technique.

used in the "Eisenhower Answers America" series, the answers written by the advertising executives were recorded by Eisenhower first. Only later were citizens recruited to ask staged questions, which were then matched up in the editing process with Eisenhower's answers. The end product misleads the viewer into thinking that Eisenhower is actually answering directly the questions of citizens in the spots.

Almost all spots use editing of some kind, but it is not difficult to abuse the techniques, as Richard Nixon's 1968 campaign did when it juxtaposed Humphrey's laughing face with scenes of Vietnam War carnage and American poverty. In a Bush 1992 anti-Clinton ad, video sequences in fast motion of supporters clapping their hands at Clinton's signing of Arkansas tax bills are interspersed with accusations about Clinton's taxation tendencies.

The most frequent type of abuse shown in Table 7.3 is "computerized alterations in video," used in over half the 475 spots (56%). Computerized alterations occur in a number of ways. Color can be changed to black-and-white, filters can shade and distort images, a candidate who was smiling can be made to frown. New digital techniques have opened up unlimited possibilities for creativity.

There are many examples of computerized alterations in the 1992 and 1996 spots, both primary and general election. In a 1992 primary spot, Republican Pat Buchanan attacked George Bush's 1988 "no new taxes" pledge by including footage from the actual Bush statement, but Bush's voice is accelerated and modulated to sound high and whiny. Clinton's "Remember" ad from the general election in 1992 distorted Bush's lips from this same sequence. In one Bush anti-Clinton ad from 1992, Clinton's faces are replaced by circles of dots to disguise his identity while the voice-over makes claims about two-sidedness. A frequent recurrence in 1996 spots, particularly the Republican primary ads, was the use of computer-generated or manipulated newspaper clippings designed to serve as "proof" for many claims offered by the spots. This technique was prevalent in many positive spots as in well as negative spots.

The 1996 spots were much more likely to use technology to alter actual features or images. For example, in the 1996 primary, Dole used numerous ads that distorted, blurred, and manipulated Steve Forbes's face/image. The previously described sequences in the Clinton general election ads that distorted Dole and Gingrich into slow-motion, black-and-white shaded images are also good examples. Morphing is another example of computerized techniques that has become a common manipulation in spots.

Special effects of various kinds were used in many spots, since 41% of the distortions fit this category. The Clinton slow-motion sequences with Dole and Gingrich are also examples of special effects techniques.

Over one-third (37%) of the distortions were specialized audio techniques. Some of the 1976 Carter spots, for instance, accelerated his voice to make it less slow and halting. The 1992 Buchanan spot mentioned earlier made a part of its distortion from the alteration of audio. In a 1988 positive spot, George Bush's handlers modified his own voice to make it sound less high and more "Reaganesque."

Table 7.3 indicates that dramatizations make up 22% of the distortions. The famous Daisy Girl ad from 1964 comes immediately to mind. In fact, many of Johnson's anti-Goldwater ads from 1964 fit this category. The "packaging the candidate" ad series by Dukakis in 1988, described earlier, also takes advantage of this technique to make the audience believe they are listening in on a Bush strategy session. In the 1996 Republican primaries, Dick Lugar's dramatization ads on nuclear terrorism were filled with the false impressions of terrorist acts, impending danger, and heightened emotions. In the "Day 1," "Day 2," and "Day 3" dramatic series, these images reach a peak that ends with a small child asking her mother, "Mommy, won't the bombs wake people up?"

SUMMARY

In this examination of a specialized aspect of the production component of videostyle, the most disturbing finding is clearly the trend to higher and higher percentages of technological distortions in recent presidential campaigns. While 19% of ads from 1952 through 1996 use some type of manipulative technique in the video production of presidential spots, the most recent 1992 and 1996 campaigns have been replete with such distortions (42–43%). The fact that these distortions occur most frequently in negative ads fuels concerns about the potentially negative consequence of attack ads in the political system, although it is only fair to note that the distortions are not unique to negative ads.

The findings do, however, indicate that the video production component of videostyle requires far more consideration and analysis. The potential for manipulation in the presentation of both candidate and opponent videostyle may be greatest in this area and could potentially offer the greatest risks to the values and goals of an informed electorate. This may be particularly true since recent research has documented that the presence of such distortions may be having the desired effects on voters—that is, distorted spots are more likely to enhance the sponsor's evaluation and vote likelihood while decreasing that of the opponent in negative spots (Kaid, Lin, & Noggle, 1999; Kaid & Noggle, 1998).

NOTES

1. This panel consisted of the following experts who were assembled in the fall of 1992 to discuss and formulate preliminary guidelines: (1) Richard Johannesen (Northern Illinois University), author of several books and articles on ethics in human communication; (2) Franklyn Haiman (Northwestern University), author of several well-known works on freedom of speech and democratic ideals; and (3) Lee Wilkins (University of Missouri-Columbia), author of several books on journalism and communication ethics.

2. The guidelines used to determine if a particular technology had been used in a potentially unethical way are as follows:

a. Video or audio editing techniques in which cutting or re-positioning is used to create a false or misleading impression. This may include video/audio techniques that juxtapose mismatched pictures and/or audio; use of video or audio technology to alter the actual features or characteristics on the screen as in computer alteration of physical features of an individual or of settings; use of voice acceleration techniques in audio; and any other editing or special effects techniques, including morphing, animation, sound effects or music, slow or fast motion, and so on.

b. Audio or video technology used in a spot to create "pseudo-neutrality" or "pseudo-actuality" (examples: false news sets, false press conferences or news reporter questioning, false or staged debate formats, dramatizations).

c. Audio or video technology used in a spot to evoke an irrelevant or unjustified emotional response. In judging whether the use of the technology to create emotional response is ethically suspect, it is important to consider the relevance of the emotion elicited and the degree or proportionality of the reality of the emotion. Irrelevant and disproportionate emotional responses that might be elicited by technological devices would include positive emotions (confidence, euphoria) as well as negative emotions (fear, hostility).

d. Audio or video technology that is used to ridicule an opponent or idea in an unjustified or irrelevant way. Ridicule may be more acceptable if some basis or justification is offered for the ridicule and/or if the reason for the ridicule or its basis is itself particularly relevant to electoral decision making.

e. Audio or video technology that is used to condemn or criticize any opponent, group or idea based on race, religion, ethnic origin, or gender. This category would include unjustified and irrelevant stereotyping.

Not all of these categories of potential abuses are reported here, but this list made up the initial guidelines from which the project proceeded.

3. Intercoder reliability averaged +.97 across all categories. The individual reliability for each category varied from a low of +.86 for several of the technological techniques categories and +.88 for the image/issue distinction to a high of +.99 for several categories.

4. This research was partially supported by the National Science Foundation under Awards # SBR-9729450 and SBR-9412925.

8

The Mediation of Videostyle: How Television and Newspapers Cover Political Candidate Advertising

As political advertising on television has become a more and more important aspect of how candidates present themselves to voters, journalists have recognized that in order to cover a political campaign completely they must also cover its advertising. In the early years of political television spots, coverage by the news media was quite limited. Newspapers occasionally mentioned campaign spots but provided little in-depth analysis of them. The coverage of the political advertising in the 1950s and in some instances in the early campaigns of the 1960s, concentrated mainly on how much the ads would cost, who was using them, and general statements about the growing influence of television in political campaigns. But in many ways, the early statements about advertising appearing in media signaled what the debate for the next 44 years might look like. In 1952, media described (albeit briefly and in short articles) Eisenhower's short question-and-answer spots and reported the reaction of some of Stevenson's campaign volunteers. Eisenhower was being sold in the same manner as "soap, ammoniated toothpaste, hair tonic or bubble gum," according to a Stevenson campaign officer, and this statement was reported not only in *Advertising Age*

("Ball blasts plan," 1952), but also in *Newsweek* ("Like bubble gum," 1952) and in the *New York Times* (Blair, 1952).

The era of political spot advertising on television had begun, as had the media's commentary on it. One of the first political advertisements to appear as a news item was Johnson's 1964 Daisy Girl spot, which elicited voters' fears and anxieties about nuclear war. Although this ad aired only once, the press reacted immediately with all three networks rebroadcasting the spot in its entirety (West, 1993).

However, in the 1980s journalists "discovered" that spots were a major aspect of the campaign discourse, and they began to recognize the significance of monitoring and analyzing spots in presidential campaigns. Important journalists like David Broder of the *Washington Post* called on journalists to take on a "watchdog" role, to police abuses in political spots (Broder, 1989), and a new format for political media coverage was born, the *adwatch*. Adwatches can be defined as "media critiques of candidate ads designed to inform the public about truthful or misleading advertising claims" (Kaid, Tedesco, & McKinnon, 1996, p. 297). As described by West (1993), adwatches "review the content of prominent commercials and discuss their accuracy and effectiveness" (p. 68).

Indeed, journalists can and do serve a very influential role, providing much of the background for Americans' political realities. Reporters teach us about candidates' backgrounds, personalities, strategies, and goals (West, 1993). Consequently, how the news media present and frame ads may have some impact on how voters interpret and react to a candidate's videostyle.

In this chapter, we consider how the media have presented candidate ads to voters over the past several decades, looking at trends in media coverage of ads and also at the type of ads covered and the slant given to the coverage by the three national television networks.

MEDIA COMMENTARY ON VIDEOSTYLE, 1952–1996

Without a doubt, the videostyle of negative advertising received the most attention from media from 1952 to 1996. Although some positive ads were singled out for lengthy discussion, media paid more attention to the strategies and techniques being used in negative advertising. In the early years, this commentary seemed to focus on accusations from the campaigns about the unfair tactics being used. Later the media would enter the debate and begin to provide their own analysis and critique of the merits and dangers of negative advertising. Although more comments from creative people dominated coverage in the beginning, academics and average citizens were also used as "experts" to comment on advertising in the later years. While negative advertising received the most attention from media, other aspects of videostyle were covered, including the issue content of ads, the slogans and music, the appeals of the ads, the types of attacks made, the visuals and style of language used, and the production techniques and formats used in the ads. The following discussion is not meant to provide a systematic or quantitative analysis of the media coverage of the videostyle of presidential advertising. Rather, it is meant to provide a descriptive sampling of the media commentary on that advertising.

The 1950s

It was Eisenhower's 1952 ads, not Reagan's 1980 ads as we might assume, that were first compared to product advertising. As the earlier quote indicates, media commented on this innovation of selling candidates with the techniques and styles typically associated with selling products.

In the 1950s there was no detailed discussion of videostyle, but there was discussion of the general look of the ads. In particular, the "Eisenhower Answers America" ads were described as "short, slick, compelling" ("Political spending," 1952, p. 1). An even stronger attack on the style of Eisenhower's 1952 ads was quoted in *Advertising Age* in October of 1952. A Stevenson worker and top-level volunteer blasted Rosser Reeves for trying to sell Eisenhower like a product, "The box tops this time are ballots. Send in enough of them and you get not only the general, you also get as an extra bonus a political space cadet with built-in secret code-breaker, atomic muscles made by United States Steel and smile by Barbasol" ("Ball blasts plan," 1952, p. 93).

The ads for the 1956 presidential campaign were not as exciting and as effective as those used in the 1952 campaign, according to the media. Creative types suggested they were "flops" ("'56 Campaign ads were promotional flops," 1956, p. 50), trying to reframe and resell the same old political products. Jack Gould (1956), in a *New York Times* article, suggested that television's role in political campaigns was due for a review and said, "Neither Republicans nor Democrats have used television wisely in the case of their five-minute programs" (p. 13).

Advertising Age once again was the medium most likely to comment on the "techniques" of the ads. In one column, readers were assured that advertising could not mask failings (so not to worry) although the ads in 1956 had certainly developed some gimmicks, like "the five minute speech in relaxed, low pressure surroundings; the man-on-the-street quiz; scenes at home romping with the little woman and kids; meeting the press; birthday party, 'this is your life' and a number of other little gadgets designed to sugar-coat the speech and the man" ("Agencies aren't political," 1956, p. 108).

The 1960s

The first televised political debates received lots of attention from media, but the ads were not discussed as much in the 1960 campaign. However, 1964 saw an increase in the discussion of how issues could be "stylized" in ads. The "Daisy Girl" commercial was, of course, big news and would become the first of a series of ads in the next 30 years that would be used by media to represent the strategies used and the issues presented in political advertising.

Johnson's use of the ad was blasted by politicians (mostly Republicans), and media reported on the debate about the use of the ads. The "Daisy Girl" ad was described over and over in media sources, and frames of the little girl's face and the mushroom cloud were reprinted numerous times (Hamill, 1964; "The nuclear issue," 1964; Robertson, 1964a).

The focus of the controversy about the ad, as framed by the media, was the ways in which the ad used visual images to define an issue and to accuse Goldwater of being dangerous. The reaction from the political community was a highlight of this coverage, with the *New York Times* reporting that Republicans had charged Democrats with presenting "horror type" commercials (Robertson, 1964a, p. 18). In one article, a Republican senator indicts Johnson for using visuals of a "little girl being blown to bits by an atomic bomb" (Robertson, 1964b, p. 23). There are no such visuals in the "Daisy Girl" commercial, but the *New York Times* did not correct this attribution for its readers.

Media, for the first time, discussed in some detail the production aspects of a political spot, not only explaining in more detail than before the "Daisy Girl" ad but also printing the scripts and frames from other Johnson ads, such as the "Ice Cream Girl" and the "Social Security" ad. Readers were given, in addition to scripts and frames, a description of the important aspects of the visuals of the ad to relay exactly what was being shown on the television screen. For example, the "Social Security" ad was described as "a disembodied pair of hands" ripping up a social security card ("The social security argument," 1964, p. 25) and the "Daisy Girl" (more accurately than the senator's description) as "a little girl's figure dissolves into an atomic explosion" (" 'Unfair' cry GOP," 1964, p. 141).

Perhaps more important than media's discussion of the visuals in these early campaign ads was their pronouncements that the issues mentioned in these ads were in fact the important issues of the campaign (Hamill, 1964; "The nuclear issue," 1964; "The social security argument," 1964). In fact, a frame from the "Daisy Girl" ad is featured in a montage of ads on a September 25, 1964, *Time* magazine cover. This was not necessarily good news, as the media reminded readers, but rather was an indication that "dramatized the fact that to an almost overwhelming degree, American political campaigns are being fought on TV channels of this country through advertising" (Hamill, 1964, p. 30).

The precedent in the print media of at least describing in more detail the political ads of the presidential candidates was established and continued in the final presidential campaign of the 1960s. But in 1968 media reported that it was not just politicians who were complaining about the ads; people were calling newspapers and networks to express alarm at what they were seeing in the ads. Media were covering the complaints and describing the ads more regularly for readers, but not necessarily analyzing them ("G.O.P. TV commercial evokes protests," 1968, p. 35). For example, the *New York Times* reported that NBC received protests (and the *New York Times* had received over 100 calls) against a Republican ad that featured scenes of war, rioting, and starving children interspersed with images of a grinning Hubert Humphrey ("G.O.P. TV commercial evokes protests," 1968). Complaints were also leveled against a controversial spot done by Humphrey that showed a mushroom cloud and criticized Nixon's lack of support for ratification of a nuclear treaty (Grant, 1968), as well as a Humphrey ad that featured a "laugh-track" to evoke the only possible reaction, according to Democrats, to Agnew becoming the vice president (Clarity, 1968).

The 1970s

In the 1970s, several notable ads received attention from the media and were covered not only in terms of their style but also in terms of their "effectiveness." Media seemed to become more comfortable with commenting on how the styles and strategies in the ads were connected to the themes being developed in the candidates' campaigns.

The visuals used in the ads for the 1972 presidential campaign between Richard Nixon and George McGovern received attention in several articles that described how positive or negative messages about candidates could be incorporated and suggested through video. *Time* magazine described and featured frames from the Nixon ad accusing McGovern of wanting to decrease American military might; the ad was described as featuring a hand that dramatically sweeps away the toy soldiers and airplanes as McGovern's views are voiced by an unseen narrator ("The candidates' world," 1972).

The formats, functions, and purposes of ads also received attention in the media during 1972. Media commented and reported on how the ads were going to be used to portray the candidates as being sympathetic to particular groups or to portray the characteristics and values of the candidates. For example, the *New York Times* reported (and the ads were described) that McGovern's latest ads were designed to present McGovern as a man of sympathy, compassion, decency, and candor (Weaver, 1972a). Later, media would report that McGovern was going to become more aggressive in ads that would be "straightforward, factual and contain no visual gimmicks" (Grant, 1972d, p. 8)

Positive ads for Nixon were also described, particularly those that would be used, according to reports, to highlight Nixon's experience and accomplishments, by showing footage of his trips to China and to the USSR. This "documentary" format was used, according to media, to emphasize Nixon's efforts to achieve world peace (Grant, 1972a; Weaver, 1972b).

But neither the documentary format used by Nixon nor the "unrehearsed" question-and-answer format used by McGovern was the format to receive the most attention from the media in 1972. The "turnaround" ad (taken from the name of the ad to use it: "McGovern Turnaround") was described first as a "new style" of ad; it showed a photograph of McGovern turning from one side to the other as McGovern's contradictory views are announced. The photograph eventually spins to highlight McGovern's inconsistencies (Grant, 1972e). *Advertising Age* later reported that an anti-Nixon ad called "Weathervane," shot but never shown during the 1968 campaign, may in fact have been the inspiration for the "turnaround" ad (Grant, 1972b).

In *Advertising Age*'s evaluations of the ads, Nixon's spots were judged as more effective (particularly his negative "turnaround" ad that reinforced the image of McGovern as inconsistent). McGovern's ad campaign was said to be like "a lot of street noise," with no central theme (Grant, 1972c, p. 109).

The issue in presidential ads, in 1976, according to the *New York Times*, would be "trust": Whom did you trust more? President Gerald Ford or challenger Jimmy Carter? In fact, the mood of the ads, according to *Advertising Age*, reflected the mood of the campaign. "If advertising served as the only standard by which this Presidential campaign was to be judged, the nation faces a happy choice between two fine, understanding gents of unquestionable integrity and judgment" (Donath, 1976b, p. 2).

Cinema verité was used to match Carter's style (not a Washington insider and free from the taint of Watergate) (Donath, 1976d), and Ford's presidential status and his qualities (a dependable father who inspired feelings of serenity in his family, official circle, and country at large) (Lelyveld, 1976b) were highlighted in his ads. *Advertising Age* included discussions from the campaigns of how certain character traits might be shown in advertising: Ford would be portrayed as unpretentious and down to earth and Carter as being articulate, intelligent, and photogenic (Donath, 1976a). But media reported that comparisons would be made in the ads and the "man-in-the-street" ads would be Ford's way of showing Georgia citizens expressing doubt about Carter (Donath, 1976c; Lelyveld, 1976a).

Advertising's ability to portray a mood through visuals, music, and slogans was also discussed for the 1976 campaign. Carter's and Ford's ads were seen as being more alike than different in their editing and use of music to stress that they would blend toughness and compassion in their ads. Ford wanted to stress "We're feeling good about America," and Carter suggested, through his ads, that the country needed "Leaders, for a change" (Donath, 1976b).

The 1980s

In the three 1980 elections, advertising received increased coverage from the news media, and political advertising was once again compared to product advertising. The *Washington Post* reported that different techniques had been chosen by the "admen who will be hawking these political candidates like breakfast cereal" (Kaiser, 1980a, p. A2). But in 1980, the media became more specific about how and what the ads were trying to sell. For Carter, it was to sell him as an "intelligent, decent, sensible president who deserves credit for some worthwhile accomplishments," whereas Reagan would be sold as the challenger who could make life a lot better in America and would be a strong leader for the United States with foreign powers (Kaiser, 1980a).

Coverage of the 1980 videostyle presented by challenger Ronald Reagan and President Jimmy Carter covered the themes that would present these two candidates to the American public. According to discussions with campaign managers from both sides, issues and accomplishments were supposed to be the focus of ads (Rozen & Gordon, 1980). Carter's ads sought to be "presidential," to focus on the record of his first administration, particularly his Camp David peace treaty. Carter was shown meeting with world leaders, reviewing military troops, and working late into the evening (Kaiser, 1980a; Rozen, 1980b; Rozen & Gordon, 1980). But this particular strategy was not working for Carter, according to news media, because he was an unpopular president and would not be able to exploit the strategy of focusing on his accomplishments and his record (Kaiser, 1980b).

Media discussed the use of symbols in the ads, particularly patriotic ones like the Oval Office, to represent visually a mood or feeling for the ads (Kaiser, 1980a; Weinraub, 1980c). Reagan's ads were also going to stress his accomplishments as a former California governor and would contrast his views on the economy and on how to achieve world peace with Carter's (Rozen & Gordon, 1980). Reagan's ads would use "library-like settings" (Rozen & Gordon, 1980, p. 2) or a "book-lined study" ("First Reagan ad," 1980) to intentionally encourage viewers to see the library-like setting as the Oval Office.

Media reported, once again, on the formats of the ads and how they would be used to structure the advertising message. Man-on-the-street interviews would again be used to provide the "average citizen's" take on the candidate; in 1980, Carter used it against Reagan to try to show that typical Californians were not thankful for Reagan's role in their state (Rozen, 1980a). The "turnaround" ad format was also resurrected in this campaign and renamed the "flip-flop" ad in media reports. It was used by Reagan, in an ad featuring a smiling Jimmy Carter face that flipped to a frowning Carter face as his 1976 campaign promises were contrasted with 1980 achievements ("Final vote," 1980).

Media also reported on how the formats of ads would be used to contrast prior perceptions of the candidate. For example, the news media discussed the intentional use of straightforward and direct techniques in the Reagan ads to counter the actor image and to emphasize his experience, not his show-business background (Weinraub, 1980a, 1980b).

If ads had asked voters to "know" something about the candidates' personalities and characteristics (Carter was not so bad as president and Reagan was not dangerous) in the 1980 election, then in 1984 they asked voters to "feel" something about the candidates. If the ads seemed to be more lush in the 1984 campaign, so too was the media coverage of them.

In 1984, news media discussed how ads could be used to make voters "feel" a certain way about a candidate or the emotions they were designed to evoke (the emotional appeals of ads). The *New York Times* reported that "producers" in 1984 "have spared no effort to wring the maximum emotion from every moment" (Clendinen, 1984, p. A18).

The news media talked about setting, dress, and other nonverbal components of the ads, with one *New York Times* reporter observing that the "nonverbals" in Reagan's ads were very good and had been used to make Reagan look like a leader (Dougherty, 1984). News media in 1984 discussed the campaign ads specifically in terms of the visuals and how they were constructed and designed to appeal to emotions.

Reagan's "Morning in America" ads received most of this type of coverage, with media suggestions that the visuals in the ads had turned the campaign into a battle of emotions and technique and not one of ideas and issues. In November, *Time* magazine had a lengthy article on the "Morning in America" ads and the visual lushness of the production style. "Reagan moved away from the traditional political spots . . . and embraced the sleek, atmospheric, slow dissolve appeals usually reserved for selling Coke and Almost Home cookies" (Kelly, 1984, p. 36). More so than in previous years of covering political ads, news media went to some length to visually represent and capture the feeling and mood of the ads, describing not only the visuals of the ads but the way the commercials projected the image of the candidates. Reagan was "bathed in natural light, looking relaxed," and his voice was "soft," the pitch distinctly "presidential" (Kelly, 1984, p. 36), or, "The photography has a golden quality, as if it were all shot on warm September afternoons" (Bumiller, 1984, p. D1). Readers of the *Washington Post* were even given insights into the creative minds behind these ads. "Meet the Dr. Feelgood gang, the Madison Avenue team that wants to bring a lump to your throat and goose bumps to your skin as you watch the Reagan commercials" (Bumiller, 1984, p. D1).

Mondale's ads were also analyzed and judged to be less effective than Reagan's and less coordinated with the candidate's news coverage. Mondale's "Computer" ad was discussed as an ad about an issue (nuclear weaponry) that attempted visually to show voters the power of the president and how unpredictable and dangerous the Star Wars system could be (Liff, 1984). *Newsweek* described Mondale's "Teach" ad as "a tough new ad reminiscent of 'the girl-in-the-daisy-field' ad, set to the tune of Crosby, Stills, Nash and Young" that alternated images of children with nuclear weapons being launched (Strasser, Fineman, & Warner, 1984, p. 26).

Slogans and tag lines were also discussed as representing the visions of the ads and of the candidates. Tag lines like "They're fighting for your future" and "With the whole world at stake, we must move on and must do better" used by Mondale's ads were set up in contrast to "Leadership That's Working" assertion and the "Prepared for Peace" reminder in Reagan's ads (Liff, 1984).

Another observation made by media during the final days of the 1984 campaign and in commentary afterward was the lesson of this cam-paign in terms of coordinating news media coverage and advertising. Brilliant ads, according to an article in the *New York Times*, would not win a campaign but rather had to supplement or amplify the content of the news so that voters got a unified view of the candidate (Clendinen, 1984). The media reported on such skillful coordination by Reagan's team to stage campaign events to reinforce the TV images (Kelly, 1984). This was contrasted with Mondale's ads, which were not coordinated with media coverage in the beginning but became more coordinated toward the end of the campaign. According to *Time*, this coordination of free media and ads, so skillfully done by Reagan, would probably change the standard for future presidential campaigns (Kelly, 1984).

Absent from the discussion bemoaning this coordination was any indictment or criticism of the news media that was a participant in these events. Advertising had been doing its job, but news media had not been. Attention to "watching" ads, not aggrandizing them, would increasingly become part of the media coverage of the remaining three presidential campaigns.

The honeymoon was not quite over during the 1988 presidential campaign featuring ads from Michael Dukakis and the assumed incumbent, George Bush. Media did begin to more actively report on the general "truthfulness" of ads. In fact, it was no longer the perspective that product advertising was giving political advertising a bad name. Articles in the *Washington Post* and the *New York Times* suggested that the opposite was now true. The techniques used in political ads, like using a candidates' own words to indict himself, sinister allegations, and furloughing the facts, would not be tolerated in product advertising (Latham, 1988). In addition, politicians were, according to creative experts, the only product you could sell with "misleading pitches" (Apple, 1988).

Media reports about the ads in the 1988 election seemed to assume a more TV-savvy audience and used film and television production terms like "camera zooms" and "slow-motion" freely in their descriptions of the ads (see, for example, Grove, 1988c; Rothenberg, 1988).

Children became a favorite symbol of the 1988 ads, and media reported on their use in several Bush and Dukakis ads. A general Republican ad featured a little girl to show how times for the past seven years (the girl's life span) had been good in a commercial that featured a "soothing female voiceover" (Rothenberg, 1988, p. 24). Democrats responded to this use of a little girl by using children in their ads with dire statements about how debt was up and the future was not bright for children ("The selling," 1988). Perhaps the most talked-about use of a child in an ad in 1988 was Bush's use of his granddaughter in an ad to highlight his desire for a kinder, gentler nation (Schwarz & Rezendes, 1988).

According to media, emotional appeals were again seen in the ads, in particular in the 1988 Bush ads that "assaulted the right hemisphere, the center of passion and poetry" and were trying to inspire voters, not educate them (Grove, 1988c, p. A6). The themes of the 1988 ads were once again discussed in the news media, with some judging that Dukakis's ads had too many themes that attempted to show him in too many roles, such as economic manager, successful debater, concerned father (Oreskes, 1988a). News media also talked about how Dukakis's use of facts and logical arguments (Reagan's 1980 ads had been described this way also) appealed, in contrast to George Bush's ads, to the intellect of the voter (Grove, 1988c).

Negative advertising received plenty of attention in the 1988 campaign, with the *New York Times* telling readers that experts believed that "this is the first time in a Presidential race that candidates have used advertising at least as much to bash the other side as to promote themselves" (Oreskes, 1988b, p. 1). In 1988, a new term was introduced to readers by news media. "Comparative advertising" would be the new phrase to describe what political consultants said their negative advertising did ("The selling," 1988).

Although presidential campaigns in the 1990s raised to a high art the use of ads to "respond" to charges made in other ads, presidential candidates in 1988 did use their TV ads to criticize negative attacks made in their opponent's ads. According to the media, this response to an ad "signifies the start of a constantly changing, two-sided argument that will be waged by way of paid commercials" (Rothenberg, 1988). Advertising was used in other words to respond to the opponent's attacks, and the ability to rapidly respond to an ad became critical in the campaign ("The selling," 1988). In addition, the use of footage from an opponent's campaign appearance was also discussed in the 1988 campaign, with the *New York Times* reporting that Bush had used visuals of Dukakis riding in a tank in a "Snoopy style helmet" to criticize Dukakis' defense policies (Oreskes, 1988a, p. A1).

The *Washington Post* noted that Dukakis was going after the false advertising of Bush in two ads, showing a Bush ad on a TV screen, with Dukakis then turning off the TV and "sternly addressing" the audience about the ads (Grove, 1988f). Lying in ads, according to some media reports, became a character issue in the reporting of the campaign (Grove, 1988b).

Another ad, like those used by Dukakis to address the negative advertising of Bush, were the ads on "The Packaging of George Bush," which used actors to imitate how handlers were trying to package George Bush. In most of the media accounts, these ads were first described and then were labeled ineffective and confusing and, in the end, insulting to voters' intelligence (Barone, 1988; Garfield, 1988; Grove, 1988e).

The ad receiving the most media coverage during the 1988 campaign was the "Willie Horton" ad. The "Willie Horton" ad was discussed in the news media so much that they, particularly broadcast news, were accused of adding to the exposure of the ad. News media reported that "Willie Horton" was tough in terms of the language used and had a put a racist tone into the campaign because Horton's picture was used in the ad (Engelberg, 1988). In reality, the "Willie Horton" ad, produced by an independent political action committee, at first received limited exposure, but it became more famous because of the network coverage.

Editing techniques and other "touch-ups" were also discussed by *Advertising Age* in an article on the sophisticated production techniques being used in political commercials to help "noses shrink" and "bald spots disappear." Bush's special effects person was discussed as using "subtle, almost subliminal techniques involving sound bites, color choice and more" (Skenazy, 1988, pp. 3, 91). The production aspect of videostyle received more discussion than in many previous campaigns.

As a harbinger of what was to come, media reported that ads would be more carefully scrutinized from now on (and even had been in the 1988 campaign, according to reports). The political advertising of the 1988 presidential campaign became a main campaign issue for news media, without much dissection of the claims made in the ads. There was some discussion of the "truthfulness" of claims made in ads (Grove, 1988d), but this was done in a descriptive way, not in any systematic way that characterized some later adwatches. After the election, both print and broadcast media were criticized for failing to consistently point out the distortions being made in the ads about the records of the candidates (Zuckerman, 1988).

The 1990s

During the summer before the 1992 election, *Time* primed voters for the coming campaign with a historical piece on the themes and styles of televised political commercials. Readers were told that popular strategies like the use of the biography ad, the "weathervane" commercials, and man-in-the-street spots had been favorites for a long time (Kramer, 1992).

But there would be several innovations or "new looks" in the advertising environment of presidential campaigns in the 1992 campaign. One would be that the news organizations were planning to critique the campaign ads more fully and to identify the misleading ones (Kurtz, 1992d). It was going to be more difficult, according to media reports, for candidates and their ads to dodge the media "truth squads" or the reporters who were making greater efforts to look into the claims of the candidates (Berke, 1992a). In the interest of helping voters understand ads, the *New York Times* featured an article about the persuasive techniques used in ads (such as lying, labeling, source-credibility appeals, fear appeals, attack ads, and one-sided arguments), with advice to viewers about how to recognize these techniques and how to "inoculate" themselves against them (Goleman, 1992).

According to media, the 1992 ads themselves were trying to sell their own credibility—not the candidates' truthfulness but the ads' truthfulness (Berke, 1992b). To do this, media reported that the 1992 ads were using all sorts of facts and figures that were frequently based on "disputed assumptions" (Kurtz, 1992c) or using assertions for support in the ad (like "nine Nobel prize economists say his [Clinton's] plan will create more jobs and raise taxes only for the rich") (Barrett, 1992). In order to be believed by voters, ads were featuring more statistics and attributions to get away with stretching the truth, trying to appear more credible by giving the appearance that the claims were based on documentation; quoting newspapers and ordinary-looking citizens, ending with a phone number where viewers could call to get copies of "issue blueprints" (Berke, 1992b). Adwatches appeared during this time to give voters the newspapers' assessment of the truthfulness of the claims made in the ads. Media reported on other techniques that the 1992 ads were using to make them appear believable or to call into question the opponent's claims.

The *Washington Post* reported on Clinton's use of Bush's "read my lips" statement in his negative ads (Kurtz, 1992a). In addition, the *New York Times* said that some of the ads were made to look deliberately amateurish, with hand-held cameras and images out of focus, to "fight the impression of slickness" (Berke, 1992b, p. A24). Because the news media were warning viewers about the manipulation in ads, ads had developed a new look. This year's ads were "sober, businesslike and to the point," and gone were the "warm, fuzzy, image ads of campaigns past" (Zoglin, 1992, p. 40).

Credibility could also come from the news media's negative coverage of the opposing candidate. The 1992 campaign was not the first campaign to use this approach, but Bush's use of the *Time* magazine cover of Bill Clinton and its headline, "Why voters don't trust Clinton," along with an unseen narrator giving details of Clinton's inconsistencies, was remarked on by several media, particularly when *Time* executives complained to Bush's campaign headquarters. The ad, described as a view of the *Time* cover as the "camera slowly pulls back from the stark image of Clinton's eyes" ("Ad Implies," 1992), had gone too far in using news media to help the credibility of an ad.

Although the ads seemed to have become more businesslike and news media were becoming more systematic in their coverage of ads through adwatches, media continued to cover the visuals in the ads. On Halloween in 1992, the *New York Times* asked, "What is scarier than Halloween? Tune in to candidates' ads and see." What the viewers would see were depressing images of life under the administration of each candidate's opponent. For example, Bush was using "creepy music and dreary scenes of buzzards and barren deserts" to show what the country would be like if Clinton were to become president (Berke, 1992c). Media also reported on the use of ridicule (Bush's use of hillbilly music and scenes of "comically speeded up footage" of Clinton) (Berke, 1992c) and the use of images to contrast the promises of the candidate

(Clinton's use of Bush making predictions of an economic recovery interspersed with black-and-white frames showing rising jobless rates) (Berke, 1992a).

Another innovation was the fact that candidates were producing ads for customized audiences and local and cable buys, not just national network buys (Petersen, 1992; Barrett, 1992). Ads were also produced solely for the purpose of getting network coverage (Colford, 1992). For example, media covered the fact that Clinton received news coverage by running several commercials during the Republican National Convention to blunt attacks made on him during the convention. This would start, as news media suggested, a strategy of using ads to get news coverage and not letting any charge go unanswered (Kurtz, 1992b).

If 1992 had been the year of facts and figures in ads, 1996 was the year, according to media, where ads used harsh, negative associations and images to challenge the credibility of the candidates. A new type of negative advertising was once again announced to voters and viewers of negative ads. *Newsweek* suggested that "human interest attack ads" were being used, primarily by Clinton. This "empathic negative" featured an attack on Dole, "sandwiched between heart warming spots of Clinton with dying children," so that the viewer might be persuaded the ad was actually a positive ad. The technique was "subtle, personal, moving, manipulative and incredibly effective" (Klein, 1996, p. 42).

Negative ads were also the topic of a September 30, 1996, *U.S. News and World Report* article that suggested that the negative ads were less hard hitting than they had been in the past. They were relying more on misrepresentations and distortions to attack. The candidates were "trading the meat-ax for the stiletto" (Auster, 1996, p. 44). Photographs were being used to imply what words could not, such as black-and-white photos of Dole, as a subtle reminder of his age; or pictures that placed Dole and Gingrich side by side; or photos and grainy video of kids with syringes, to attack Clinton (Auster, 1996).

The 1996 ads also were directing their messages in some cases to women and to families, according to media, in their subtle and not so subtle use of symbols (Garfield, 1996; Kurtz, 1996d). Clinton's ads used children and families to promote his stand on crime bills and family medical leave, and a Dole ad featured video of a little girl claiming to smoke pot because the president did (Garfield, 1996).

If anything, the media's coverage of the 1996 advertising indicated the growing need for news media, print and broadcast, to "watch" the ads and to comment for voters on styles, techniques, and strategies in the ads. As the description of coverage indicates, all interested parties in presidential elections—candidates, voters, and media—have, over the decades of televised presidential advertising, grown more sophisticated in their knowledge of the videostyle in political ads. In the next section, the television network adwatches are analyzed to see how they have addressed this growing need.

ANALYZING THE AD ANALYSIS

Our research on broadcast news adwatches involved a content analysis of network news coverage of television spots from 1972 through 1996. Before 1972, consistent data on network coverage were not available. The data were drawn from the *Vanderbilt Television News Index and Abstracts* and from actual videotapes of network newscasts on the three major networks: ABC, CBS, and NBC.

We examined political advertising coverage in network newscasts from the Vanderbilt Television News Archive appearing from Labor Day to Election Day in each of the presidential election years from 1972 through 1996.[1]

Trained graduate student coders analyzed the ads according to a series of categories.[2] In order to determine the intercoder reliability coefficient, coders analyzed during the training session a sample of the adwatch features; intercoder reliability was computed using the formula suggested by North, Holsti, Zaninovich, and Zinnes (1963).[3]

TRENDS IN ADWATCH COVERAGE

The fact that candidate videostyles as presented through their advertising did not receive much attention in the early days of presidential television is verified in Table 8.1. In the presidential elections from 1972 through 1996, the national networks have aired 228 stories that featured political television spots. Less than one-fourth of these (23%) were aired in the presidential elections of 1972, 1976, 1980, and 1984 combined. The year with largest number of adwatches was 1988, when more attention was given to television advertising on the networks than in the previous four elections combined. In fact, 35% of all adwatch stories for the entire period analyzed here fell into the 1988 election time span. The election in 1992 received a much smaller number, down from 79 stories in 1988 to only 44, while 1996 saw a slight increase over 1992, to 53 stories.

When the news media cover political spots, they give them high priority. As Table 8.2 shows, adwatch stories tend to come in the first 10 minutes of a network newscast (73%). The networks are pretty evenly balanced in their willingness to cover the ads. Both ABC and CBS aired 31% of the adwatches across time; NBC was out in front with 38%.

However, there are some surprising findings in Table 8.2. For instance, network news was much more likely to scrutinize the ads of

TABLE 8.1
Network Coverage of Political Ads, 1972-1996

Year	Stories Covering Ads
1972	13
1976	8
1980	24
1984	7
1988	79
1992	44
1996	53
Total	228

Republican presidential candidates (32% of adwatches across time) than those of Democratic candidates (26%). This imbalance is even more acute in some specific election years. For instance, in 1992 the Democratic candidate, Bill Clinton, was subjected to advertising scrutiny in only 6.8% of network adwatches, while his Republican opponent, George Bush, was the subject of analysis in over 20% of adwatch stories.

TABLE 8.2
Characteristics of Network News Coverage of Political Spots, 1972–1996, (N = 228)

Placement of Political Ad Stories	
1st 10 minutes	166 (73%)
Network Ad Stories	
ABC	70 (31%)
CBS	70 (31%)
NBC	88 (38%)
Party of Candidate in Ad Story	
Republican	73 (32%)
Democrat	59 (26%)
Independent	33 (14%)
Combination	63 (28%)
Spots Featured in 1988, 1992, and 1996 Stories (n = 176)	
Negative Spots	121 (69%)
Positive Spots	52 (30%)
Slant of Stories in 1988, 1992, and 1996 Stories (n = 176)	
Positive/Favorable	5 (3%)
Negative/Unfavorable	45 (26%)
Neutral	126 (71%)

Even more surprising, the 1992 stories focused heavily on the advertising of Independent candidate Ross Perot; almost half of all adwatch stories (43%) focused on Perot ads. However, this trend altered a bit in 1996, when Democratic candidate Bill Clinton's ads received more attention than did Bob Dole's spots.

Even more troubling for candidates may be the heavy focus networks place on analyzing negative ads. Fully 69% of the ads that the networks chose to cover were negative ads. Only 30% of the stories focused on positive ads, far outweighing the total negative-to-positive ratio of the ads produced during these seven election cycles (see Chapter 6).

More interesting though than the actual numerical counting of the stories and the ad types covered may be what the networks say about the ads. Here the story is a mixed one. On the one hand, it is clear from the analysis from 1972 through 1996 that the networks rarely have anything good to say about political spots. While most adwatch stories have a neutral slant (71%), Table 8.2 shows that when there is a direction to the slant, it is much more often negative (26%) toward political spots than positive (3%). In fact, in 1996, there were no stories with a positive slant toward political spots on any network during the entire campaign period.

The networks, in fact, seemed determined to make the ads the focus of the campaign and to do so in a negative way. The fact that negative ads received priority in their coverage and that the slant of their coverage was more often negative than positive lends credence to this interpretation. A good example of how the networks treated the ads is NBC's October 5, 1988, feature on spots. In this 180-second story, 93 seconds of actual spot footage was shown, with excerpts from 14 different spots. The story basically attempted to juxtapose advertising with news, saying that advertising gives the candidate "total control." An interview with an academic expert is included in which the expert basically presents a very negative view of spots, saying that you "never get a clear and complete picture" from spots and that spots sell candidates "like cornflakes."

IMPLICATIONS OF ADWATCHES FOR CANDIDATES

Overall, the news about the news on ads is both good and bad from a presidential candidate's viewpoint. The bad news, of course, is that the news media may be critical of the candidate's advertising or may try to point up fallacies in the message. On this score, however, candidates have so far had little to worry about. Almost all studies of adwatches have shown that the news media, both print and television, rarely provide in-depth analysis of candidate spot messages (Kaid, Tedesco, & McKinnon, 1996; McKinnon, Kaid, Murphy, & Acree, 1996; Tedesco, McKinnon, & Kaid, 1996). According to Jamieson (1992a), only 1.7% of the content of coverage about ads deals with the accuracy of the ad claims. In her comparison of print and broadcast adwatches from 1992 and 1996, Bennett (1997) indicates that the percentages of advertising reports with in-depth analysis of spots dropped 68% for the networks and 20% for print sources from 1992 to 1996.

Experimental studies of adwatches have tended to verify that candidates have little to fear from current adwatch approaches. A number of studies have suggested the candidate may actually benefit from the adwatch, whatever the intent of the journalist may be (Cappella & Jamieson, 1994; McKinnon & Kaid, 1999; Pfau & Louden, 1994).

Thus, the negative aspect of the news media coverage may actually turn into a positive for the candidate, or at least do no permanent negative harm. In fact, the news media's presentation and coverage of political spots may serve to reinforce the candidate's advertising message. Some researchers have suggested that the playing and replaying of a candidate's spot as part of a news story may work to the candidate's advantage, providing free airtime for the message. Adwatches may therefore provide unpaid access to millions of voters. In fact, many candidates have developed strategies to assure that their message is aired in the news, producing and promoting controversial ads for the mere sake of news exposure.

For this reason, many scholars have suggested the need for adwatches to present ads in a more careful way, avoiding the playing of ads in a full-screen and labeling them to be sure viewers understand the point of the analyses. Because adwatches focus on ads that are likely to be both emotionally and cognitively involving, Cappella and Jamieson (1994) suggest interrupting the ads. Journalists have used voice-overs, on-screen graphics, and downsized video in hopes of lessening the advertisement's effect by interrupting the viewers' short-term memory. Such strategies are important because they help to undercut the advertisement's visual impact (West, Kern, & Alger, 1992).

Beyond the free exposure time itself, the presentation of a candidate's ad during television news may aid in the presentation of videostyle in another way. News is generally a more credible environment than the advertising message itself, and this credibility may carry over to the ad (Jamieson, 1992a; West, 1993). The presentation of the ad in the news environment may even serve to legitimize the ad, assuring voters that if ads are important enough to be covered by the news, they are important enough to consider in making voting decisions (Kaid, Gobetz, Garner, Leland, & Scott, 1993).

NOTES

1. The unit of analysis for the content analysis was a news story featuring campaign advertising. Only adwatches covering presidential candidates were analyzed. Researchers used the *Vanderbilt Television News Abstracts* to identify stories to be examined. For the stories from 1972 through 1984, coding of basic categories was done from the printed abstracts. For the years 1988, 1992, and 1996, the coders worked directly from full videotapes of the newscasts.

2. Categories included: whether video of the spot was shown, the number of ads shown, whether the entire ad was shown, the time the entire or partial advertisement appeared on screen, and the candidate's political party (Republican, Democrat, Independent, other, or combination). Coders also recorded the dominant type of advertisement (positive, negative, or combination). In the latter case, the same definition of positive and negative ads was used as the definition we used to distinguish negative and positive ads in Chapter 6. Other categories were also developed, including ad placement within the newscast (first, second, or third 10 minutes of newscast) and type of experts cited, if any (independent political consultant, campaign's media or political consultant, campaign or party official, candidate or running mate, journalist, or academic resource). Moreover, coders determined the dominant approach of the adwatch. The coders were instructed to code the tone of the coverage as "positive" if the adwatch favored the candidate's ad, as "negative" if the report implicitly or explicitly criticized the candidate or the campaign for advertising strategies, as "neutral" when the adwatch was extremely balanced between positive and negative critiques, and as "unable to determine" if the coder could not tell from the information given.

3. Across all years, the intercoder reliability averaged +.89; individual category reliability ranged from +.77 to +1.00.

9

Videostyle in International Perspective

Political candidates and parties in most democratic systems face the fundamental problem of how to communicate with and persuade voters to accept their leadership. Televised political ads or party political broadcasts have become important to many democratic systems because they provide a solution to this problem that also has the advantage of being under the direct control of the candidate or party. American presidential candidates are not the only ones to recognize that with political television advertising, candidates/parties determine the content and style of their messages and increase their chances to influence the outcome of the election.

Despite this fundamental advantage to political advertising, the roles of such messages, their content and style, vary across democratic systems. In *Political Advertising in Western Democracies*, Kaid and Holtz-Bacha (1995) discuss the various media, cultural, and political system differences that affect the role such messages play in a number of democratic systems. These differences often prompt researchers to throw up their hands in despair, lamenting that the differences are so great that no meaningful comparison is possible. Videostyle analysis, however, has rejected that premise and attempts to provide a comparison across democracies of the styles and effects of modern political television broadcasts. Consequently, this chapter provides some comparisons of videostyle in an international perspective, applying some of the same classifications of verbal, nonverbal, and production characteristics to political television broadcasts in a number of other countries.

AMERICANIZATION DESPITE DIFFERENT MEDIA AND POLITICAL SYSTEMS

American presidential candidates have relied on television advertising for several decades, but "American-style" advertising has only recently become an important part of the political process in other democracies (Gurevitch & Blumler, 1990; Tak, Kaid, & Lee, 1997). There are, however, many differences among the institutional and political systems and among the media structures of other democracies that affect how television is used in elections. For instance, France, Germany, Italy, and Great Britain are characterized by multiparty systems, shorter campaign periods, greater emphasis on the political parties themselves, parliamentary electoral systems, and publicly controlled media systems. Despite these differences there are increasing similarities between the campaigning processes. Researchers have verified that television has become a dominant force in German politics (Noelle-Neumann, 1978; Holtz-Bacha, 1990; Schoenbach, 1987; Semetko & Schoenbach, 1994) and is a major electoral information medium in France (Blumler, Cayrol, & Thoveron, 1978; Cayrol, 1988). Asian countries such as Korea are also adopting electoral advertising that is more like American standards (Tak, Kaid, & Lee, 1997; Lee, Tak, & Kaid, 1998). New and emerging democracies in East and Central Europe are also facing the challenge of incorporating television advertising into their electoral systems (Kaid, 1999).

A consideration of videostyle in other countries does, however, require a broader definition of "political television advertising" than the American system uses. The term is used here to encompass, as Kaid and Holtz-Bacha (1995) define it, "all moving image programming that is designed to promote the interests of a given party or candidate" (p. 2). Thus, political television advertising would include any broadcast controlled by the party or candidate and for which time is given or purchased. Sometimes this advertising time is given free of charge to the parties and candidates, and sometimes the time is purchased. The United States remains the major representative of a commercial and private media system where most candidate advertising is purchased. The growth, particularly in Europe, of dual media systems, with both public and private outlets, has also led to more opportunities for parties and candidates to purchase time for election advertising in these democracies. Greater detail about the differences in the media systems and the relationship to the electoral process is provided by Kaid and Holtz-Bacha (1995) and Kaid (1999).

Clearly, then, the most distinguishing aspect of the American system is its commercial nature; because television stations are primarily private entities selling advertising time, American candidates at every level of elective office are free to buy almost unlimited amounts of advertising time on television. Also distinctive to the American system is the almost unregulated nature of the message content; candidates and parties can say or do almost anything in political spots because the value placed on free speech rights in the United States insists that political speech be unfettered (Kaid, 1991b). These system differences do result in some variations in how candidates and parties can develop a videostyle for television campaigning. Probably the most noticeable difference is in the quantity of spot advertising allowed, since most other countries allow no or limited purchase of time, providing instead free time on public channels to candidates and parties (Kaid & Holtz-Bacha, 1995). While in many countries this free-time system may allot commonly three or five or ten spots per candidate in an election campaign, the two major-party U.S. presidential candidates in 1996 purchased time in the general election campaign for over 100 spots, costing nearly $200 million (Devlin, 1997). American spots also tend to be shorter, since time blocs given to candidates on public systems in other countries are often much longer than 20-30 seconds.

Despite the fact that the United States uses a private system model of television in which political advertising is generally purchased by candidates and parties, many observers have suggested that the characteristics of the American system and its consequences can be observed in many other democratic systems. Gurevitch and Blumler have made this case most directly, suggesting that "the practices and ideologies of the American political communications industry are taking hold worldwide" and that "American-style 'video-politics' seems to have emerged as something of a role model for political communicators in other liberal democracies" (Gurevitch & Blumler, 1990, p. 311). This Americanization, although sometimes seen as merely modernization or professionalization or globalization, seems to encompass a number of factors, including the dominance of television as an electoral information medium, the supplanting of issue discussions with candidate image considerations, a reduction in the direct influence of the political party organization, a professionalization (use of political consultants) of the campaign process, and reliance on sophisticated technologies, including polling and other computerized techniques (Blumler, Kavanaugh, & Nossiter, 1996; Kaid & Holtz-Bacha, 1995; Mancini & Swanson, 1996).

RESEARCH ON CONTENT AND EFFECTS IN
OTHER DEMOCRACIES

Most research on political television advertising has been conducted in the United States, where television spots are the dominant form of communication between candidates and voters; it is summarized in Chapter 2. However, the past two decades have seen an increased interest in research on political broadcasts in other countries. Like the American research, these analyses fall into two categories, content/style research and effects research.

Content and Style

Research on the content and style of political party/candidate broadcasts in other countries has been much less comprehensive or systematic than that done in the United States. A few studies have compared content in British spots and have found a similar dominance of issue content in British Party Election Broadcasts (PEBs) (Johnson & Elebash, 1986; Kaid & Holtz-Bacha, 1995; Kaid & Tedesco, 1993). Similar findings validate the importance of issue content in political broadcasts in France (Johnston, 1991a). In Germany, however, the 1990 campaign spots showed a strong emphasis on candidates and image content (Holtz-Bacha & Kaid, 1993; Holtz-Bacha, Kaid, & Johnston, 1994).

Democracies outside the United States have not often measured precisely the effects of political spots on voters. As with other aspects of political television and the possible "Americanization" of their systems, most countries have preferred to assume that party broadcasts were not very important to voters. However, research on early PEBs in Britain suggested that they did affect voter knowledge levels (Blumler & McQuail, 1968) and may have had some effects on undecided or low-interest voters. Research on the 1988 French presidential election also indicated that exposure to party broadcasts affected images of French presidential candidates Chirac and Mitterrand (Kaid, 1991a). Kaid and Holtz-Bacha have measured experimentally the reactions to German chancellor candidates after viewing election spots during the 1990 and 1994 national elections (Kaid & Holtz-Bacha, 1993; Holtz-Bacha & Kaid, 1996).

With this background in mind, the chapter tries to describe the videostyle used in several other democracies and to compare it with the findings about videostyle from American campaigns. This attempt to apply the videostyle concept across cultures is not possible in the comprehensive way that is possible with the American system. For one thing, archives do not exist in every country to provide sets of political broadcasts for analysis. Difficulties in language often make comparisons difficult, as well. Consequently, this analysis is limited to selected countries.

The same basic coding and category system used to analyze videostyle for U.S. commercials, described in Chapter 3, was applied to the international spots to provide comparisons. Because a large sample of spots from every country was not available, this analysis concentrates on spots from campaigns during the past ten years, 1988-1997. While some attempt is made to compare with all American spots, it seemed most important to concentrate the comparison on recent U.S. campaigns, where the comparability of issues and electoral contexts might be more similar.

The videostyle comparison concentrates on 410 spots from eight countries: the United States (1996 presidential election), France (1988 presidential campaign), Germany (1994 national election), Italy (1992 national election), Britain (1992 and 1997 general election spots for the Labour and Conservative parties only), Poland (1995 presidential election), Korea (1992 national election), and Israel (1992 national election).[1] The number of spots from each country varied; the samples were composed as follows:

United States—120 spots (43 Dole and 77 Clinton)

France—20 spots (10 each for Mitterrand and Chirac)

Germany—52 spots from all parties allocated TV time

Italy—sample of 41 spots from various parties

Israel—sample of 60 spots from Labour and Likud

Korea—20 spots from two major candidates

Britain—16 broadcasts from Labour and Conservative (4 each for each election in 1992 and 1997)

Poland—81 spots from all parties allocated TV time

The categories developed for videostyle coding, set forth in Chapter 3, were followed in the international analyses as well.

The content analysis was done by trained student coders who were native speakers.[2]

OVERALL TRENDS AND COMPARISONS IN INTERNATIONAL VIDEOSTYLE

Comparison of Verbal Content of Spots

Across the eight countries analyzed here, the most common element of the spots is that the majority of ads concentrate on issues, rather than images of candidates or parties. As Table 9.1 indicates, issues are the dominant content of spots in the United States in 1996 (79%), in France in 1988 (100%), in Germany in 1994 (69%), in Italy in 1992 (71%), in Poland in 1995 (56%), and in Britain in 1992 and 1997 (88%). The split is 50/50 in Israel, and only in Korea (30% issues) is there a substantial tilt toward an image orientation. Even in the Korean election this finding is unusual, because overall advertising, including newspapers, and the campaign in general focused more on issues in 1992 (Tak, Kaid, & Lee, 1997). However, Korean campaigns since 1987 have used more sophisticated campaign strategies based on marketing techniques, and personal candidate image was particularly important in 1992 for President Kim Young-Sam, the first civilian president in 30 years, who focused on personal characteristics in all of his television commercials in order to emphasize the image of a "New Korea" throughout his campaign.

A few other differences are apparent when examining the specific party/candidate emphasis within each individual country. This type of comparison tells more about individual candidate videostyles. For instance, although the Israel split is 50/50 overall, the Labour Party concentrated 59% of its spots on issues, while Likud emphasized images in 58% of its spots. In the 1997 British election, the Conservatives placed far more emphasis on issues in their spots, while the Labour

TABLE 9.1
Content and Appeals of International Political TV Broadcasts

	U.S. 1996	France 1988	Germany 1994	Italy 1992	Britain 1992 & 1997	Israel 1992	Korea 1992	Poland 1995
N	120	20	52	41	16	60	20	81
Emphasis of the Ad								
Issues	79%	100%	69%	71%	63%	50%	30%	56%
Image	21%	0	12%	23%	37%	50%	70%	30%
Combination	0	0	19%	0	0	0	0	14%
Focus of Ad								
Positive	35%	75%	NA	85%	69%	58%	55%	93%
Negative	65%	25%	NA	15%	31%	42%	45%	7%
Dominant Type of Appeal								
Logical	37%	80%	23%	15%	56%	25%	30%	21%
Emotional	38%	10%	33%	54%	25%	40%	20%	67%
Source Credibility	25%	10%	4%	31%	19%	35%	50%	12%
Combination	0	0	40%	0	0	0	0	0
Political Party Emphasized in Ad	6%	5%	44%	7%	50%	7%	NA	4%

Party concentrated on the image of their popular young leader Tony Blair.

Table 9.1 also shows that another commonality across countries is the positive focus of the ads. The United States is the outlier here, of course. In the 1996 election, as in the 1992 one, the spots were predominantly negative (65%). The percentage was even higher for Bill Clinton since 68% of his spots were negative ones. In the other six countries the dominant focus of the ads was positive, ranging from 93% of the ads in Italy to 58% in Israel. In Germany the coding for spot focus was not comparable, since there the coding did not dichotomize between positive and negative, as a dominant ad emphasis, but rather reported whether or not an attack was made in the ad, whether the ad was negative or positive. On this measure, about two-thirds of the German spots included some type of negative attack, whether or not the spot itself was predominantly positive or negative. For instance, in one of the general promotional spots by the Christian Democrats (CDU, Helmut Kohl's party), a male voter says: "Die Linken können nicht mit Geld umgehen" [the left can't be trusted with money].

As with the United States, there are a few differences when individual parties or candidates within a country are considered. In Israel, 48% of the Labour Party's spots were negative. In Italy, the challenging parties (those not in power at the time of the election) used a much higher percentage of negative ads than the overall totals would indicate.

There has been discussion that the use of television in campaigns has deemphasized political parties in many democracies. Table 9.1 indicates that this is certainly true in political spots in most countries studied here. The number of spots whose content focused primarily on the political party in each country was generally quite small. Only in Britain, where the contest seems to be more sharply fought as a battle between two party philosophies, were even half of the spots focused on the party itself. In 1997 this took on particular meaning in Britain as Labour Party spots sought to reinforce for voters the notion that the party was offering a "New Labour" Party. In France only one spot emphasized political party over issue, image, or interest group concerns (5%). In Italy and Israel (7%), the United States (6%), and Poland (4%), the percentages were also small. This trend may provide some evidence that spots are contributing to a declining emphasis on parties in democratic systems, resulting in a more personalized campaign system.

Spots were also categorized according to whether the dominant type of appeal or proof offered in the ad was logical, emotional, or ethical, corresponding to Aristotle's original distinctions among logos, pathos, and ethos. The French spots were the most likely to use logical proof, relying on this form of persuasion in 80% of their ads. British spots also made frequent use of logical reasoning, which was used in 56% of the

British broadcasts. Other countries found emotional proof to be more attractive. Emotional proof was dominant in the Italian spots (54%), Israeli spots (40%), Polish spots (67%), and American spots (40%). However, the Israeli and American spots showed more balance among the three types of proof. British spots also used some emotional proof (25%), a good example being the famous "Jennifer's Ear" spot used by the Labour Party in 1992. Spots in the United States were high in emotional appeals, partly because of a tendency to use fear appeals in negative spots, a tactic that was prevalent in a great many Clinton spots that attempted to cast Bob Dole as an old, somewhat sinister figure. Korean ads are, like their focus on personalities in 1992, somewhat unique in their concentration on ethical proof. There may be a cultural factor at work here, as well as the fact that the Korean president, Kim Young-Sam, used his own qualifications and personal qualities as a great deal of the content in his spots.

Nonverbal and Production Aspects of Spots

One of the most interesting nonverbal aspects of spots is the subtlety conveyed by whether or not the candidate is the speaker in the spot. As the earlier analysis of American videostyle has indicated, the appearance of the candidate as the main speaker in political spots has declined dramatically in the United States in recent years. This trend is not unique to American candidates, however. As Table 9.2 shows, French candidates were the only ones in this set of over 400 spots across eight countries likely to be the dominant speakers in their spots, but even then the candidate is the main speaker at most 50% of the time (France in 1988). American and German broadcasts trail all others in this regard, with the party spokesperson being the main speaker only 6% and 8% of the time, respectively. In the 1996 U.S. ads, for instance, Bill Clinton almost never spoke or appeared in his ads, let alone being the main spokesperson. Since 68% of Clinton's ads were negative ads, it is not surprising that he left the speaking to anonymous announcers. Apparently, however, many other presidential or prime-minister/chancellor candidates in other countries make the same choice.

The setting of a spot is also an important nonverbal indicator. Formality is a major distinction in settings, and in this sense there are major differences among the eight countries compared. French settings in 1988 were very formal (95%), as were over half the Israeli (55%) and American settings (50%). The Polish (19%), British (19%), and Italian (9%) spots use formal settings much less frequently. The Korean case is again interesting with its heavy emphasis on informal settings (67%), which is probably related again to the personality emphasis in the ads. The French tendency toward formal settings is partly explained by the

TABLE 9.2
Nonverbal and Television Production Aspects of TV Broadcasts across Countries

	U.S. 1996	France 1988	Germany 1994	Italy 1992	Britain 1992 & 1997	Israel 1992	Korea 1992	Poland 1995
N	120	20	52	41	16	60	20	81
Setting								
Formal	50%	95%	34%	9%	19%	55%	32%	19%
Informal	19%	5%	8%	37%	44%	13%	67%	25%
Combination	13%	0	10%	27%	38%	3%	0	56%
Not applicable	18%	0	48%	27%	0	29%	0	0
Candidate the Speaker	6%	50%	8%	27%	25%	27%	NA	31%
Production Technique								
Cinema verité	24%	0	NA	34%	50%	3%	NA	4%
Slides w/print, voice-over	48%	0	NA	7%	0	2%	NA	2%
Head-on	13%	25%	11%	15%	12%	62%	NA	16%
Animation & special prod.	10%	0	8%	17%	0	3%	NA	0
Combination	5%	75%	NA	27%	38%	31%	NA	78%

NA: Not available

more stringent controls on the content of French ads. The tendency toward informal settings in the British examples are partly a result of the style of the 1997 British ads. In particular, the Labour Party relied a great deal on "dramatizations" in their spots or in the cinema verité style used to chronicle Tony Blair's ideas in the 1997 10-minute PEB often referred to as "Blair, the Movie."

These differences in style also relate to the classification of spots according to production techniques. With so few spots relying on the candidate as the dominant speaker, it is not surprising that very few spots use the traditional candidate statement or "head-on" production technique. Table 9.2 displays the various production techniques. In most countries (a different system of coding this category was used in Germany and Korea), the production techniques are marked by the combination of various types of production. This multiplicity of production techniques, over the straight candidate statement style, is a mark of the growing sophistication in technology available in all countries and considered by some to be a mark of Americanization. Even less developed democracies like Poland found such production techniques desirable as a way to hold viewer attention. The "head-on" technique was dominant in Israel (62%). Although the total category of "head-on" production was only 12% in Britain, the notable examples were the direct candidate statements on European Union issues by John Major in the 1997 campaign. In Germany, the majority of the spots using this technique were those from the smaller parties (not the CDU/CSU or SPD parties) whose production budgets often did not allow for more varied and sophisticated production techniques.

The types of spot formats used are also quite similar across cultures. Because of the differences in spot lengths, it was difficult to categorize international spots in the same way as American ones. The longer formats of most international spots meant that many are combinations of many different formats. For instance, the French spots of Mitterrand often began with pre-produced clips of music and video images for a full two minutes and then proceeded to three or more minutes of talking heads. Other spots might be combinations of music and voice-over announcers interspersed with other techniques. For example, the German spots for the CDU (Helmut Kohl's party) often relied on testimonials from ordinary people about the great things Kohl had done. One woman voter proclaims: "Kohl und Adenauer haben das Meiste für Deutschland getan" [Kohl and Adenauer have done the most for Germany]. Bill Clinton proclaims: "Amerika steht an Ihrer Seite" [America stands on your side]. In this case perhaps the visual image of Bill and Hillary Clinton strolling down the street with the Kohls in front of Berlin's Brandenburg Gate said more than Clinton's awkward German.

Another point of interest related to production techniques has been the increasing use of special-effects video techniques in spots. The use of special sounds and music is one aspect of this trend. In some countries, for instance, music was used in 100% of all political advertising productions (Israel and Britain). One spot in the 1997 British Labour Party's arsenal relied solely on pictures, music, and words printed on the screen; there were no verbal or spoken messages in the entire spot, which attacked and ridiculed the Conservative Party. In a Polish spot for the Solidarity Party, a popular singer belts out specific points in Lech Walesa's platform. The United States led in the use of special-effects techniques, with frequent use of computer graphics, superimpositions, slow- and stop-motion techniques. British ads also capitalized on such techniques, using slow motion, montages, superimpositions, and computer graphics in several broadcasts. The French broadcasts were also notable for their use of such techniques, primarily as part of pre-produced clips contained within the spots. Several of these French segments were actually more like American MTV (Music Television) productions than political spots.

One of the most interesting sets of spots from a production standpoint were the spots produced for the Polish 1995 presidential election. Poland is one of the former East European countries that has perhaps had a longer history of adapting to Western styles. In this campaign, it was in fact the former Communist leader Alexander Kwasniewski who put Western techniques to best advantage by capitalizing on television's ability to convey style. In press coverage of the campaign, Walesa was often cited as the less telegenic of the two candidates. Some observers called Kwasniewski "a television producer's dream: composed, affable, and unflappable. . . . good looking and a smooth talker, . . . one of those candidates who looks even better and performs better on television than in person" (Perlez, 1995, p. A8).

Although it is not captured specifically in the categories used for the videostyle analysis, one thing that an analyst quickly notes when looking at spots from different countries is the similarity of the "bio spot" seen in many different countries. The Tony Blair spot mentioned from the 1997 British campaign, although it received a lot of emphasis in the press, was hardly unique. During the same campaign, Liberal Democratic candidate Paddy Ashdown displayed his life story with scenes from his background, partially narrated by his former nanny. British Labour candidate Neil Kinnock stirred many voters in 1987 with his moving biographical broadcast, produced by "Chariots of Fire" movie producer Hugh Hudson.

In his "Man from Hope" bio in 1992, Bill Clinton told the American people that he had been born in the small town of Hope, Arkansas, and gone on to meet President Kennedy and to scale his own hopes to a high level. In the most widely used political spot of the Social Democrats (SPD) party in Germany in 1994, SPD candidate Rudolph Scharping narrates his bio spot, telling how he was born in Lahnstein, but grew up in a small village in the Westerwald area of Germany. His mother and wife help out with the storytelling; in one scene, borrowed almost exactly from George Bush's 1988 "The Future" ad, Scharping thrusts one of his children skyward, as George Bush did one of his granddaughters. Scenes like this are so similar and so appealing across cultures that they make a stronger case for cultural similarity than the numbers and categories of analysis alone.

Across the different countries, it is also clear that some spots are dependent for interpretation on the symbolism inherent in a political culture. During the 1997 British campaign, one of Labour's most successful spots was one that used a bulldog, a longtime symbol of British determination, to encourage British voters to think about the need for a "New Labour" government after long years of having the Conservatives as their "masters." Country colors and flags and other government symbols are prevalent in many spots. Thus, spots also provide cultural and ritualistic symbols that help bind voters together in a common understanding of their histories and, of course, invite voters to see the party or leader in the spots as one with the values represented.

SUMMARY COMPARISONS OF VIDEOSTYLE

Despite differences in media and political system variables, these comparisons across several democratic systems of the advertising styles and effects of exposure show some striking similarities across cultures. Summary findings indicate:

1. Most countries concentrate the content of their ads on issues, although in 1992 Korea was an exception.
2. The political broadcasts across countries are overwhelmingly positive, not negative in their focus. The United States is the notable exception.
3. Despite the emphasis on issues and positivity, most leaders and parties rely on emotional, rather than logical proof to make their points. Exceptions are France and Britain, where logical proof is dominant, and Korea, where ethical proof is stressed.
4. Candidates and leaders across all countries are rarely the main speakers in their own or their party's broadcasts, relying instead on anonymous announcers to make their pitch.
5. Most parties and leaders have deemphasized the political party in their ads. Germany and Britain are exceptions.
6. While earlier research (Kaid & Holtz-Bacha, 1995) found substantial differences in production styles, there is an increasing similarity in these across countries as well. This may extend in some cases to the actual copying of formats and styles among countries.

Certainly more work needs to be done to compare videostyles across countries and across political and cultural contexts. However, these results do indicate that there is considerable evidence for the idea that American-style "videostyle" translates quite well across borders. The United States may not be exporting merely democratic traditions of government and American television programming but American approaches to candidate and party marketing as well.

NOTES

1. The authors wish to express appreciation to Jacques Gerstlé for work on the content analysis of the French ads; Gianpietro Mazzoleni and Cindy Roper for the provision and content analysis of the Italian spots; Holli Semetko for assistance in obtaining the British 1992 ads and John Tedesco for his assistance in the content analysis process; Sarah Oates (Glasgow) and Stephan Henneberg and Nick O'Shaughnessy (Cambridge) and Robin Hodess for assistance in obtaining copies of the 1997 British election PEBs; Andrzej Falkowski and Wojciech Cwalina for the content analysis of the Polish spots; Christina Holtz-Bacha for assistance with the German spots; Akiba Cohen for providing copies of the Israeli ads and Keely Cormier for the content analysis work on these ads; and Jinyoung Tak and Soobum Lee (Korea) for assistance in analyzing the Korean spots.

2. Intercoder reliabilities were calculated using the formula suggested by Holsti (North et al., 1963) and averaged +.84 across all categories for all samples.

10

Recurring Elements of Videostyle and the Future of Presidential Candidate Presentation

In the preceding chapters, we have examined videostyle from a number of different perspectives. Some elements of the verbal, nonverbal, and production aspects of presidential candidate presentation on television seem to stand out as particularly characteristic of presidential videostyle. These elements are summarized in Figure 10.1, which displays the recurring elements of presidential videostyle from 1952 through 1996.

In terms of the *verbal component*, presidential candidate spots are issue oriented and candidate positive, while relying on emotional appeals. The content of presidential spots are weighted toward economic concerns, stress the aggressive and competency qualities of the candidate, and emphasize the values of a comfortable life, a sense of accomplishment, change and progress, and patriotism. The *nonverbal component* of videostyle is characterized by the use of anonymous announcers, as fewer and fewer candidates speak for themselves in their spots. When they do appear, however, they are in formal indoor settings, dressed formally, looking attentive and serious, maintaining eye-contact with the viewer, and speaking fluently and without a monotone.

Verbal Elements	Nonverbal Elements	Production Elements
*Issue-oriented (66%) *Candidate-positive (62%) *Uses Emotional Appeals *Stresses Economic Concerns *Stresses Personal Qualities of Aggressiveness and Competence *Stresses Values of Comfortable Life/ Material Comfort, Sense of Accomplishment, Change and Progress, and Patriotism	*Uses Anonymous Announcer *Formal Indoor Settings *Candidate Dress: Formal *Candidate Looks Attentive and Serious *Candidate Maintains Eye Contact with Viewer *Candidate Speaks Fluently and with Pitch Variety	*Short spot length (under 60 seconds) *Introspective Production Style *Frequent Use of Cinema Verité Style and Head-On Style *Uses Tight Camera Shots *Frequent Use of Special Production Techniques *Frequent Use of Technological Distortions

Figure 10.1 Recurring Elements of Presidential Videostyle

The *video production techniques* used by presidential candidates are somewhat varied, of course, but they are composed of short spot lengths (under 60 seconds). While a head-on style is sometimes used, there is also a frequent use of introspective style and of a cinema verité approach to production. Candidates like to be caught in tight camera shots, close-ups that give an intimate feel. Videostyles are also increasingly characterized by the use of specialized production techniques and by a growing use of technological distortions that may mislead voters, particularly in negative spots.

VIDEOSTYLES OF WINNERS AND LOSERS

While videostyle has been used primarily as a descriptive concept, any such organizing concept suggests the possibility of characterizing a successful or unsuccessful style. While videostyle does not pretend to provide a retrospective explanation of why some presidential candidates succeeded and others did not, it is possible to consider whether specific elements of videostyle distinguish winning and losing presidential candidates. In order to make such a comparison, the presidential candidates who won the 12 elections analyzed here were grouped as winners and their opponents as losers. Figure 10.2 summarizes the characteristics that distinguish these two groups, providing statistically different elements when subjected to chi-square tests.

Winner	Loser
1. Uses More Logical Appeals	1. Makes More Specific Policy Proposals
2. Emphasizes Competency	2. Stresses Personal Character More
3. Emphasizes More Values, Particularly a "Comfortable Life/Material Comfort," "Change and Progress," and "Patriotism"	3. Emphasizes Partisanship
4. Attacks Record of Opponent	4. Stresses Optimism
5. More Likely to Attack Opponent on Issues, Not Personality	5. Emphasizes Fewer Values
6. Calls for Change	6. Puts More Values Stress on "Puritanism," "Science and Rationality," and "Family Security"
7. Uses Endorsements	7. Uses Anonymous Announcers
8. More Likely to Speak in Spots	8. Uses Moderate and Frequent Body Movement in Spots
9. Has Limited Body Movement in Spots	9. Uses Longer Commercials
10. Uses Shorter Spots (under 60 seconds)	10. Uses a More Introspective Production Format
11. Uses More Testimonials, More Documentaries, and More Opposition-Focused Formats	
12. Uses More Special Effects and Varied Production Techniques	

Figure 10.2 Videostyles of Winners and Losers

An initial observation is in order about what is not different about winners and losers. Both winners and losers illustrate some of the recurring elements of videostyle: Their spots are primarily issue oriented and candidate positive. While it would be tempting, given the current condemnation of "negative advertising," to credit losers with a surfeit of negative spots, this is simply not the case. In fact, losers actually have a slightly higher percentage of positive spots over time; 63% of loser spots are positive, compared to 60% for winners. There is no statistically significant difference between winners and losers in the degree of negativity.

However, it is quite clear, from the analysis in Chapter 4, that both winners and losers do not hesitate to criticize their opponents. Winners, in fact, are more likely to attack the record of their opponent than are losers. However, when they attack, winners attack the opponent's record and issue stances; losers are more likely to attack an opponent's personal qualities. Clearly, this de facto finding lends some credence to the experimental research that shows negative ads are more effective when they focus on issues, rather than images of the opponent (Kahn & Geer, 1994; Pfau & Burgoon, 1989; Roddy & Garramone, 1988).

While both winners and losers do favor issue spots over personality presentations, there are some differences in how they handle specific aspects of content presentation in their spots. Most significant is the fact that losers make more specific policy proposals, perhaps verifying the old wisdom that the more specific a candidate is, the more likely it is that someone will take offense. Winners have apparently steered a more careful path through such potential minefields. While both winners and losers sponsor more issue-oriented commercials, losers also stress more personality and character qualities in their spots than do winners. Losers also remind voters of their partisanship more frequently than do winners. Winners apparently desire to rest their case to the voter more on issues and values that do not reside in partisan representations.

Values are themselves another clear way in which differences between winners and losers can be isolated. The presence of more value representations is a characteristic of winning presidential candidate videostyle; losers simply talk less about values in general. There are also differences in what specific values are stressed. Winners endorse the values of "a comfortable life/material comfort," "change and progress," and "patriotism." Losers are more likely to stress "puritanism," "family security," and the more abstract notion of "science and rationality."

Winners are also characterized by their reliance on logical appeals. While both winners and losers certainly use emotional appeals, winners are more likely to beef up their presentations with facts and figures, statistics, and logical reasoning examples. Both winners and losers make equal use of fear appeals.

While the verbal content of videostyle seems to offer more distinctions between winners and losers, Figure 10.2 also itemizes some of the nonverbal and production components that differentiate these two types of videostyle. Winners are more likely to speak in their spots, whereas losers make more use of anonymous announcers. Winners, when they appear and speak, restrict their body movements, but there are no significant differences in formality of dress, in eye contact or facial expressions, or in voice pitch or fluency. From a production standpoint, winners use shorter spots and rely on testimonial and documentary formats, as well as more special effects and varied production techniques.

INDIVIDUAL CANDIDATE VIDEOSTYLES

Most of our discussion throughout this book has been on overall trends of videostyle and on the effects of political positioning, partisan affiliation, and negativity in spots. Individual candidates have been used as examples, but each presidential candidate has his own videostyle, made up of a combination of the three components of the overall concept. While space does not allow an item by item analysis of each candidate on each and every aspect of videostyle, the major characteristics of the videostyle of each presidential candidate are considered.

In classifying the videostyle of individual candidates, we have developed a classification system that relates to the videostyles of the presidential candidates considered in this volume. The first level of classification relates to whether the candidate has a direct or indirect style. Candidates with a direct style tended to speak for themselves in their spots, used production techniques such as head-on productions, and demonstrated corresponding nonverbal behavior such as frequent eye contact. The second recurring element seemed to be the type of proof offered by the candidate in making his points in spots. Here the use of the distinctions among logical, emotional, and ethical standards of proof as used and illustrated throughout the volume were used in the classification. Tone of the spots, the positive or negative content, also distinguished the videostyle of many candidates and also often related to production and nonverbal categories, and thus we distinguish between a positive and a negative style. Figure 10.3 classifies presidential candidates according to the combinations, and the following discussion mentions some of the style highlights that resulted in these classifications. No attempt is made here to incorporate every single aspect of videostyle, but rather to emphasize those that are particularly characteristic of a particular classification or candidate.

Dwight Eisenhower

In Eisenhower's initial campaign in 1952, he found himself in a clear challenger situation. Democrats had held the White House for the past two decades, and his own experience was in the military, not politics. His videostyle in 1952 might be characterized as *direct-logical-negative*. Most of the spots use a straightforward question-and-answer format in which Eisenhower himself appears (80%). The spots demonstrate aggressiveness and competency, focusing on issues (91%) and using logical proof (51%). The spots are also attack spots, but they assault the

Direct-Logical-Negative	Indirect-Logical- Negative	Indirect-Emotional-Negative
Eisenhower 1952	Bush 1992	Stevenson 1952
		Johnson 1964
		Mondale 1984
		Dukakis 1988
		Clinton 1992
		Clinton 1996
		Dole 1996
Indirect-Ethical-Positive	**Indirect-Emotional-Positive**	**Direct-Emotional-Positive**
Eisenhower 1956	Nixon 1968	Stevenson 1956
Carter 1980	Nixon 1972	Kennedy 1960
Bush 1988	Humphrey 1968	Nixon 1960
	Ford 1976	McGovern 1972
	Carter 1976	
	Reagan 1984	
Direct-Emotional-Negative	**Direct-Logical-Positive**	
Goldwater 1964	Reagan 1980	

Figure 10.3 Classification of Individual Candidate Videostyles

opposition party, not the individual opponent. Nonetheless, they are direct attacks and made by Eisenhower himself in head-on productions with formal settings.

The 1956 Eisenhower videostyle demonstrates one of the clearest examples of the difference between an incumbent style and a challenger style. In 1956 Eisenhower's spots illustrate an *indirect-ethical-positive* videostyle. Eisenhower does not speak for himself, and he relies on ethical/source credibility as proof for the arguments offered. This approach is reinforced by the fact that, instead of stressing aggressiveness, the spots emphasize Eisenhower's honesty and his strength. The spots are primarily positive and use a variety of different production techniques.

Adlai Stevenson

In his 1952 race, Stevenson was the assumed incumbent because his party had been in office for so many terms. However, Stevenson did not endorse a national ad campaign, and the spots that represent his videostyle were produced without his active participation. They are *indirect-emotional-assaultive* in that they are quite negative (67%), but Stevenson himself does not appear in them or make the attacks himself. The ads are characterized by music and video clips, yet try to convey aggressiveness.

The 1956 spots may provide a better representation of Stevenson's style. Running as a challenger, he demonstrates a *direct-emotional-positive* videostyle. He is the main speaker in most of his ads, stressing issues but relying on emotional proof.

John F. Kennedy

Kennedy was a challenger in 1960, and his style was much like that of his Democratic predecessor, a *direct-emotional-positive* videostyle. Kennedy appeared as the main speaker in most of his spots (71%), emphasizing issues but using emotional proof (53%). His ads are primarily positive (88%). The production formats are simple and straightforward, with Kennedy himself speaking in many head-on productions (with a serious/attentive facial expression and maintaining direct eye contact with the viewer). He called for change and progress. He stressed his own competency and demonstrated aggressiveness.

Richard Nixon

Richard Nixon provides one of the most interesting studies in videostyle because he is the only presidential candidate to run on three different occasions, first as a presumed incumbent in 1960, then as a challenger in 1968, and finally as a true incumbent in 1972. In 1960 his videostyle was, like his opponent's, *direct-emotional-positive*. He was the main speaker in his ads (46%), using emotional proof as the major form of evidence and persuasion in his spots (71%). Like most candidates he emphasized issues (83%). He had the all-time high percentage of positive ads (92%) for any candidate. While he often relied on somewhat informal settings for his ads, his expression was serious, with direct eye contact. He stressed foreign affairs and defense issues, a Nixon mainstay throughout all three of his campaigns.

The 1968 and 1972 campaigns demonstrate an *indirect-emotional-positive* videostyle. In these two years, one as challenger and another as incumbent, Nixon rarely spoke directly and was not the dominant visual figure in the spots, although his voice is often heard. Much has been written elsewhere about how and why Nixon chose this strategy in his later campaigns (McGinniss, 1969). In both campaigns, the ads are also primarily positive (85% in 1968 and 80% in 1972). There are marked production differences, however, in that the 1968 ads use slides and stills with lots of montages and specialized graphics—techniques designed to convey action and dynamism without the candidate actually being present in the ads. In 1972, however, the production style used greater variety of production approaches and particularly relied on documentary style.

Lyndon Johnson

While Lyndon Johnson's style was clearly *indirect-emotional-negative*, it was also a bit discomforting. The emotional tone (70%) was the dominant aspect of the campaign, and fear appeals played a significant role in nearly half of the spots (48%). Johnson rarely delivered any message himself during the entire advertising campaign; anonymous announcers did the job in 70% of the ads. Negative ads played a major role in this campaign, as Johnson assaulted Goldwater over and over, often in issue dramatizations about foreign policy/nuclear weapons use.

Barry Goldwater

In his challenger role, Barry Goldwater used a *direct-emotional-negative* style. One major difference in his style, compared to opponent Lyndon Johnson, was that Goldwater appeared and spoke for himself in 60% of his spots. The production style was frequently candidate head-on, with a formal indoor setting and Goldwater speaking with a serious expression, maintaining eye contact with viewers. Production styles emphasized tight shots of Goldwater, emphasizing again his directness. But the message, while a bit less ominous than Johnson's and focused on issues, was often negative (46%), and the proof offered was usually emotional (73%).

Hubert Humphrey

In 1968, Hubert Humphrey was often uncomfortable in his role as the presumed incumbent and tried frequently to distance himself from the incumbent president (Johnson) he served. Humphrey's videostyle best fits the *indirect-emotional-positive* mode. Like his opponent in this race, Richard Nixon, Humphrey was not the main speaker in his spots; anonymous announcers took on the job most of the time. Humphrey relied primarily on emotional proof (50%). Although he primarily used positive ads (67%), his percentage of negative ads (33%) was more than double the percentage used by his opponent (15%). The most noticeable aspect of Humphrey's videostyle that distinguishes him from other presidential candidates over the years is his heavy emphasis on candidate image. While most candidates have emphasized issues in their ads, Humphrey's style emphasized image qualities in 61% of his spots. His issue choices were also somewhat atypical, focusing on Medicare and Social Security and civil rights concerns.

George McGovern

In 1972 George McGovern found himself in the challenger role against Richard Nixon, who had honed his videostyle in previous campaigns. The major difference in the McGovern style was in its directness, a *direct-emotional-positive* videostyle. Unlike Nixon, McGovern appeared in his spots and was the main speaker in 62% of them. He

used primarily emotional proof but also frequently relied on ethi-
cal/source, credibility proof as he tried to contrast his own character
with that of his opponent. McGovern emphasized issues (72%) and
used primarily positive ads (60%). The production style of his ads is
somewhat distinctive as well. Production was largely the responsibility
of award-winning producer Charles Guggenheim, who crafted a cinema verité format that often showed McGovern in natural-seeming,
confrontational situations with voters. These settings allowed McGovern to demonstrate a knowledge of issues, as well as competence and
an aggressive personal style.

Gerald Ford

While Gerald Ford's 1976 campaign positioned him as an incumbent
in the literal sense, his assumption of the presidency in the aftermath
of Nixon's resignation in 1974 and his own abrupt appointment as
vice-president following Spiro Agnew's demise did not leave him much
opportunity to take advantage of the perks of incumbency. His
videostyle falls into the *indirect-emotional-positive* mode. He used an
anonymous announcer more often than he spoke himself; and, when he
did speak in his spots, he almost never maintained direct eye contact
with viewers. The primary type of proof used in his spots was emotional
(52%), although like McGovern he tried to emphasize his own good
character through ethical proof. Interestingly, this need to establish his
own good character came from the need to distinguish himself from his
own party's predecessor (Richard Nixon), rather than from his opponent, Jimmy Carter. Nonetheless, his spots were mostly positive ones
(73%). Attacks on his opponent were presented mostly as testimonials
by others, often in a "man-on-the-street" style. Ford's spots were also
noticeable for the infrequent emphasis on values.

Jimmy Carter

Jimmy Carter is, of course, another president who ran as both incumbent and challenger, and his style demonstrates clearly some of the
differences that political positioning can make. As a challenger in 1976,
Carter used a style that was primarily *direct-emotional-positive*. He was
the main speaker in 77% of his ads, using a head-on production style in
over half of all spots (51%). Despite the directness of his style, it is worth
noting that his vocal patterns, perhaps attributable to his Southern
roots, were unusual in a presidential candidate. He was not particularly
fluent, his delivery was often stumbling and halting, and his vocal pitch
was often a droning monotone. An emotional style of proof dominated
his spots (47%).

As an incumbent in 1980, however, Carter's style was quite different, most easily classified as *indirect-ethical-positive*. Like most incumbents, Carter chose to let others speak for him more than he spoke for himself. Adopting an indirect style, he used anonymous announcers in 51% of his spots. Abandoning the head-on production format, his video production style was more cinema verité. While still positive (64%), his ads were actually more negative than they had been in 1976. Even more different was his use of proof. As an incumbent, he chose not logical or emotional proof to make his points, but relied instead on ethical or source credibility. His own character and competence became the underlying evidence for most of his claims as an incumbent.

Ronald Reagan

Ronald Reagan provides another test of a candidate who ran as both a challenger and a true incumbent. In 1980, his style was a *direct-logical-positive* one, a style not seen so clearly since Eisenhower's 1952 campaign. The distinguishing feature, of course, was the reliance on logical proof, perhaps emanating from a need to avoid further criticism for being an actor and a nonsubstantive candidate. Reagan's 1980 campaign emphasized Reagan himself as the speaker in many ads (40%); others were done by testimonials and endorsements of other officials. The spots were also primarily positive (65%). In his role as direct speaker, Reagan often used a head-on format. Speaking in a formal indoor setting, he almost always maintained eye-contact with the viewer and a serious/attentive facial expression.

As an incumbent in 1984, however, Reagan felt free to emphasize a more emotional tone in his spots, and his style became more *indirect-emotional-positive*. Emotional proof was dominant in 58% of the 1984 spots, and most spots were positive (73%). While Reagan still appeared in a substantial number of his spots (42%), anonymous announcers took over for 48% of them in 1984. When he did appear, however, he maintained eye contact and a serious/attentive expression. The 1984 spots also demonstrated more varied production techniques, relying less on Reagan as the dominant speaker and more on special effects.

Walter Mondale

In his 1984 role as challenger to incumbent Ronald Reagan, Walter Mondale's videostyle can best be characterized as *indirect-emotional-negative*. Mondale relied heavily on anonymous announcers (68%) in his spots. When he did appear in his spots, the camera shots often made unusual use of low-angle shots designed to give him a more commanding appearance. While he emphasized issues heavily (93%), his ads were very negative. Assaults on Ronald Reagan made up over half of his ads (54%). Issue dramatizations comprised a large number of his spots, again making an indirect appeal. Mondale also relied on an unusually heavy amount of emotional proof (68%) and fear appeals (64%).

George Bush

George Bush was in the interesting position of being an incumbent both times he ran for president. In 1988 he was the assumed incumbent, as a result of serving two terms as vice-president to Ronald Reagan, and in 1992 he stood for re-election as an incumbent in his own right. In neither case does his style match that of a typical incumbent, departing in some ways from both the general recurring videostyle pattern and from the characteristics of an incumbent style. In both campaigns, Bush's spots are much less issue-oriented than the norm for presidential candidates (only 57% in 1988 and 50% in 1992). However, other characteristics make more difference in his style between the two years. In 1988 Bush's videostyle was *indirect-ethical-positive*. He relied on anonymous announcers in 57% of his 1988 spots. The production styles were primarily issue dramatizations (26%), like the famous "Revolving Door" ad criticizing Dukakis's prison furlough program or cinema verité ads that capitalized on Bush qualifications and history. This latter style reinforced the use of ethical or source-credibility proof for the spots. The most involving theme here was the emphasis on George Bush's qualifications and experience, his character. This emphasis on ethical proof is, of course, one reason for the lower use of issues in Bush's 1988 campaign, and it is also one of the reasons that his overall mix of ads is primarily positive (64%) in 1988, despite the frequent criticism of his negativity in that campaign.

In 1992 Bush was defending his own record, and he did it in a way that was somewhat different from most candidates. As a result of this campaign, Bush stands alone as the sole example of *indirect-logical-negative* videostyle. In 1992 Bush was not the main speaker in his spots, using an indirect style with anonymous announcers or others speaking for him. His mix of issues and images was 50/50. However, his negative advertising rate was much higher than it had been in 1988; two-thirds of the 1992 Bush ads (66%) were negative assaults on Bill Clinton. However, the ads rely primarily on logical proof to make their case. Bush mounted his offensive against Clinton with facts and figures, with logical and analytical reasoning. While many of the ads used fear appeals of some kind, this was not the dominant proof used.

Michael Dukakis

Dukakis's 1988 campaign against presumed incumbent George Bush can be classified as an *indirect-emotional-negative* videostyle. Dukakis did not speak for himself very often in his spots. When he did appear in his ads, he used eye contact frequently, but he often showed an unusual smiling facial expression (48%) despite the seriousness of the topic. Production techniques were also unusual, using a surprising number of low-angle shots and long shots, rather than close-ups or tight shots that might have conveyed a warmer, more intimate and direct personality. Dukakis used a high number of negative ads (54%). While most ads emphasized issues (73%), they also relied primarily on emotional proof (51%). This use of emotional proof and a smiling face may have presented a difficult credibility problem for Dukakis, contrasting with a man often characterized in other formats as wooden and unemotional.

Bill Clinton

Bill Clinton's first campaign as a challenger and his second as an incumbent represent the clearest examples of a consistent videostyle not affected by political positioning. In both campaigns, Clinton's style is consistently *indirect-emotional-negative*. In both campaigns, Clinton himself is rarely the main speaker. In 77% of the 1992 spots and 79% of the 1996 ones, an anonymous announcer makes the argument. Because of this indirect style, production formats are varied in both years and characterized by special effects (computer graphics, superimpositions, slow motion, etc.). Clinton almost never appears at all in the 1996 ads. When he does, he rarely has any eye contact with the viewer. The ads for these two campaigns are the most negative in the history of presidential ads: 69% in 1992 and 68% in 1996. Clinton's videostyle is one of attack, attack, attack. In 1996 this is offset somewhat by the comparative tone in some ads, but the overwhelming message is still a negative assaultive one. In both campaigns, while the attacks are based on issues, the type of proof used is repeatedly emotional, relying on feelings and the evoking of emotional responses. Fear appeals are present in nearly half (48%) of the 1996 ads.

Robert Dole

While Robert Dole certainly speaks and appears more frequently in his spots than does Bill Clinton in 1996, his style is still an indirect one. Given the emotional proof (44%) and the high number of negative spots (61%), his style also must be classified as *indirect-emotional-negative*.

Dole's spots did emphasize issues (65%), but their indirect nature meant that he used a lot of specialized production techniques (computer print/graphics and a mixture of ad formats).

IMPLICATIONS OF VIDEOSTYLE FOR FUTURE PRESIDENTIAL CAMPAIGNS

It is not difficult to suggest that future presidential candidates may develop new combinations of videostyle components. Our analysis has already classified some common elements of videostyle that may relate to political positioning, to political parties, or to successful campaigns.

But what will the presidential videostyles of the next millennium be like? Trends and cycles are always difficult to predict, and our analysis is not meant to be predictive or prescriptive. However, it is likely that there will be some differences in the videostyles of the presidential candidates in 2000. It seems likely that the trend toward indirect and assaultive styles has peaked. The next presidential campaign will surely see one or more of the candidates demonstrating a videostyle that is more direct, although it is unlikely that a candidate will suddenly devote his entire arsenal of political spots to head-on, direct candidate statements. It is also likely that the percentage of attack spots will decline, but whether it will decline sufficiently to put the balance back to the positive side is not a certainty. Finally, there seems little likelihood that emotional proof will disappear from presidential videostyle.

Of increasing interest is the possibility that a candidate's videostyle may be affected by the use of the Internet for campaigning. At this point, much of the use of the Internet for political advertising is as a delivery mechanism. However, innovations in the use of the Internet for political advertising promise to provide the first potential for interactive political advertising messages. Exciting new possibilities are raised by the potential for the voter to play a role in how a candidate's videostyle may evolve.

Videostyle may be affected in other ways in the future if Congress succeeds in enacting campaign reform legislation. Many reformers are anxious to further restrict a candidate's ability to determine his or her own videostyle in campaign spots. For instance, proposals such as the proposed Danforth/Hollings "Clean Campaign Act" have received some attention. This legislation proposed sweeping changes, which would have included guarantees of free response time for candidates opposed by "independent expenditures" or by negative ads in which the sponsoring candidate did not appear (Hoff & Bernstein, 1988; Clinger, 1987). Other proposals have suggested that candidates be given free blocs of time in lengths of at least 5 minutes (Hoff & Bernstein, 1988), would require candidates to appear and address the camera for the duration of their ads (S. 340, 1989; S.577, 1987), or would require that when negative attacks are made, the candidate must make the attacks in person (S.2, 1987). In the 1996 campaign the free-time proposal was, in fact, tried on a voluntary basis by several television networks and cable channels. Since they gave candidates the time free, the sponsoring entity did prescribe the format and approach that could be taken in the broadcast segments. These spots did change somewhat the videostyles of both Dole and Clinton. For instance, although both did appear as the major speakers in the free time segments, some negative attacks were still made, and the use of emotional proof did not disappear (Kaid, McKinney, & Tedesco, 2000).

Many of these proposed changes would seem to be obviously unconstitutional (Clinger, 1987), but there are many viable arguments on both sides of these issues. Some contend these regulations only affect the format of ads and thus meet the constitutional tests of being "contentneutral" regulations (Dugan, 1989). However, the visual aspects of a television ad (its format, techniques, style, etc.) are just as much "content" as words are. It seems equally certain that any attempt to regulate based on "negativity" in ads would itself be a content-based regulation and not likely to withstand constitutional tests. Despite disclaimer and source disclosure laws, the courts also have not been particularly sympathetic to attempts to outlaw the right to anonymity in making attacks (Clinger, 1987; Jones & Kaid, 1976), calling into question even the constitutionality of "talking head"/candidate appearance restrictions.

In the aftermath of alleged campaign finance violations in the 1996 campaign, there are new proposals for campaign finance regulation that might affect political advertising in other ways in the future. It looks at this point unlikely that any major changes or restrictions will be in effect for the 2000 campaign. For the present at least, candidates remain the captains of their own videostyles; and, as our analysis in Chapter 9 suggests, these videostyles have a great deal in common with the self-presentations of political leaders around the world.

Appendix: Videostyle Codesheet

Coder Name: _____

Commercial ID: _____

1. **Candidate name**:

2. **Length of commercial**:
   (1) Two to five minutes
   (2) 20 to 30 seconds
   (3) 60 seconds
   (9) Other (specify) _____
3. **Who sponsored the ad**?
   (1) Committee for election/re-election
   (2) Citizens for good government group

(3) Issue based group

(4) Independent third party group

(5) National Party (Rep. or Dem.)

(6) Free Time provided by network

(8) Cannot determine

(9) Other (specify)

4. **Format of commercial?**

(0) Documentary

(1) Video Clip/Music Video

(2) Testimonial (reaction)

(3) Introspection

(4) Issue Statement

(5) Staged Press Conference

(6) Opposition focused

(7) Issue Dramatization

(8) Question and Answer/Confrontation

(9) Other (specify) _____

5. **Is there any music present in the commercial?**
(Code 1 if present, 0 if not present)

5a. **If music is present, style of music?**

(0) not present

(1) classical

(2) modern (pop, rock, jazz)

(3) Instrumental (background but cannot be defined as classical or modern)

(4) marching music

(5) trumpet or announcing music

(6) folk music/country/western

(7) national anthem

(8) other

(9) combination

6. **What is the relationship between music and text?**

(1) more music than text

(2) more text than music

(3) balance between text and music

7. **Is the ad candidate or opponent focused?**

(1) Candidate-positive focused

(2) Opponent-negative focused

8. **Is there a negative attack made in the ad**:

(0) No

(1) Yes

9. **If an attack is made, who makes the attack?**

(1) Candidate attacks opponent.

(2) Surrogate attacks opponent.

(3) Anonymous announcer attacks opponent.

(0) no attack

10. **If a negative attack is made, what is the purpose or nature of the attack?**

(Code 1 if present, 0 if not present)

(1) Attack on personal characteristics of opponent.

(2) Attack on issue stands/consistency of opponent.

(3) Attack on opponent's group affiliations or associations.

(4) Attack on opponent's background/qualifications.

(5) Attack on opponent's performance in past offices/positions.

10a. **If negative attack is made, is it**

(1) direct attack against another politician/cand.

(2) direct attack against another party

(3) more general, indirect attack against government and other parties

(4) indirect/implicit attack without specific mention of the object of the attack

(0) no attack is made in ad

11. **What strategies are used in making the negative attack?**

(Code 1 if present, 0 if not present)

(1) Use of humor/ridicule

(2) Negative association

(3) Name-calling (using negative labels)

(4) Guilt by association

12. **Production technique** (code for dominant technique):

(1) Cinema verité

(2) Slides with print and voice-over or slides with movement, print, and voice-over

(3) Candidate head-on

(4) Somebody other than candidate head-on

(5) Animation and special production

(6) Combination (specify)

13. **Setting of the ad** (code for dominant setting):

(1) Formal indoors

(2) Informal indoors

(3) Formal outdoors

(4) Informal outdoors

(5) Combination (specify)

(8) Not applicable

14. **Any dominant inanimate object with which the candidate inter-acts?** (Code 1 if yes, 0 if no) If yes, describe below:

14a. **Can American symbols be seen in the ad?**
      (0) no
      (1) yes
14b. **If yes, mark present or absent for the following:**
      (1) flag
      (2) national colors/red/white/blue
      (3) national bird—eagle
      (4) famous American landscapes
      (5) famous documents (such as Const./Dec. of Indep.)
      (6) representations of prior presidents/famous fig.
      (7) other famous patriotic symbols
15.   **Who is speaking?** (code for dominant speaker)
      (1) Candidate
      (2) A government official or office-holder
      (3) An anonymous announcer
      (4) Non-government celebrity
      (5) Spouse or family member
      (6) Combination (specify) _____
      (9) Other
15a. **Does a candidate or party representative appear in the spot?**
      (0) no
      (1) yes; candidate or party sponsoring ad
      (2) yes; opponent(s) of candidate or party sponsoring ad
      (3) both appear
15b. **If yes, is the candidate or party member presented:**
      (1) positively
      (2) negatively
      (3) neutrally
      (4) both positive and negative
15c. **Does family appear in spot?**
      (1) spouse
      (2) other family member
      (3) children
      (4) spouse and children
      (5) spouse, children, and other family member(s)
      (6) other combination of family
      (0) no family
16.   **Does candidate have eye contact directly with the viewer?**
      (Code for overall eye contact)
      (1) Almost always
      (2) Sometimes
      (3) Almost never
      (8) Not applicable

17. **Is candidate usually**: (code dominant expression)
    (1) Smiling
    (2) Attentive/serious
    (3) Frowning/glaring
    (8) Not applicable/candidate not present
    (9) Other (specify)
18. **Body movement of candidate**:
    (1) Never
    (2) Moderate
    (3) Frequent
    (8) Not applicable
19. **Fluency**: (code for candidate only)
    (1) Fluent
    (2) Stumbling/hesitant/non-fluent
    (8) Not applicable
20. **Rate of speech**: (code for candidate only)
    (1) Slow
    (2) Moderate
    (3) Fast
    (8) Not applicable
21. **Pitch variety**: (code for candidate only)
    (1) Monotone
    (2) Pitch variety
    (3) Combined monotone and pitch variety
    (8) Not applicable
22. **Dress**: (code dominant attire for candidate only)
    (1) Formal
    (2) Casual
    (3) Varied
    (8) Not applicable
23. **Staging of ad**:
    (1) All obviously staged
    (2) Natural appearing
    (8) Cannot be determined
    (9) Other (specify) _____
24. **Candidate or commercial (if candidate not present) sound characteristics:** (code for dominant characteristics)
    (1) Live—sound is live and on-video directly from person speaking
    (2) Sound-over—sound is placed over video
    (8) Not applicable
25. **Special effects/production techniques used**:
    (Code 1 if present, 0 if not present)
    (0) Computer graphics

    (1) Slow motion
    (2) Fast motion
    (3) Reversed motion
    (4) Freeze frame
    (5) Split screen
    (6) Superimpositions
    (7) Montage
    (8) Stop-motion photography
    (9) Use of stills
Any other special effects? (Describe)

---

26. **Is the emphasis of this ad/broadcast on:**
    (1) Issues
    (2) Image
27. **Types of appeals used in ads:**
    (Code 1 if present, 0 if not present)
    (1) Logical appeals (use of evidence in ads)
    (2) Emotional appeals
    (3) Source credibility/ethos appeals (appealing to qualifications as
        candidate)

    List the dominant appeal used in the ad

28. **Are fear appeals used in the ad?**
    (Code 1 if present, 0 if not present)
29. **Content of appeal of the ad:**
    (Code 1 if present, 0 if not present)
    (1) Emphasis on partisanship of candidate
    (2) Issue-related appeal: candidate's issue concern
    (3) Issue-related appeal: vague policy preference
    (4) Issue-related appeal: specific policy proposals
    (5) Personal characteristics of candidate
    (6) Linking of candidate w/certain demographic groups

    Code for the dominant content of the ad.

30. **Is there a particular issue emphasized in this ad?**
    From the following list, mark present or absent for each issue listed:
      1. International or foreign affairs
      2. Military or defense spending
      3. Economic concerns (inflation, unemployment, jobs)
      4. Deficit/need to balance budget

5. Crime/prisons/penalties/gun control
6. Drugs
7. Concern for children or children's issues
8. Medicare/Social Security/problems of Elderly
9. Other social policies (ex. family leave)
10. Abortion
11. Environmental concerns
12. Health care
13. Problems with immigrants
14. Smoking/tobacco abuse
15. Taxes
16. Welfare reform
17. Education
18. Civil rights/affirmative action/special rights for special groups

30a. **Which of these issues is dominant in the spot?**
(list number of issue from above list) _____

Which strategies are present in the ad?
(Code 1 if strategy is present, 0 if not present)
31. Use of symbolic trappings to transmit importance of office
32. Incumbency stands for legitimacy
33. Competency and the office
34. Charisma and the office
35. Calling for changes
36. Emphasizing optimism for the future
37. Speaking to traditional values
38. Appearing to represent the philosophical center of the party
39. Consulting or negotiating with world leaders
40. Using endorsements by party and other important leaders
41. Emphasizing accomplishments
42. Creating and maintaining "above the trenches" posture
43. Depending on surrogates to speak
44. Taking the offensive position on issues
45. Attacking the record of the opponent
46. Other (specify) _____

What candidate characteristics are emphasized in the ad?
(Code 1 if present, 0 if not present)
47. Honesty/integrity
48. Toughness/strength
49. Warmth/compassion
50. Competency
51. Performance/success
52. Aggressiveness
53. Activeness

54. Qualifications
55. **Dominant camera angle used in ad:** (code for candidate only)
    (1) High
    (2) Straight-on
    (3) Low
    (4) Movement combination (specify) _____
    (8) Candidate not present
56. **Dominant type of camera shot used in ad**: (code for candidate only)
    (1) Tight (head and shoulders)
    (2) Medium (waist up)
    (3) Long (full length)
    (4) Movement combination (specify) _____
    (8) Candidate not present
57. **Is a candidate or party slogan used in the ad?**
    (0) no   (1) yes
    If yes, what is it? _____
58. **Is the term "values" used explicitly in the spot?**
    (0) no   (1) yes
59. **Does the spot actually discuss or relate to values?**
    (0) no (1) yes
60. **From the following list of values, mark present or absent if the value appears or is mentioned in the spot, verbally or visually or both.** These values come from Rokeach (1973).

	verbally	visually	both
1. a comfortable life	____	____	
2. a sense of accomplishment	____		____
3. a world at peace	____		____
4. family security	____		____
5. an exciting life	____		____
6. a world of beauty	____		____
7. equality	____		____
8. happiness	____		____
9. national security	____		____
10. freedom	____		____
11. pleasure	____		____
12. self-respect	____		____
13. true friendship	____		____
14. wisdom	____		____

Of the values marked above, rank order the three that are the most dominant or important in the ad; there is no need to distinguish here between verbal or visual dominance; simply consider the significance or dominance of the value to the ad's message:

1. (most important value)   _____
2. (second most important)   _____
3. (third most important)   _____

61. **Is a sense of alienation or cynicism referred to in the spot in any way? Mark any references or statements that apply.** Mark present (1) or absent (0) for each statement.
    (1) feelings that ordinary people are not able to influence government or politics
    (2) politicians are not responsive to what the people want; politicians aren't willing to do what people want
    (3) distrust of government or politicians in general
    (4) reference to consequences of alienation—might not vote, might as well not bother, no need to participate
62. **Below is a list of American values**, outlined by Steele & Redding (1962). For each one, mark if it is present in the spot.
    See Codebook for definitions of each value.

    Puritan and Pioneer Morality
    Value of the Individual
    Achievement and Success
    Change and Progress
    Ethical Equality
    Equality of Opportunity
    Effort and Optimism
    Efficiency, Practicality, and Pragmatism
    Rejection of Authority
    Science and Secular Rationality
    Sociality
    Material Comfort
    Quantification
    External Conformity
    Humor
    Generosity and Considerations
    Patriotism

References

'56 campaigns were promotional flops, ex-adman writes. (1956, November 26). *Advertising Age*, p. 50.

Abramowitz, A. I. (1980). A comparison of voting for U.S. Senator and Representative in 1978. *American Political Science Review, 74*, 633–640.

Ad implies Clinton lied about draft. (1992, October 12). *Washington Post*, p. A14.

Agencies aren't political masterminds. (1956, November 5). *Advertising Age*, p. 108.

Agranoff, R. (1976). *The management of election campaigns*. Boston: Holbrook.

Aguinis, H., Simonsen, M. M., & Pierce, C. (1998). Effects of nonverbal behavior on perceptions of power bases. *Journal of Social Psychology, 138*, 455–469.

Albert, J. A. (1986). The remedies available to candidates who are defamed by television or radio commercials of opponents. *Vermont Law Review, 11*, 33–73.

Alexander, H. E. (1972). *Financing the 1968 election*. Lexington, NH: Lexington Books.

Alexander, H.E. (1983). *Financing the 1980 election*. Lexington, NH: Lexington Books.

Angell, T. (1988). Video image generators. In J. L. Swerdlow (Ed.), *Media technology and the vote* (pp. 37–40). Washington, DC: Annenberg Washington Program.

Ansolabehere, S., & Iyengar, S. (1995). *Going negative: How political advertisements shrink and polarize the electorate*. New York: Free Press.

Ansolabehere, S., Iyengar, S., Simon, A., & Valentino, N. (1994). Does attack advertising demobilize the electorate? *American Political Science Review, 88*, 829–838.

Apple, R. W., Jr. (1988, November 6). State by state: Old pros appraise the '88 campaign. *New York Times*, Section 1, p. 1.

Atkin, C. K., Bowen, L., Nayman, O. B., & Sheinkopf, K. G. (1973). Quality versus quantity in televised political ads. *Public Opinion Quarterly, 37*, 209–224.

Atkin, C., & Heald, G. (1976). Effects of political advertising. *Public Opinion Quarterly, 40*, 216–228.

Auster, B. B. (1996, September 30). Accentuating the negative—quietly. *U.S. News & World Report*, p. 44.

Ball blasts plan to fill airwaves with Ike spots. (1952, October 6). *Advertising Age*, p. 93.

Barone, M. (1988, October 11). These Dukakis ads just don't work. *Washington Post*, p. A19.

Barrett, L. I. (1992, October 5). As Bush struggles to catch up to Clinton, Perot's threat to leap in from the sidelines complicates the race in its final stretch. *Time*, p. 28.

Basil, M., Schooler, C., & Reeves, B. (1991). Positive and negative political advertising: Effectiveness of ads and perceptions of candidates. In F. Biocca (Ed.), *Television and political advertising, Volume 1: Psychological processes* (pp. 245–262). Hillsdale, NJ: Lawrence Erlbaum Associates.

Baukus, R. A., Payne, J. G., & Reisler, M. C. (1985). Negative polispots. In J. R. Cox, M. O. Sillars, & G. B. Walker (Eds.), *Argumentation and social practice* (pp. 236–252). Annandale, VA: Speech Communication Association.

Becker, L. B., & Doolittle, J. C. (1975). How repetition affects evaluations of and information seeking about candidates. *Journalism Quarterly, 52*, 611–617.

Bennet, J. (1996a, September 5). Dole camp breaks the mold, try an ad that will last a full five minutes. *New York Times*, p. B9.

Bennet, J. (1996b, September 11). Dole campaign says it has hardly begun to fight as Clinton storms the airwaves. *New York Times*, p. B9.

Bennett, C. (1997). Assessing the impact of ad watches on the strategic decision-making process: A comparative analysis of ad watches in the 1992 and 1996 presidential elections. *American Behavioral Scientist, 40*, 1161–1182.

Benoit, W. L., Pier, P. M., & Blaney, J. R. (1997). A functional approach to televised political spots: Acclaiming, attacking, defending. *Communication Quarterly, 45*, 1–20.

Berelson, B. (1966). Democratic theory and public opinion. In B. Berelson & M. Janowitz (Eds.), *Reader in public opinion and communication* (pp. 489–504). New York: Free Press.

Berke, R. L. (1992a, September 27). Cooking up some ideas for negative campaigns. *New York Times*, Section 3, p. 4.

Berke, R. L. (1992b, October 29). Volleys of data replace blatant attacks of 1988. *New York Times*, p. A24.

Berke, R. L. (1992c, October 31). What is scarier than Halloween? Tune in to candidates' ads and see. *New York Times*, Section 1, p. 7.

Blair, W. M. (1952, October 2). Stevenson aides hit rival TV plan. *New York Times*, p. 22.

Bloom, M. H. (1973). *Public relations and presidential campaigns: A crisis in democracy*. New York: Thomas Y. Crowell Company.

Blumler, J. G., Cayrol, R., & Thoveron, G. (1978). *La télévision fait-elle l'élection? Une analyse comparative: France, Grande-Bretagne, Belgique*. Paris: Presses de la Fondation Nationale des Sciences Politique.

Blumler, J. G., Kavanaugh, D., & Nossiter, T. J. (1996). Modern communications versus traditional politics in Britain: Unstable marriage of convenience. In D. L. Swanson & P. Mancini (Eds.), *Politics, media, and modern democracy* (pp. 49–72). Westport, CT: Praeger.

Blumler, J. G., & McQuail, D. (1968). *Television in politics*. London: Faber and Faber.

Bowen, L. (1994). Time of voting decision and use of political advertising: The Slade Gorton–Brock Adams senatorial campaign. *Journalism and Mass Communication Quarterly, 71*, 665–675.

Bowers, T. A. (1977). Candidate advertising: The agenda is the message. In D. L. Shaw & M. E. McCombs (Eds.), *The emergence of American political issues*. St. Paul, MN: West Publishing.

Broder, D. A. (1989, January 19). Should news media police accuracy of ads? *Washington Post*, p. A22.

Brody, R., & Sigelman, L. (1983). Presidential popularity and presidential elections: An update and extension. *Public Opinion Quarterly, 47*, 325–328.

Buckley v. Valeo, 424 U.S. 1, 60–84 (1976).

Bumiller, E. (1984, October 18). Reagan's ad aces: The Tuesday Team, making America feel good about itself. *Washington Post*, p. D1.

Burgoon, J. K., Buller, D. B., & Woodall, W. Gill (1989). *Nonverbal communication: The unspoken dialogue*. New York: Harper & Row.

Burgoon, J. K., & Le Poire, B. A. (1999). Nonverbal cues and interpersonal judgments: Participant and observer perceptions of intimacy, dominance, composure and formality. *Communication Monographs, 66*, 105–124.

Buss, T., & Hofstetter, C. R. (1976). An analysis of the logic of televised campaign advertisements: The 1972 presidential campaign. *Communication Research, 3*, 367–392.

Bystrom, D. G. (1995). *Candidate gender and presentation of self: The videostyles of men and women in U.S. Senate campaigns*. Unpublished doctoral dissertation, University of Oklahoma, Norman.

Bystrom, D. G., & Miller, J. L. (1999). Gendered communication styles and strategies in campaign 1996: The videostyles of women and men candidates. In L. L. Kaid & D. G. Bystrom (Eds.), *The electronic election: Perspectives on the 1996 campaign communication* (pp. 293–302). Mahwah, NJ: Lawrence Erlbaum.

Campbell, A., Converse, P., Miller, W., & Stokes, D. (1960). *The American voter*. New York: John Wiley & Sons.

The candidates' world. (1972, October 16). *Time*, pp. 18–19.

Cappella, J. N., & Jamieson, K. H. (1994). Broadcast adwatch effects: A field experiment. *Communication Research, 21*, 342–365.

Cayrol, R. (1988). The electoral campaign and the decision-making process of French voters. In H. R. Penniman (Ed.), *France at the polls, 1981 and 1986*. Durham, NC: Duke University Press.

Center for Media and Public Affairs (1996, May-June). Whose campaign did you see? *Media Monitor, 10*(3), 1–4.

Clarity, J. F. (1968, October 30). G.O.P. cancels commercial showing Humphrey grinning amid distress. *New York Times*, p. 28.

Clendinen, D. (1984, September 14). Actor as president: Half-hour commercial wraps in advertising's best. *New York Times*, p. A18.

Clinger, J. H. (1987). The Clean Campaign Act of 1985: A rational solution to negative campaign advertising which the One Hundredth Congress should reconsider. *Journal of Law and Politics, 3*(4), 727–748.

Colford, S. W. (1992, August 24). Clinton's forces score with "tactical" use of ad. *Advertising Age*, p. 3.

Cundy, D. T. (1986). Political commercials and candidate image: The effects can be substantial. In L. L. Kaid, D. Nimmo, & K. R. Sanders (Eds.), *New perspectives on political advertising* (pp. 210–234). Carbondale: Southern Illinois University Press.

Cundy, D. T. (1990). Image formation, the low involvement voter, and televised political advertising. *Political Communication and Persuasion, 7*, 41–59.

Devlin, L. P. (1977). Contrasts in presidential campaign commercials of 1976. *Central States Speech Journal, 28*, 238–249.

Devlin, L. P. (1982). Contrasts in presidential campaign commercials of 1980. *Political Communication Review, 7*, 1–38.

Devlin, L. P. (1986). An analysis of presidential television commercials, 1952–1984. In L. L. Kaid, D. Nimmo, & K. R. Sanders (Eds.), *New perspectives on political advertising* (pp. 21–54). Carbondale: Southern Illinois University Press.

Devlin, L. P. (1989). Contrasts in presidential campaign commercials in 1988. *American Behavioral Scientist, 32*, 389–414.

Devlin, L. P. (1993). Contrasts in presidential campaign commercials of 1992. *American Behavioral Scientist, 37*(2), 272–290.

Devlin, L. P. (1997). Contrasts in presidential campaign commercials of 1996. *American Behavioral Scientist, 40*, 1058–1084.

Diamond, E., & Bates, S. (1984). *The spot: The rise of political advertising on television*. Cambridge, MA: MIT Press.

Diamond, E., & Bates, S. (1988). *The spot: The rise of political advertising on television* (2nd ed.). Cambridge, MA: MIT Press.

Diamond, E., & Bates, S. (1992). *The spot: The rise of political advertising on television* (3rd ed.). Cambridge, MA: MIT Press.

Diamond, E., & Marin, A. (1989). Spots. *American Behavioral Scientist, 32*, 382–388.

Donath, B. (1976a, July 12). The adman behind Jimmy Carter: A decade of dedication paying off. *Advertising Age*, p. 1.

Donath, B. (1976b, October 4). Candidate ads take high tone; smiles outweigh accusations. *Advertising Age*, p. 2.

Donath, B. (1976c, October 25). Ford ads to get tougher on Carter, as challenger reverts to "sincerity." *Advertising Age*, p. 3.

Donath, B. (1976d, August 23). Ford's adman plans election turnaround strategy. *Advertising Age*, p. 1.

Donohue, T. R. (1973). Impact of viewer predispositions on political TV commercials. *Journal of Broadcasting, 18*, 3–15.

Dougherty, P. H. (1984, November 8). Advertising: Reagan's emotional campaign. *New York Times*, p. D29.

Dugan, J. R. (1989). Secondary effects and political speech: Intimations of broader governmental regulatory power. *Villanova Law Review, 34*, 995–1033.

Edelman, M. (1974). The politics of persuasion. In J. D. Barber (Ed.), *Choosing the president* (pp. 149–173). Englewood Cliffs, NJ: Prentice-Hall.

Edmonds, R. (1982). *The sights and sounds of cinema and television: How the aesthetic experience influences our feelings*. New York: Teachers College Press.

Elebash, C., & Rosene, J. (1982). Issues in political advertising in a deep South gubernatorial race. *Journalism Quarterly, 59*, 420–423.

Engelberg, S. (1988, November 3). Bush, his disavowed backers and a very potent attack ad. *New York Times*, p. A1.

Erickson, K. V., & Schmidt, W. V. (1982). Presidential political silence: Rhetoric and the rose garden strategy. *Southern Speech Communication Journal, 47*, 402–421.

Erickson, R. S. (1971). The advantage of incumbency in congressional elections. *Polity, 3*, 395–405.

Faber, R. J., & Storey, M. C. (1984). Recall of information from political advertising. *Journal of Advertising, 13*(3), 39–44.

Faber, R. J., Tims, A. R., & Schmitt, K. G. (1993). Negative political advertising and voting intent: The role of involvement and alternative information sources. *Journal of Advertising, 22*(4), 67–76.

Federal Election Campaign Act (1971). 2 U.S.C. § 441(d)(1982).

Ferejohn, J. A. (1977). On the decline of competition in congressional elections. *American Political Science Review, 71*, 166–176.

Final vote drives a free-for-all. (1980, November 3). *Advertising Age*, p. 1.

Fiorina, M. P. (1977). The case of the vanishing marginals: The bureaucracy did it. *American Political Science Review, 71*, 177–181.

First Reagan ad of fall campaign appears on TV. (1980, August 30). *Washington Post*, p. A3.

Garfield, B. (1988, October 10). With ads like these, Duke's going home. *Advertising Age*, p. 76.

Garfield, B. (1992, October 12). Bush/Quayle ads lose thread of any strategy. *Advertising Age*, p. 50.

Garfield, B. (1996, October 28). President uses Klaas killing to hone crime fighting image. *Advertising Age*, p. 50.

Garramone, G. M. (1983). Image versus issue orientation and effects of political advertising. *Communication Research, 10*, 59–76.

Garramone, G. M. (1984a). Voter responses to negative political ads. *Journalism Quarterly, 61*, 250–259.

Garramone, G. M. (1984b). Motivational models: Replication across media for political campaign content. *Journalism Quarterly, 61*, 537–541.

Garramone, G. M. (1985). Effects of negative political advertising: The roles of sponsor and rebuttal. *Journal of Broadcasting and Electronic Media, 29*, 147–159.

Garramone, G. (1986). Candidate image formation: The role of information processing. In L. L. Kaid, D. Nimmo, & K. R. Sanders (Eds.), *New perspectives on political advertising*. Carbondale: Southern Illinois University Press.

Garramone, G. M., Atkin, C. K., Pinkleton, B. E., & Cole, R. T. (1990). Effects of negative political advertising on the political process. *Journal of Broadcasting and Electronic Media, 34*, 299–311.

Garramone, G. M., & Smith, S. J. (1984). Reactions to political advertising: Clarifying sponsor effects. *Journalism Quarterly, 61*, 771–775.

Geiger, S. F., & Reeves, B. (1991). The effects of visual structure and content emphasis on the evaluation and memory for political candidates. In F. Biocca (Ed.), *Television and political advertising* (Vol. 1, pp. 125–144). Hillsdale, NJ: Lawrence Erlbaum Associates.

Gertz v. Robert Welch, Inc., 418 U.S. 323, 339–40 (1974).

Ghorpade, S. (1986, August/September). Agenda setting: A test of advertising's neglected function. *Journal of Advertising Research*, 23–27.

Goffman, E. (1959). *The presentation of self in everyday life*. New York: Doubleday Anchor Books.

Goleman, D. (1992, October 27). Voters assailed by unfair persuasion. *New York Times*, p. C1.

G.O.P. TV commercial evokes protests on image of Humphrey. (1968, October 29). *New York Times*, p. 35.

Gould, J. (1956, October 28). Medium's effect on election regarded as less important than in 1952. *New York Times*, p. 13.

Grant, D. (1968, October 21). Nixon intensifies ad efforts; fund lack hurts HHH. *Advertising Age*, p. 206.

Grant, D. (1972a, August 28). Believe Nixon can win with smaller ad budget. *Advertising Age*, p. 1.

Grant, D. (1972b, October 9). Did '68 anti-Nixon spot inspire anti-McGovern ad? *Advertising Age*, p. 3.

Grant, D. (1972c, November 11). Effective advertising let Nixon keep low profile in campaign. *Advertising Age*, p. 3.

Grant, D. (1972d, October 23). McGovern ads hitting harder in final drive against Nixon. *Advertising Age*, p. 1.

Grant, D. (1972e, October 2). Nixon Dems' TV ad raps McGovern. *Advertising Age*, p. 1.

Grove, L. (1988a, November 13). Attack ads trickled up from state races. *Washington Post*, pp. A1, 18–19.

Grove, L. (1988b, October 26). Bush ad and surrogates attack Dukakis' credibility. *Washington Post*, p. A14.

Grove, L. (1988c, September 27). Candidate ads: Emotional vs. cerebral. *Washington Post*, p. 16.

Grove, L. (1988d, October 21). Campaign ads play fast and loose with the truth. *Washington Post*, p. A1.

Grove, L. (1988e, October 5). Dukakis counterpunches at Bush's handlers in television spots. *Washington Post*, p. A1.

Grove, L. (1988f, October 22). Dukakis TV blitz targets "false advertising." *Washington Post*, p. A8.

Gurevitch, M., & Blumler, J. G. (1990). Comparative research: The extending frontier. In D. Swanson & D. Nimmo (Eds.), *New directions in political communication: A sourcebook* (pp. 305–325). Newbury Park, CA: Sage.

Haiman, F. S. (1958). Democratic ethics and the hidden persuaders. *Quarterly Journal of Speech, 44*, 385–392.

Hale, J. F., Fox, J. C., and Farmer, R. (1996). Negative advertisements in U.S. Senate campaigns: The influence of campaign context. *Social Science Quarterly, 77*, 329–343.

Hamill, P. (1964, October 25). When the client is a candidate. *New York Times Magazine*, p. 30.

Harwood, J. (1996, September 17). Political ad makers struggle to preserve their slice of the pie. *Wall Street Journal*, pp. 1, 10.

Hill, R. P. (1989). An exploration of voter responses to political advertisements. *Journal of Advertising, 18*, 14–22.

Hoff, P. S., & Bernstein, K. (1988). *Congress and the media: Beyond the 30–second spot: Enhancing the media's role in Congressional campaigns.* Washington, DC: Center for Responsive Politics.

Hofstetter, C. R., & Buss, T. F. (1980). Politics and last-minute political television. *Western Political Quarterly, 33*, 24–37.

Hofstetter, C. R., & Zukin, C. (1979). TV network news and advertising in the Nixon and McGovern campaigns. *Journalism Quarterly, 56*, 106–115, 152.

Hofstetter, C. R., Zukin, C., & Buss, T. F. (1978). Political imagery and information in an age of television. *Journalism Quarterly, 55*, 562–569.

Holtz-Bacha, C. (1990). Videomalaise revisited: Media exposure and political alienation in West Germany. *European Journal of Communication, 5*, 73–85.

Holtz-Bacha, C., & Kaid, L. L. (Eds.). (1993). *Die Massenmedien im Wahlkampf.* Opladen, Germany: Westdeutscher Verlag.

Holtz-Bacha, C., & Kaid, L. L. (1995). Television spots in German national elections: Content and effects. In L. L. Kaid & C. Holtz-Bacha (Eds.), *Political advertising in western democracies* (pp. 61–88). Thousand Oaks, CA: Sage.

Holtz-Bacha, C., & Kaid, L. L. (Eds.). (1996). *Wahlen und Wahlkampf in den Medien: Untersuchungen aus dem Wahljahr 1994.* Opladen, Germany: Westdeutscher Verlag.

Holtz-Bacha, C., Kaid, L. L., & Johnston, A. (1994). Political television advertising in Western democracies: A comparison of campaign broadcasts in the U.S., Germany, and France. *Political Communication, 11*, 67–80.

Jackson, J. S. (1994). Incumbency in the United States. In A. Somit, R. Wildenmann, B. Boll, & A. Rommele (Eds.), *The victorious incumbent: A threat to democracy?* (pp. 29–70). Aldershot, England: Dartmouth Publishing Company Limited.

Jacobson, G. C. (1981). Incumbents' advantages in the 1978 U.S. Congressional elections. *Legislative Studies Quarterly, 6*, 183–200.

Jamieson, K. H. (1984). *Packaging the presidency.* New York: Oxford University Press.

Jamieson, K. H. (1986). The evolution of political advertising in America. In L. L. Kaid, D. Nimmo, & K. R. Sanders (Eds.), *New perspectives on political advertising* (pp. 1–20). Carbondale: Southern Illinois University Press.

Jamieson, K. H. (1992a). *Dirty politics: Deception, distraction, and democracy.* New York, London: Oxford University Press.

Jamieson, K. H. (1992b). *Packaging the presidency* (2nd ed.). New York: Oxford University Press.

Jamieson, K. H. (1996). *Packaging the presidency* (3rd ed.). New York: Oxford University Press.

Jamieson, K. H., & Campbell, K. K. (1997). *The interplay of influence: News, advertising, politics, and the mass media* (4th ed.). Belmont, CA: Wadsworth.

Johannesen, R. L. (1990). *Ethics in human communication* (3rd ed.). Prospect Heights, IL: Waveland Press.

Johnson, K. S., & Elebash, C. (1986). The contagion from the right: The Americanization of British political advertising. In L. L. Kaid, D. Nimmo, & K. R. Sanders (Eds.), *New perspectives on political advertising* (pp. 293–313). Carbondale: Southern Illinois University Press.

Johnson-Cartee, K. S., & Copeland, G. (1989). Southern voters' reaction to negative political ads in 1986 election. *Journalism Quarterly, 66*, 888–893, 986.

Johnson-Cartee, K. S., & Copeland, G. A. (1991). *Negative political advertising: Coming of age*. Hillsdale, NJ: Lawrence Erlbaum.

Johnson-Cartee, K. S., & Copeland, G. A. (1997). *Manipulation of the American voter*. Westport, CT: Praeger.

Johnston, A. (1991a). Political broadcasts: An analysis of form, content, and style in presidential communications. In L. L. Kaid, J. Gerstlé, & K. R. Sanders (Eds.), *Mediated politics in two cultures: Presidential campaigning in the United States and France* (pp. 59–72). New York: Praeger.

Johnston, A. (1991b). Trends in political communication: A selective review of research in the 1980s. In D. L. Swanson & D. Nimmo (Eds.), *New directions in political communication: A resource book*. Newbury Park, CA: Sage Publications.

Johnston, A. (1999). Political advertising during the 1996 North Carolina Senate race: The Helms and Gantt rematch. In L. L. Kaid & D. G. Bystrom (Eds.), *The electronic election: Perspectives on the 1996 campaign communication* (pp. 303–315). Mahwah, NJ: Lawrence Erlbaum.

Johnston, A., & Gerstlé, J. (1995). The role of television broadcasts in promoting French presidential candidates. In L. L. Kaid & C. Holtz-Bacha (Eds.), *Political advertising in Western democracies: Parties and candidates on television* (pp. 44–60). Thousand Oaks, CA: Sage.

Johnston, A., & White, A. B. (1994). Communication styles and female candidates: A study of the political advertising during the 1986 senate elections. *Journalism Quarterly, 71*, 321–329.

Jones, C. A., & Kaid, L. L. (1976). Constitutional law: Political campaign regulation and the Constitution. *Oklahoma Law Review, 29*, 684–711.

Joslyn, R. A. (1980). The content of political spot ads. *Journalism Quarterly, 57*, 92–98.

Joslyn, R. A. (1984). *Mass media and elections*. Reading, MA: Addison-Wesley.

Joslyn, R. A. (1986). Political advertising and meaning of elections. In L. L. Kaid, D. Nimmo, & K. R. Sanders (Eds.), *New perspectives on political advertising* (pp. 139–184). Carbondale: Southern Illinois University Press.

Just, M., Crigler, A., & Wallach, L. (1990). Thirty seconds or thirty minutes: What viewers learn from spot advertisements and candidate debates. *Journal of Communication, 40*, 120–133.

Kahn, K. F., & Geer, J. G. (1994). Creating impressions: An experimental investigation of political advertising on television. *Political Behavior, 16*, 93–116.

Kaid, L. L. (1981). Political advertising. In D. D. Nimmo & K. R. Sanders (Eds.), *Handbook of political communication* (pp. 249–271). Beverly Hills, CA: Sage.

Kaid, L. L. (1982). Paid television advertising and candidate name identification. *Campaigns and Elections, 3*, 34–36.

Kaid, L. L. (1991a). The effects of television broadcasts on perceptions of political candidates in the United States and France. In L. L. Kaid, J. Gerstlé, & K. R. Sanders (Eds.), *Mediated politics in two cultures: Presidential campaigning in the United States and France*. New York: Praeger.

Kaid, L. L. (1991b). Ethical dimensions of political advertising. In R. Denton (Ed.), *Ethical dimensions of political communication* (pp. 145–169). New York: Praeger.

Kaid, L. L. (1994). Political advertising in the 1992 campaign. In R. E. Denton, Jr. (Ed.), *The 1992 presidential campaign* (pp. 111–127). Westport, CT: Praeger.

Kaid, L. L. (1996). Technology and political advertising: The application of ethical standards to the 1992 spots. *Communication Research Reports, 13*, 129–137.

Kaid, L. L. (1997). Effects of the television spots on images of Dole and Clinton. *American Behavioral Scientist, 40*, 1085–1094.

Kaid, L. L. (1998). Videostyle and the effects of the 1996 presidential campaign advertising. In R. E. Denton (Ed.), *The 1996 presidential campaign: A communication perspective* (pp. 143–159). Westport, CT: Praeger.

Kaid, L. L. (Ed.). (1999). *Television and politics in evolving European democracies*. Commack, NY: Nova-Science Publishers.

Kaid, L. L., & Boydston, J. (1987). An experimental study of the effectiveness of negative political advertisements. *Communication Quarterly, 35*, 193–201.

Kaid, L. L., & Chanslor, M. (1995). Changing candidate images: The effects of television advertising. In K. Hacker (Ed.), *Candidate images in presidential election campaigns* (pp. 83–97). New York: Praeger.

Kaid, L. L., Chanslor, M., & Hovind, M. (1992). The influence of program and commercial type on political advertising effectiveness. *Journal of Broadcasting and Electronic Media, 36*, 303–320.

Kaid, L. L., & Davidson, J. (1986). Elements of videostyle: Candidate presentation through television advertising. In L. L. Kaid, D. Nimmo, & K. R. Sanders (Eds.), *New perspectives on political advertising* (pp. 184–209). Carbondale: Southern Illinois University Press.

Kaid, L. L., & Garner, J. (1995). Political advertising and the elderly. In J. Nussbaum & J. Coupland (Eds.), *Handbook of communication and aging research* (pp. 343–357). Hillsdale, NJ: Erlbaum Publishers.

Kaid, L. L., Gobetz, R. H., Garner, J., Leland, C. M., & Scott, D. K. (1993). Television news and presidential campaigns: The legitimization of television political advertising. *Social Science Quarterly, 74*(2), 274–285.

Kaid, L. L., Haynes, K. J. M., & Rand, C. E. (1996). *The Political Communication Center: A catalog and guide to the collections*. Norman, OK: Political Communication Center.

Kaid, L. L., & Holtz-Bacha, C. (1993). Audience reactions to televised political programs: An experimental study of the 1990 German national election. *European Journal of Communication, 8*, 77–99.

Kaid, L. L., & Holtz-Bacha, C. (Eds.). (1995). *Political advertising in Western democracies*. Thousand Oaks, CA: Sage.

Kaid, L. L., & Johnston, A. (1991). Negative versus positive television advertising in presidential campaigns, 1960–1988. *Journal of Communication, 41*, 53–46.

Kaid, L. L., Leland, C., & Whitney, S. (1992). The impact of televised political ads: Evoking viewer responses in the 1988 presidential campaign. *Southern Communication Journal, 57*, 285–295.

Kaid, L. L., Lin, Y., & Noggle, G. (1999). The effects of technological distortions on voter reactions to the televised political advertising. In L. L. Kaid & D. G. Bystrom (Eds.), *The electronic election: Perspectives on the 1996 campaign communication* (pp. 247–256). Mahwah, NJ: Lawrence Erlbaum.

Kaid, L. L., McKinney, M., & Tedesco, J. C. (2000). *Civic dialogue in the 1996 campaign: Candidate, media, and public voices.* Cresskill, NJ: Hampton Press.

Kaid, L. L., & Noggle, G. (1998). Televised political advertising in the 1992 and 1996 elections: Using technology to manipulate voters. *Southeastern Political Review, 26 ,* 889–906.

Kaid, L. L., & Sanders, K. R. (1978). Political television commercials: An experimental study of the type and length. *Communication Research, 5,* 57–70.

Kaid, L. L., & Tedesco, J. (1993). A comparison of political television advertising from the 1992 British and American campaigns. *Informatologia, 25,* 1–12.

Kaid, L. L., & Tedesco, J. C. (1999). Presidential candidate presentation: Videostyle in the 1996 presidential spots. In L. L. Kaid & D. G. Bystrom (Eds.), *The electronic election: Perspectives on the 1996 campaign communication* (pp. 209–221). Mahwah, NJ: Lawrence Erlbaum.

Kaid, L. L., Tedesco, J., Chanslor, M., & Roper, C. (1993). Clinton's videostyle: A study of the verbal, nonverbal, and video production techniques in campaign advertising. *Journal of Communication Studies, 12*(1), 11–20.

Kaid, L. L., Tedesco, J. C., & McKinnon, L. M. (1996). Presidential ads as nightly news: A content analysis of 1988 and 1992 televised adwatches. *Journal of Broadcasting and Electronic Media, 40*, 297–308.

Kaiser, R. G. (1980a, September 9). Candidates on TV: Reagan goes low-key, Carter goes dramatic. *Washington Post*, p. A2.

Kaiser, R. G. (1980b, October 12). Carter and Reagan media strategies. *Washington Post*, A2.

Kelley, S., Jr. (1960). *Political campaigning: Problems in creating an informed electorate.* Washington, DC: Brookings Institution.

Kelly, J. (1984, November 12). Packaging the presidency: How to coordinate campaigning and commercials. *Time*, p. 36.

Kern, M. (1989). *30–second politics: Political advertising in the eighties.* New York: Praeger.

Kern, M., & Just, M. (1995). The focus group method, political advertising, campaign news, and the construction of candidate images. *Political Communication, 12*, 127–145.

Kessel, J. (1980). *Presidential campaign politics: Coalition strategies and citizen response.* Homewood, IL: Dorsey Press.

Kessler, M. S. (1981). The roles of surrogate speakers in the 1980 presidential campaign. *Quarterly Journal of Speech, 67*, 146–156.

Kitchens, J. T., & Stiteler, B. (1979). Challenge to the "rule of minimum effect": A case study of the in man–out man strategy. *Southern Speech Communication Journal, 44,* 176–190.

Klapper, J. (1960). *The effects of mass communication.* New York: Free Press.

Klein, J. (1996, September 23). The limits of negativity: Voters hate attack ads, so Clinton has finessed that—with "human interest" attack ads. *Newsweek,* p. 42.

Knapp, M. L. (1978). *Nonverbal communication in human interaction* (2nd ed.). New York: Holt, Rinehart and Winston.

Knapp, M. L., & Hall, J. A. (1992). *Nonverbal communication in human interaction* (3rd ed.). New York: Harcourt Brace Jovanovich College Publishers.

Koop, R. F. (1980). Evolving standards of broadcast journalism. In L. Thayer (Ed.), *Ethics, morality and the media* (pp. 165–173). New York: Hastings House.

Kramer, M. (1992, July 13). On TV, it's all déjà vu. *Time,* p. 27.

Kraus, S.(Ed.). (1962). *The great debates.* Bloomington: Indiana University Press.

Kurtz, H. (1992a, September 23). Clinton, Bush ads go separate ways; while Democrat targets specific states, Republican uses nationwide approach. *Washington Post,* p. A12.

Kurtz, H. (1992b, August 19). Clinton rebuts GOP attacks with TV ads. *Washington Post,* p. A27.

Kurtz, H. (1992c, October 2). Democrats decry Bush ad on taxes; GOP acknowledges TV spot relies on disputed assumptions. *Washington Post,* p. A1.

Kurtz, H. (1992d, July 28). Past brings perspective to negative ads; risks seen high for Bush if topics stray from governor's record. *Washington Post,* p. A8.

Kurtz, H. (1996a, October 22). An emotional pitch for Clinton; TV spot features father of murder victim; Dole aide calls it "cynical." *Washington Post,* p. A11.

Kurtz, H. (1996b, September 19). Candidates get a charge from negative ads. *Washington Post,* p. C1.

Kurtz, H. (1996c, October 25). Clinton's team's early offensive blunted effect of Dole ad blitz. *Washington Post,* p. A19.

Kurtz, H. (1996d, September 12). Democrats' ad blitz echoes Bush theme of change as "risk." *Washington Post,* p. A1.

Lang, A. (1991). Emotion, formal features, and memory for televised political advertisements. In F. Biocca (Ed.), *Television and political advertising* (Vol. 1, pp. 221–243). Hillsdale, NJ: Lawrence Erlbaum.

Lang, A., & Krueger, E. (1993). Candidates' commercials and the law: The public perception. *Journal of Broadcasting & Electronic Media, 37,* 209–218.

Lang, A., & Lanfear, P. (1990). The information processing of televised political advertising: Using theory to maximize recall. *Advances in Consumer Research, 17,* 149–158.

Latham, A. (1988, November 6). This mud's for you: What if they advertised products the way they do candidates? *Washington Post,* p. C5.

Latimer, M. K. (1984). Policy issues and personal images in political advertising in a state election. *Journalism Quarterly, 61,* 776–784, 852.

Latimer, M. K. (1989a). Legislators' advertising messages in seven state campaigns in 1986. *Journalism Quarterly,66,* 338–346, 527.

Latimer, M. K. (1989b). Political advertising for federal and state elections: Issues or substance? *Journalism Quarterly, 66,* 861–868.

Lee, S., Tak, J., & Kaid, L. L. (1998). Americanization of Korean political adver-
    tising: A comparative perspective on televised political spots in the 1992
    presidential campaign. *Asian Journal of Communication, 8*(1), 73–86.
Lelyveld, J. (1976a, October 22). New ads for Ford show man in street expressing
    doubt about Carter. *New York Times*, p. 117.
Lelyveld, J. (1976b, September 29). President's latest TV commercials portray
    him as father figure who inspires quiet confidence. *New York Times*, p. 22.
Leroy, D. L., & Smith, F. L. (1973). Perceived ethicality of some television news
    production techniques by a sample of Florida legislators. *Speech Mono-
    graphs, 40*, 326–329.
Lichter, S. R., & Noyes, R. (1996). *Campaign '96: The media and the candidates.* First
    Report to the Markle Foundation. Washington, DC: Center for Media and
    Public Affairs.
Liff, M. (1984, November 5). Reagan, Fritz use whips at wire. *Advertising Age*, p. 3.
Like Bubble Gum. (1952, October 3). *Newsweek*, pp. 33–34.
Maarek, P. J. (1995). *Political marketing and communication.* London: John Libbey.
Mancini, P., & Swanson, D. L. (1996). Politics, media, and modern democracy:
    Introduction. In D. L. Swanson & P. Mancini (Eds.), *Politics, media, and
    modern democracy* (pp. 1–26). Westport, CT: Praeger.
Mandell, L. M., & Shaw, D. L. (1973). Judging people in the news—uncon-
    sciously: Effect of camera angle and bodily activity. *Journal of Broadcast-
    ing, 17*, 353–362.
Mann, T. E. (1978). *Unsafe at any margin: Interpreting Congressional election.* Wash-
    ington, DC: American Enterprise Institute for Public Policy Research.
Mann, T. E., & Wolfinger, R. E. (1980). Candidates and parties in Congressional
    elections. *American Political Science Review, 74*, 617–632.
Martinelli, K. A., & Chaffee, S. H. (1995). Measuring new-voter learning via three
    channels of political information. *Journalism and Mass Communication
    Quarterly, 72*, 18–32.
Martinez, M. D., & Delegal, T. (1990). The irrelevance of negative campaigns to
    political trust: Experimental and survey results. *Political Communication
    and Persuasion, 7*(1), 25–40.
Mayhew, D. R. (1974). Congressional elections: The case of the vanishing mar-
    ginals. *Polity, 6*, 295–317.
Mazzoleni, G., & Roper, C. S. (1995). The presentation of Italian candidates and
    parties in television advertising. In L. L. Kaid & C. Holtz-Bacha (Eds.),
    *Political advertising in Western democracies: Parties and candidates on televi-
    sion* (pp. 89–108). Thousand Oaks, CA: Sage.
McCain, T. A., Chilberg, J., & Wakshlag, J. (1977). The effect of camera angle on
    source credibility and attraction. *Journal of Broadcasting, 21*, 35–46.
McClure, R. D., & Patterson, T. E. (1974). Television news and political advertis-
    ing: The impact of exposure on voter beliefs. *Communication Research,
    1*(1), 3–31.
McGinniss, J. (1969). *The selling of the president 1968.* New York: Trident.
McKinnon, L. M., & Kaid, L. L. (1999). Exposing negative campaigning or
    enhancing advertising effects: An experimental study of adwatch effects
    on voters' evaluations of candidates and their ads. *Journal of Applied
    Communication Research, 27*, 217–236.

McKinnon, L. M., Kaid, L. L., Murphy, J., & Acree, C. K. (1996). Policing political ads: An analysis of five leading newspapers' responses to 1992 political advertisements. *Journalism and Mass Communication Quarterly, 73*, 66–76.

Meadow, R. G., & Sigelman, L. (1982). Some effects and noneffects of campaign commercials: An experimental study. *Political Behavior, 4*(2), 163–175.

Merritt, S. (1984). Negative political advertising, *Journal of Advertising, 13*, 27–38.

Messaris, P. (1990, Fall). Ethics in visual communication. *Feedback, 31*, 2–5, 22–24.

Metallinos, N. (1996). *Television aesthetics: Perceptual, cognitive, and compositional bases.* Mahwah, NJ: Lawrence Erlbaum.

Meyer, T. P., & Donohue, T. R. (1973). Perceptions and misperceptions of political advertising. *The Journal of Business Communication, 10*(3), 29–40.

Millerson, G. (1972). *The technique of television production.* New York: Hastings House Publishers.

Millerson, G. (1990). *The technique of television production* (12th ed.). Boston, MA: Focal Press.

Minow, N. N., Martin, J. B., & Mitchell, L. M. (1973). *Presidential television.* New York: Basic Books.

Monaco, J. (1981). *How to read a film: The art, technology, language, history, and theory of film and media* (rev. ed.). New York: Oxford University Press.

Mulder, R. (1979). The effects of televised political ads in the 1975 Chicago mayoral election. *Journalism Quarterly, 56*, 336–340.

National Association of Broadcasters. (1988). *Political broadcast handbook* (3rd ed.). Washington, DC: NAB.

Nesbitt, D. (1988). *Videostyle: In Senate campaigns.* Knoxville: University of Tennessee Press.

Newhagen, J. E., & Reeves, B. (1991). Emotion and memory responses for negative political advertising: A study of television commercials used in the 1988 presidential election. In F. Biocca (Ed.), *Television and political advertising* (Vol. 1, pp. 197–220). Hillsdale, NJ: Lawrence Erlbaum Associates.

Nichols, B. (1981). *Ideology and the image: Social representation in the cinema and other media.* Bloomington: Indiana University Press.

Nimmo, D. (1974). *Popular image of politics.* Englewood Cliffs, NJ: Prentice-Hall.

Nimmo, D., & Combs, J. E. (1990). *Mediated political realities* (2nd ed.). New York: Longman.

Noelle-Neumann, E. (1978). The dual climate of opinion: The influence of television in the 1976 West German federal election. In M. Kaase & K. von Beyme (Eds.), *Elections and parties.* Beverly Hills, CA: Sage.

North, R. C., Holsti, O., Zaninovich, M. G., & Zinnes, D. A. (1963). *Content analysis: A handbook with applications for the study of international crisis.* Evanston, IL: Northwestern University Press.

Norton, R. (1983). *Communicator style.* Beverly Hills, CA: Sage.

Norton, R., & Brenders, D. (1996). *Communication and consequences: Laws of interaction.* Mahwah, NJ: Lawrence Erlbaum.

The nuclear issue. (1964, September 25). *Time*, pp. 15–16.

Nugent, J. F. (1987, March/April). Positively negative. *Campaigns and Elections, 7*, 47–49.

Oreskes, M. (1988a, October 19). Dukakis ads: Blurred signs, uncertain path. *New York Times*, p. A1.

Oreskes, M. (1988b, October 30). TV's role in '88: The medium is the election. *New York Times*, Section 1, p. 1.

Parker, D. (1988). Ethical implications of electronic still cameras and computer digital imaging in the print media. *Journal of Mass Media Ethics, 3*, 47–59.

Parker, G. R. (1980). The advantage of incumbency in House elections. *American Politics Quarterly, 8*, 449–464.

Patterson, T. E. (1983). Money rather than TV ads judged "root cause" of election costliness. *Television/Radio Age, 44*, 130–132.

Patterson, T. E., & McClure, R. D. (1976). *The unseeing eye: Myth of television power in politics*. New York: Putnam.

Payne, J. G., & Baukus, R. A. (1985, April). *Trend analysis of the 1984 GOP senatorial spot*. Paper presented at the McElroy Symposia: Current Trends in Broadcast Advertising, University of Northern Iowa.

Payne, J. G., Marlier, J., & Baukus, R. A. (1989). Polispots in the 1988 presidential primaries. *American Behavioral Scientist, 32*(4), 365–381.

Payne, J. L. (1980). The personal electoral advantage of House incumbents, 1936–1976. *American Politics Quarterly, 8*, 465–482.

Penniman, H. R. (1985). U.S. elections: Really a bargain? In M. J. Robinson & A. Ranney (Eds.), *The mass media in campaign '84*. Washington, DC: American Enterprise Institute for Public Policy Research.

Perlez, J. (1995, November 16). The televised debate meets politics in Poland. *New York Times*, p. A8.

Petersen, L. M. (1992, October 12). Presidential candidates start snapping up spot cable avails. *Mediaweek*, p. 4.

Pfau, M., & Burgoon, M. (1988). Inoculation in political campaign commercials. *Human Communication Research, 15*, 91–111.

Pfau, M., & Burgoon, M. (1989). The efficacy of issue and character attack message strategies in political campaign communication. *Communication Research Reports, 2*, 52–61.

Pfau, M., & Kenski, H. C. (1990). *Attack politics: Strategy and defense*. New York: Praeger.

Pfau, M., & Louden, A. (1994). Effectiveness of adwatch formats in deflecting political attack ads. *Communication Research, 21*, 325–341.

Political spending makes admen pikers. (1952, October 27). *Advertising Age*, p. 1.

Polsby, N. W., & Wildavsky, A. (1980). *Presidential elections: Strategies of electoral politics* (5th ed.). New York: Charles Scribner's Sons.

Polsby, N. W., & Wildavsky, A. (1991). *Presidential elections: Contemporary strategies of American electoral politics*. New York: Free Press.

Powell, L., & Shelby, A. (1981). A strategy of assumed incumbency: A case study. *Southern Speech Communication Journal, 46*, 105–123.

Primeau, R. (1979). *The rhetoric of television*. New York: Longman.

Ragsdale, L. (1981). Incumbent popularity, challenger invisibility, and congressional voters. *Legislative Studies Quarterly, 6*, 201–218.

Regan, R. J., Jr. (1986). *The moral dimensions of politics*. New York: Oxford University Press.

Rivers, W. L., & Mathews, C. (1988). *Ethics for the media*. Englewood Cliffs, NJ: Prentice-Hall.

Rivers, W. L., Schramm, W., & Christians, C. G. (1980). *Responsibility in mass communication* (3rd ed.). New York: Harper and Row Publishers.

Roberts, M., & McCombs, M. (1994). Agenda-setting and political advertising: Origins of the news agenda. *Political Communication, 11,* 249–262.

Robertson, N. (1964a, September 15). Johnson and Goldwater open television campaigns with both planning big outlays. *New York Times,* p. 18.

Robertson, N. (1964b, October 15). "Smear" tactics alleged by G.O.P. *New York Times,* p. 23.

Roddy, B. L., & Garramone, G. M. (1988). Appeals and strategies of negative political advertising. *Journal of Broadcasting and Electronic Media, 32*(4), 415–427.

Rokeach, M. (1973). *The nature of human values.* New York: Free Press.

Rose, E. D. (1983). Moral and ethical dilemmas inherent in an information society. In J. L. Salvaggio (Ed.), *Telecommunications: Issues and choices for society* (pp. 9–23). New York: Longman.

Rosenstone, S. J., Kinder, D. R., Miller, W. E., & the National Election Studies (1997). *American national election study, 1996: Pre- and post-election survey* [Computer file]. Ann Arbor: University of Michigan, Center for Political Studies [producer], 1997. Ann Arbor, MI: Inter-university Consortium for Political and Social Research [distributor].

Rothenberg, R. (1988, August 7). Political marketing: TV's new age of thrust and parry. *New York Times,* Section 1, p. 24.

Rothschild, M. L., & Ray, M. L. (1974, July). Involvement and political advertising effect: An exploratory experiment. *Communication Research, 1,* 264–285.

Rozen, L. (1980a, October 13). Candidates start final ad blitz. *Advertising Age,* p. 1.

Rozen, L. (1980b, August 18). Carter forces plan battle: Will ads take high road? *Advertising Age,* p. 2.

Rozen, L., & Gordon, R. L. (1980, September 8). Pols break ads—rather gently. *Advertising Age,* p. 2.

Rudd, R. (1986). Issue as image in political campaign commercials. *Western Journal of Speech Communication, 50,* 102–118.

S.340. 1989, 2 February. *Congressional Record*—Senate, p. S1093.

S.577. 1987, 23 February. *Congressional Record*—Senate, p. S2389.

S.2. 1987, 3 June. *Congressional Record*—Senate, p. S7526–7565.

Sabato, L. J. (1981). *The rise of political consultants: New ways of winning elections.* New York: Basic Books.

Schenck-Hamlin, W. J., Procter, D. E., & Rumsey, D. J. (2000). The influence of negative advertising frames on political cynicism and politician accountability. *Human Communication Research, 26,* 53–74.

Schleuder, J. (1990). Effects of commercial complexity, party affiliation and issue vs. image strategies in political ads. *Advances in Consumer Research, 17,* 159–168.

Schleuder, J., McCombs, M., & Wanta, W. (1991). Inside the agenda-setting process: How political advertising and TV news prime viewers to think about issues and candidates. In F. Biocca (Ed.), *Television and political advertising* (Vol. 1, pp. 263–310). Hillsdale, NJ: Lawrence Erlbaum Associates.

Schoenbach, K. (1987). The role of mass media in West German election campaigns. *Legislative Studies Quarterly, 12,* 173–394.

Schwartz, M., & Rezendes, M. (1988, September 7). Both sides begin the battle of broadcast ads. *Washington Post*, p. A6.

Schwartz, T. (1973). *The responsive chord*. Garden City, NY: Anchor Press/Doubleday.

Schwartz, T. (1984). *Media: The second God*. New York: Anchor Press.

Seiter, J. S. (1999). Does communicating nonverbal disagreement during an opponent's speech affect the credibility of the debater in the background? *Psychological Reports, 84*, 855–861.

Seiter, J. S., Abraham, J. A., & Nakagama, B. T. (1998). Split screen versus single screen formats in televised debates: Does access to opponent's nonverbal behaviors affect viewers' perceptions of a speaker's credibility? *Perceptual & Motor Skills, 86*, 491–497.

The selling of the President: 1988. (1988, September 5). *Broadcasting*, pp. 27–29.

Semetko, H. A., & Schoenbach, K. (1994). *Germany's "Unity Election": Voters and the media*. Cresskill, NJ: Hampton Press.

Shannon, M. R. (1990, February/March). Glass houses for sale—cheap. *Campaigns & Elections, 10*, 18.

Sheinkopf, K. G., Atkin, C. K., & Bowen, L. (1972). The functions of political advertising for campaign organizations. *Journal of Marketing Research, 9*, 401–405.

Sheinkopf, K. G., Atkin, C. K., & Bowen, L. (1973). How political party workers respond to political advertising. *Journalism Quarterly, 50*, 334–339.

Sheridan, D. (1990, January/February). The trouble with Harry: High technology can now alter a *moving* video image. *Columbia Journalism Review, 28*(5), 4–6.

Shyles, L. (1983). Defining the issues of a presidential election from televised political spot advertisements. *Journal of Broadcasting, 27*, 333–343.

Shyles, L. (1984a). Defining "images" of presidential candidates from televised political spot advertisements. *Political Behavior, 62*(2), 171–181.

Shyles, L. (1984b). The relationship of images, issues and presentational methods in televised spot advertisements for 1980's American presidential primaries. *Journal of Broadcasting, 28*, 405–421.

Shyles, L. (1988). Profiling candidate images in televised political spot advertisements for 1984: Roles and realities of presidential jousters at the height of the Reagan era. *Political Communication and Persuasion, 5*, 15–31.

Sigelman, L. (1979). Presidential popularity and presidential elections. *Public Opinion Quarterly, 43*, 532–534.

Sinclair, J. R. (1995). Reforming televisions role in American political campaigns: Rationale for the elimination of paid political advertisements. *Communication and the Law, 17*(1), 65–97.

Skenazy, L. (1988, April 18). Political touch-ups: Special effects benefit Bush. *Advertising Age*, p. 3.

The social security argument. (1964, October 23). *Time*, p. 25.

Spero, R. (1980). *The duping of the American voter*. New York: Lippincott & Crowell Publishers.

Steele, E. D., & Redding, W. C. (1962). The American value system: Premises for persuasion. *Western Speech, 26*(2), 83–91.

Stovall, J. G. (1984). Incumbency and news coverage of the 1980 presidential election campaign. *Western Political Quarterly, 37*, 621–631.

Strasser, S., Fineman, H., & Warner, M. G. (1984, November 5). Battle of the political ads. *Newsweek*, p. 26.

Surlin, S. H., & Gordon, T. F. (1976). Selective exposure and retention of political advertising. *Journal of Advertising, 5,* 32–44.

Surlin, S. H., & Gordon, T. F. (1977). How values affect attitudes toward direct reference political advertising. *Journalism Quarterly, 54,* 89–98.

Swanson, D. (1991). Theoretical dimensions of the U.S.-French presidential campaign studies. In L. L. Kaid, J. Gerstlé, & K. R. Sanders (Eds.), *Mediated politics in two cultures: Presidential campaigning in the United States and France* (pp. 9–23). Westport, CT: Praeger.

Tak, J., Kaid, L. L., & Lee, S. (1997). A cross-cultural study of political advertising in the United States and Korea. *Communication Research, 24,* 413–430.

Taylor, P. (1989, January 17). Consultants rise via the low road. *Washington Post,* pp. A1, A14.

Tedesco, J. C., McKinnon, L. M., & Kaid, L. L. (1996). Advertising watchdogs: A content analysis of print and broadcast adwatches. *Harvard International Journal of Press/Politics, 1*(4), 76–93.

Tenpas, K. D. (1997). *Presidents as candidates: Inside the White House for the presidential campaign.* New York: Garland Publishing.

Thorson, E., Christ, W. G., & Caywood, C. (1991a). Effects of issue-image strategies, attack and support appeals, music, and visual content in political commercials. *Journal of Broadcasting and Electronic Media, 35,* 465–486.

Thorson, E., Christ, W. G., & Caywood, C. (1991b). Selling candidates like tubes of toothpaste: Is the comparison apt? In F. Biocca (Ed.), *Television and political advertising* (Vol. 1, pp. 145–172). Hillsdale, NJ: Lawrence Erlbaum.

Tiemens, R. K. (1970). Some relationships of camera angle to communicator credibility. *Journal of Broadcasting, 14,* 483–490.

Tiemens, R. K. (1978). Television's portrayal of the 1976 presidential debates: An analysis of visual content. *Communication Monographs, 45,* 362–370.

Tinkham, S. F., & Weaver-Lariscy, R. A. (1995). Incumbency and its perceived advantage: A comparison of 1982 and 1990 congressional advertising strategies. *Political Communication, 12,* 291–304.

Trent, J. S. (1973). Image building strategies in the 1972 presidential campaign. *Speaker and Gavel, 10,* 39–45.

Trent, J. S., & Friedenberg, R. V. (1983). *Political campaign communication: Principles and practices.* New York: Praeger.

Trent, J. S., & Friedenberg, R. V. (1995). *Political campaign communication: Principles and practices* (3rd ed.). Westport, CT: Praeger.

"Unfair," cry GOP, Democrats at TV efforts. (1964, September 21). *Advertising Age,* p. 1.

Wadsworth, A. (Johnston). (1986). Incumbent and challenger strategies in presidential communication: A content analysis of television campaign ads from 1952 to 1984. Unpublished doctoral dissertation. University of Oklahoma, Norman.

Wadsworth, A. J., & Kaid, L. L. (1987, May). *Incumbent and challenger styles in presidential advertising.* Paper presented at the International Communication Association Convention, Chicago, IL.

Weaver, W., Jr.. (1972a, October 10). McGovern talks tougher in latest TV com-
    mercial. *New York Times*, p. 35.
Weaver, W., Jr. (1972b, September 26). Nixon's TV drive opens with film on
    Soviet. *New York Times*, p. 36.
Weinraub, B. (1980a, October 19). Carter and Reagan go on attack in ads. *New
    York Times*, Section 1, p. 38.
Weinraub, B. (1980b, November 10). Reagan's adman savoring "dull" success.
    New York Times, p. D8.
Weinraub, B. (1980c, October 8). TV battlefield tests presidential strategies. *New
    York Times*, p. B8.
West, D. (1993). *Air wars: Television advertising in election campaigns, 1952–1992.*
    Washington, DC: Congressional Quarterly.
West, D. (1994). Political advertising and news coverage in the 1992 California
    U.S. Senate campaigns. *Journal of Politics, 56*, 1053–1075.
West, D. M., Kern, M., & Alger, D. (1992). *Political advertising and ad watches in
    the 1992 presidential nominating campaign.* Paper presented at the annual
    meeting of the American Political Science Association, Chicago, IL.
Williams, W., Shapiro, M., & Cutbirth, C. (1983). The impact of campaign
    agendas on perception of issues in 1980 campaign. *Journalism Quarterly,
    60*, 226–231.
Winsbro, J. (1987). Misrepresentation in political advertising: The role of legal
    sanctions. *Emory Law Journal, 36*, 853–916.
Wood, S. C. (1990). Television's first political spot ad campaign: Eisenhower
    Answers America. *Presidential Studies Quarterly, 20*(2), 265–283.
Zettl, H. (1976). *Television production handbook* (3rd ed.). Belmont, CA: Wadsworth
    Publishing.
Zettl, H. (1997). *Television production handbook* (6th ed.). Belmont, CA: Wadsworth
    Publishing.
Zhao, X., & Bleske, G. L. (1995). Measurement effects in comparing voter learning
    from television news and campaign advertisements. *Journalism and Mass
    Communication Quarterly, 72*, 72–83.
Zhao, X., & Chaffee, S. M. (1995). Campaign advertisements versus television
    news as sources of political issue information. *Public Opinion Quarterly,
    59*, 41–65.
Zoglin, R. (1992, October 19). As the TV battle intensifies, lectures loaded with
    facts, figures and issues have replaced the slick image and propaganda
    productions of elections past. *Time*, p. 40.
Zuckerman, L. (1988, November 14). The made-for-TV campaign: A year when
    candidates—not reporters—controlled the images. *Time*, p. 66.

Index

ABOUT THE AUTHORS

Lynda Lee Kaid is Professor of Communication and George Lynn Cross Research Professor at the University of Oklahoma, where she also serves as the Director of the Political Communication Center and supervises the Political Commercial Archive. She is the author or editor of 14 books, including *The Electronic Election, New Perspectives on Political Advertising, Mediated Politics in Two Cultures, Political Advertising in Western Democracies,* and *Political Campaign Communication: A Bibliography and Guide to the Literature.*

Anne Johnston is an associate professor in the School of Journalism and Mass Communication at the University of North Carolina, Chapel Hill. She has authored and co-authored work on cross-cultural studies of political broadcasting, styles and strategies in political advertising, and on women and the media. Her articles have appeared in the *Journal of Applied Communication Research, Journalism Quarterly, Journal of Communication,* and *Political Communication.*